THE UNITED STATES IN THE WORLD

A series edited by Mark Philip Bradley, David C. Engerman, Amy S. Greenberg, and Paul A. Kramer

For God and Globe

Christian Internationalism in the United States
between the Great War and the Cold War

Michael G. Thompson

Cornell University Press
Ithaca and London

First published 2015 by Cornell University Press

Printed in the United States of America

Library of Congress Cataloging-in-Publication Data

Thompson, Michael G. (Michael Glenn), author.
    For God and globe : Christian internationalism in the United States between the Great War and the Cold War / Michael G. Thompson.
        pages cm. — (The United States in the world)
    Includes bibliographical references and index.
    ISBN 978-0-8014-5272-7 (cloth : alk. paper)
    1. Christianity and international relations—History—20th century.
2. Christianity and politics—United States—History—20th century.
3. Protestantism—United States—History—20th century.
4. United States—Church history—20th century.   I. Title.
    BR115.I7T46 2015
    261.8'7—dc23   2015009583

Cornell University Press strives to use environmentally responsible suppliers and materials to the fullest extent possible in the publishing of its books. Such materials include vegetable-based, low-VOC inks and acid-free papers that are recycled, totally chlorine-free, or partly composed of nonwood fibers. For further information, visit our website at www.cornellpress.cornell.edu.

Cloth printing   10 9 8 7 6 5 4 3 2 1

For Nikki, Evie, Willem, and Joey

Contents

Acknowledgments

This book, like most, has been a communal project. Colleagues, friends, and family have all lent encouragement and support, given insights, or sparked changes of direction that I hope are as visible to them as they are to me. First, the project owes a great debt to the ever-buzzing and intellectually stimulating History Department at Sydney University—an extraordinary place to work on U.S. and international history. I must thank Neville Meaney for originally helping pique my interest in Reinhold Niebuhr and American nationalism years ago. For both her generosity as a mentor and her intellectual leadership in developing international and transnational history at Sydney, I am grateful to Glenda Sluga. Alison Bashford's own suggestive and field-shaping approach to international history has always been matched by her sincere interest in others' work and welfare, my own included. Clare Corbould's encouragement and her welcome asking of hard questions have helped shape this project at vital points. Enormous thanks are due to Stephen Robertson, whose commitment to methodological rigor and innovation I aspire to. For his collegiality and support I owe Stephen far more gratitude than I can adequately communicate. And, Penny, Andrew, Frances, Mike, James, Cindy, Gab, and everyone else: What a pleasure to work alongside you these last years!

The United States Studies Centre at the University of Sydney has provided much support and a hospitable environment in which to conduct research for this book. I thank CEO Bates Gill, Brendon O'Connor and Rebecca Sheehan in particular for their ongoing personal support, and I thank the Centre for its support in providing vital funding in the final stages of the work.

Several others beyond the sandstone confines of Sydney University have offered invaluable guidance. Prominent among these is Ian Tyrrell, whose far-reaching and diverse interests in U.S. history has left a deep impression on my thinking. I trust he knows also what his personal support means to me. Andrew Preston—whose own work has set the benchmark in this field—has been of similar encouragement, generously offering valuable direction in later stages. Mark T. Edwards's collegiality and insight on all things mainline Protestant has also assisted me greatly. The Sydney EHA/CTE crowd, including Stuart Piggin, Geoff Treloar, Steve Chavura, Meredith Lake, and Robert Linder, has provided welcome friendship and a valuable hub for trialing ideas. I thank Michael McGandy at Cornell University Press for prescient criticism and sound advice, all of which, I trust, has made my writing sharper than it would otherwise have been. Finally, this book may not have materialized without Paul Kramer. Aside from the considerable impact of his own thinking in the field of the United States in the world scholarship, Paul's generosity, friendship, and help have been unwavering.

Portions of the Introduction have been reproduced and adapted from my article, "Sherwood Eddy, the missionary enterprise, and the rise of Christian internationalism in 1920s America," *Modern Intellectual History* 12, no. 1 (2015): 65–93. I thank Cambridge University Press for their permission to reproduce this material.

In the research process, I accrued several debts to librarians and archivists. Special thanks must be made to Ruth Tonkiss Cameron of Burke Library, Union Theological Seminary, for guidance and suggestions on the records of the Theological Discussion Group and Fellowship of Socialist Christians. Martha Smalley at Yale Divinity School Library provided a warm welcome to an Australian and untrammeled access to the excellent Special Collections held at Yale. Thanks also to Barbara Addison at the Swarthmore College Peace Collection, who not only offered access to the Devere Allen Papers but also shared her own research into Allen's work. Staff at the Library of Congress were outstandingly helpful in providing rapid and streamlined access to the Reinhold Niebuhr Papers. The Seeley G. Mudd Manuscript Library, Princeton, and especially Jennie Cole, are to be thanked for their great patience in processing large volumes of copying for shipment to Australia.

Family tend to bear the brunt of projects such as these, but I could not possibly have asked for more supportive people around me. For helping at various stages with research, my sister Briar deserves special mention. My parents, Glenn and Roz, have remained not merely benignly interested but—perhaps supernaturally—positively supportive throughout the process. Pieter and Sue:

Great thanks are due to you for all your warm and generous help expressed in innumerable ways. I thank Norma Hardy for support that has been vital to this project's survival. To Evie, Will, and Joey, gifts who arrived during the course of writing: Your mischief and sense of fun cheer the soul! Most of all I must thank my dear wife, Nikki, my chief editor, fellow discussant, coach, critic, and best friend. I could not have done this without her.

For God and Globe

Introduction

Missionaries, Mainliners, and the Making of a Movement

Writing in 1928 in *The World Tomorrow*, the New York-based magazine that he helped finance, Sherwood Eddy poured scorn on his earlier views of the missionary enterprise. Having been in the field since 1896, Eddy was still, in the 1920s, a YMCA missionary of extraordinary international standing—a celebrity evangelist to a generation of mainline, ecumenical Protestants. But what he confessed now, with embarrassment, was the way that back "then," in the prewar days, "we felt a divine call to go from our own favored 'Christian' nation to the backward 'heathen' nations"; he cringed to think of the way he felt called to "take up 'the white man's burden' and go out from our 'superior' race to the backward peoples of the world."[1] Now, he noted, Christians would be better to adopt a posture of being "deeply disturbed" by the "semi-pagan order at home." How could Americans claim to be of a "superior" race when "we still lead the world in our record of lynching, in race and color prejudices"? How could Anglo-Saxon democracies claim to be superior when their imperialism "has conquered or exploited over half of Asia and all but one-thirtieth of Africa," and when together they spend more on naval armaments than the rest of the world combined?[2]

Not only did Eddy's article exemplify the far-ranging blend of antiracism, anti-imperialism, and antimilitarism that characterized Christian internationalism in the interwar period, his expression highlighted that something striking had happened to the grammar of the typical missionary sentence. New qualifiers, quotation marks, and distancing devices pervaded articles, reports, and deliberations of missionaries like Eddy, all with the function of conveying missionaries' self-conscious eschewal of a notion most of them had until recently taken for granted: namely, the idea that America and other Western countries were "Christian" nations. The same year, John R. Mott, a close confidant of Eddy's in the YMCA, and still then arguably America's most globally influential Protestant missionary and ecumenist, distanced himself from earlier language by referring to "our so-called western Christian civilization" and "the so-called non-Christian world" in his address to the landmark world conference of the International Missionary Council in Jerusalem.[3] American Quaker theologian Rufus Jones, who wrote a major preparatory paper used at that same conference, was more direct: Delegates went to Jerusalem "not as members of a Christian nation to convert other nations which are not Christian, but as Christians within a nation far too largely non-Christian."[4] At a later Student Christian Movement (SCM) conference, Dutch theologian Willem Adolph Visser 't Hooft—a figure close to Mott and a leader of the new ecumenism—reflected on the changed speech-rules. "There was a time, and that not so very long ago, when the expression 'The Christian West' seemed no less natural and self-evident than platitudes like 'The Sunny South.'" Now, he believed, people had to speak differently. In an address carefully billed "The 'Christian' West," he remarked that if "it were not for the inverted commas, our title would have been taken for a cynical joke."[5]

Ecumenists' and missionaries' rejection of the language of Christian nationhood was part of their attempted expression of a new Christian internationalist consciousness; it was the negative voicing of their positive argument for wider solidarities. Sherwood Eddy, for example, did not restrict himself to criticizing old nationalist notions, but set about deploying his missionary credentials to help create a new internationalist viewpoint in American Protestant life. He took the format of his traditional missionary report-letters and applied it to reporting on international affairs—letting readers of the *Churchman*, *Christian Century*, or *New York Times* know about nationalist reform efforts in China, the features of Japanese imperialism in Korea, or the hopes of the new Czechoslovakian government in the 1920s, for example.[6] And, he used the wide contacts and facility with travel he had developed as a YMCA missionary to create a new innovation: his annual "traveling seminar."

Eddy's seminar—an iconic interwar Christian internationalist institution in its own right—was an annual study tour through Europe, led by Eddy, but with major British and European political and church leaders appearing as guest lecturers.[7] By giving shapers of Protestant thought exposure to world conditions, the seminar was Eddy's attempt, in his words, to create an "avenue to international understanding and peace."[8] Certainly participants saw its significance in such terms. Having freshly returned from Eddy's 1927 tour, F. Ernest Johnson, director of the Department of Research and Education in the U.S. Federal Council of Churches, claimed, "No other single factor has been more potent in securing recognition in America of an international viewpoint."[9] The *Christian Century*, a key liberal Protestant magazine whose editor, Charles Clayton Morrison, was also an Eddy Seminar participant, wondered at the "enormous significance of . . . American minds of many types who return to their homes bearing the inspiration of new international understanding."[10] Aided by its selective enrollment policy—restricted to those who could "exert wide influence on American public opinion"—the seminar had a notable ripple effect in American public life.[11] A "who's who" of Progressive leaders and thinkers were influenced by their time on Eddy's steamship. The first tour in 1921 began with less than a dozen participants. By 1926 the tour consisted of 140 people. By 1927 the cumulative total of alumni was nearly one thousand.[12] Hubert Herring, head of the Committee on Cultural Relations with Latin America, was inspired to start his own "Latin American Seminar" after his experience of Eddy's seminar.[13] Ben M. Cherrington, a YMCA figure, later International Relations scholar, and still later, the first head of the U.S. State Department's Culture division, was also an early seminar traveller.[14] And it was on a trip through the Ruhr with the Eddy Seminar in 1923 that Reinhold Niebuhr turned to pacifism, confessing in his journal that he was finally "done with the war business"—a position he later famously reversed.[15]

Both the negative and positive articulations of Eddy's 1920s work—his critiques of nationalism, imperialism, and racism on one hand, and his efforts to promote internationally minded study and publicity via his seminars on the other—were representative of the wider movement of which he was a part. That movement, its ideas, enterprises, and legacies, is the subject of this book. In the 1920s and 1930s, as the following chapters show, Christian internationalism in the United States was characterized by three factors. First, as a movement of thought, it consisted in large part in the proliferation of new enterprises devoted to producing Christian reflection on the ethics of "international relations"—world conferences, traveling seminars like Eddy's, new forms of print and periodical culture, ecumenical study commissions, and more. As socially concerned Protestants discovered international life as their newest sphere of reform, the number and scale of such activities mushroomed. Such a development dovetailed with the rapid development of secular "international relations" institutions—whether private groups such as the Council on Foreign Relations and Foreign Policy Association, or new International Relations university departments.[16] But more than merely producing knowledge, Christian internationalists sought to deploy it to shape the engagement of fellow Protestants with the deliberations of the foreign policy public and, in fact, to crystallize new public formations altogether.

A second defining characteristic of Christian internationalism in the interwar period was its distinct *structure of thinking* that held Christian universalism to be a check against nationalism rather than a boon for it. This basic normative commitment—together with the fact that the very question of the relationship between Christianity and nationalism became an unprecedentedly conscious one in the 1920s and 1930s—helped set interwar Christian internationalism apart from that of other periods. Unlike liberal Protestant arguments justifying the Wilsonian "war for righteousness" in 1917, and counter to the crusading rhetoric offered by many mainline or evangelical Protestants in the early Cold War, Christian internationalists in the interwar decades rejected outright the notion that God's universal cause could be seen as immanent within the nation's cause. Such a claim was "idolatrous." Rather, Christian universalism was to be a check against the tendencies of nationalism to make falsely religious claims. Nationalism represented, in the words of famed New York preacher Harry Emerson Fosdick, "a competing religion . . . the most dangerous rival of Christian principles on earth."[17] Historians have found no shortage of material to illustrate the ways American Protestantism has offered a "yes" to the state—functioning as an ideological ancillary to expansionism and imperialism—but have taken comparatively little stock of movements and moments that were characterized by "no."[18] The Christian internationalism examined in this book was a movement animated by a "no." Indeed, not only did its proponents answer in the negative, they often went further than recent scholars have in asking fellow American Christians whether they had mistaken for religion the cult of their own national sovereignty.[19]

Thirdly, interwar Christian internationalism consisted of a holistic, oppositional, and at times radical political orientation that in many enterprises actually united realists and pacifists, setting them apart from their legalist and institutionalist counterparts. As such, the movement's shape, as examined in the case studies that follow, does not fit the reductive narrative strategies with which historians have tended to identify Protestant thinking in the 1920s to 1940s. For one, the interests of the movement ranged far beyond the issues of peace versus war, or pacifism versus realism. Christian internationalists of both pacifist and realist persuasions together sought to agitate against the influences of American capitalism, imperialism, nationalism, and racism in world affairs, against what Sherwood Eddy and others had called the "white peril."[20] The movement's wide-ranging character owed much to it roots in the missionary enterprise. These origins gave it an intellectual history related to, but distinct from, that of other internationalisms of the period. Like liberal international-ism, Christian internationalism was implicitly defined as an alternative to Com-munist internationalism. And, like liberal internationalism, Christian interna-tionalism was suffused with a cosmopolitanism that, though unacknowledged, owed some debt to Kant's vision of "perpetual peace."[21] But, unlike main-stream liberal internationalism, such missionary-rooted Christian internation-alism was distinguished by its lack of focus on international law and interna-tional institutions. Its protagonists stressed instead cultural causality in international relations and the importance of nonstate, person-to-person in-ternational relations—emphases that reflected missionaries' positioning as agents of cultural diplomacy and nonstate international relations by nature of their vocation. Retaining this orientation, interwar Christian internationalists insisted throughout the 1920s to 1940s that cultural relations—especially race relations—were constitutive of international relations, the domestic intertwined with the global. On this they were far from conservative internationalists in the in-ternational law tradition, for whom international relations meant regulating conduct between discretely defined nation-states.[22]

By way of definition, it should be clarified that my use of the term "Chris-tian" internationalist is not intended to imply a greater membership than this movement actually had. Used here, it refers to the substantive impulse of these particular subjects—using their language, and that of scholars since—rather than their demographic and denominational scope.[23] Christian international-ism was largely, but not entirely, liberal Protestant in its base, with a notable Quaker influence through related peace organizations such as the Fellowship of Reconciliation. Notably absent from the following narrative are Catholic Christians and conservative evangelical Christians—or, in the parlance of the 1920s, "fundamentalists." Further work could indeed be done on parallel efforts among American Catholic organizations. For instance, the Catholic Associa-tion for International Peace, founded around 1926, aimed to help Catholic Americans in "ascertaining more fully the facts of international life."[24] Rel-ative to the size and influence of Protestant groups at the time, however, such groups were marginal, and neither shared with Protestants the institutional basis in missionary agencies nor, at that point, the mixed blessing of constituting a de facto national establishment.[25]

Conservative evangelicals, on the other hand, are not examined here as, on the whole, they less often engaged in such discourse. Across denomi-nations, they were imbued with what Markku Ruotsila shows was a relatively consistent "anti-internationalism."[26] The rising influence of premillennial dispensationalist teaching among fundamentalist churches—a belief that contemporary history as interpreted through biblical prophecy revealed the activity of the anti-Christ and the end of the world—lent itself to a fear of international conspiracy that did not sit naturally with the preference for international organization held by those examined here.[27] But it is not that interwar Christian internationalism was merely a fruit of liberalism and modernism in religion, nor that evangelical theology was incapable of producing similar kinds of antimilitarism and antinationalism, as David Swartz's history of the 1970s evangelical Left has shown.[28] Indeed, as this book aims to show, Mott and Eddy's style of YMCA-rooted liberal evangelicalism, which retained strands of Christocentrism, intense piety, and revivalistic preaching, was a major and shaping influence on interwar internationalism. Mott's arguments for racial equality—like those of many of his ecumenical colleagues—were couched in the most evangelical of terms, focusing, in Pauline terms, on the reconciliation among races achieved by the sacrificial death of Jesus Christ. Aside from Mott, the influence of other major ecumenical figures like Mott's British missionary counterpart, Joseph Oldham, or Dutchman Willem Adolph Visser 't Hooft, respectively the research director of the Oxford 1937 conference and the first general secretary of the World Council of Churches, should not be overlooked. These figures of enormous international influence were neither fundamentalist nor modernist, but presented a conciliatory and astute blend of neo-orthodoxy and traditional evangelicalism that arguably helped American mainline ecumenism transcend such dichotomies.

As for "internationalism," scholars have, for good reason, been inconsistent in their definitions. Perhaps the best attempt to provide an essential definition of the term has come from international relations scholar Fred Halliday, who sees it containing an empirical observation—the world is interconnected—linked to a normative claim: people should better realize their interconnectedness. "In its simplest terms," he suggests, "internationalism is the idea that we both are and should be a part of a broader community than that of the nation or state."[29] Yet, as Halliday himself acknowledges, such a definition tells us little about the political behavior or outlook of internationalists, who might be engaged variously in revolutionary Marxist internationalism, classical liberal internationalism, or Islamic revolutionary internationalism. Positing an abstract and static meaning for the term is of little utility and even less validity. Glenda Sluga's excellent recent work reminds us not to confuse or conflate the Enlightenment genealogy of Kant, Mazzini, and others with the mid-nineteenth-century "class-based political imaginary," for which the name "internationalism" was first coined in French and English. The former saw an ongoing place for the nation in humanity's apparent evolution toward increasingly wider planes of conscious-ness and solidarity—world community as a federation of nations. The latter was "specifically opposed to nationalism, supporting instead transnational, non-state-bound class interests as the stepping-stone to radical economic egalitarianism."[30] The Christian internationalists examined here by and large stressed the federal vision of the Enlightenment strand, but also, in many im-portant ways, in their critiques of nationalism, racism, and capitalism, echoed the radical class-based tradition. Internationalism is best understood, then, as Micheline Ishay argues, as "a process *sui generis* rather than a static concept, shaped and transformed by progressive thinkers and historical events."[31] The definition of internationalism depends at least on the nature of the agent (whether individuals or organizations, state or non-state, etc.) and on a variety of relational and discursive contingencies, particularly who or what the inter-nationalism was defined against.

One task of this book is to disentangle Christian internationalism from American internationalism. That is, it aims to show that historically they were in fact disentangled for much of the 1920s to 1930s, until in World War II the two became increasingly one. But, conceptually too, the need to distinguish Christian internationalism from state-based internationalism arises from the in-stability of the term in American politics. Almost all the major foreign policy debates of the early to mid-twentieth century had so-called "internationalists" on both sides. Not only Wilson, but also his chief opponent in the Senate, Henry Cabot Lodge, was, as noted by historian Manfred Jonas, an "archetypal American internationalist."[32] Both advocates of the Outlawry of War pro-gram, who often despised the League of Nations, and those who supported the League of Nations were internationalists—and their conflict, like others, was a struggle between rival internationalisms. Similarly, many pacifists who opposed American intervention in wars from 1939 to 1941 did not do so be-cause they were "isolationist" in a nationalistic sense (as some of their allies on the far Right indeed were). Rather, they combined their internationalism with a strong opposition to war, which led them to believe neutralism represented the better way to achieve international peace. They and their political oppo-nents both counted themselves internationalists—as did both Henry Wallace and President Truman in the late 1940s. With internationalists found on all sides of key, definitive debates in American foreign relations history, it becomes impossible to define the term by any one specific policy position.

My use of the term "internationalism" in this book is much closer to the impulse of Sondra Herman's classic work of decades ago, *Eleven against War: Stud-ies in American Internationalist Thought, 1898–1921*.[33] Drawing on the theoretical groundwork of German thinker Ferdinand Tönnies (famous for making the distinction between *gemeinschaft* and *gesellshaft*), Herman distinguished between "political" and "community" approaches in internationalist thought. The former, usually propounded by figures close to the state such as Elihu Root and Nicholas Murray Butler, stressed the development of a legal or institutional apparatus as the way to a peaceful, nonrevolutionary world order—a world order, incidentally, in which American interests and power might peacefully expand. "Community internationalism" was more often propounded by intellectuals and radicals such as Jane Addams, Thorstein Veblen, or Josiah Royce— intellectual heroes of *The World Tomorrow* magazine, the periodical that will be examined in part 1 of this book. Those intellectuals did not ignore the need for legal or institutional changes but saw such reform as insufficient for the prevention of war. What they felt was needed, explains Herman, "was the development of a more organic world consciousness, a sense of international community among the peoples of different nations."[34] Herman's approach, sensitive to the depth and breadth of her subjects' own projects, is what set her work apart from classic policy-oriented (but still helpful) narratives like Robert Divine's, or the relatively pragmatic and institutionalist approach offered by others, most notably, Warren Kuehl.[35] In key ways, this inquiry owes more to Herman's impulse than Divine's in that it takes internationalist thought as its subject, rather than policy influence, although the latter is definitely part of the story.

Organizing Logics

The problem of defining and locating internationalism is closely related to the methodological problem of narrating a movement. What organizational logics best allow historians to capture wider patterns? How, indeed, can empirical connections assist us in making intellectual connections? Existing scholarship on Reinhold Niebuhr, one of the figures discussed in this book, reveals the challenges of such a task. As one of the most significant intellectuals to emerge from interwar Christian internationalism, Niebuhr is a figure that has long drawn the attention of historians. One approach, exemplified by Richard Pells's classic intellectual history of the 1930s, has been to place Niebuhr among other big thinkers who wrote big books and to paint a picture of an American intellectual struggle.[36] While helpful in many ways, such an approach tends to extract Niebuhr from the immediate milieu in which he wrote, placing him instead in an artificial context.[37] Another option has been the group biography. In Niebuhr's case, this approach has tended to reinforce the dominance of the realism versus pacifism dyad in historiography. The terms of realists' self-definition, which arose largely out of Niebuhr's own polemical writings (and from contemporary historians such as E. H. Carr) were adopted as controlling categories for many historians.[38] For example, though he denied offering Niebuhr's views as normative, Donald Meyer's classic, *The Protestant Search for Realism*, held out Niebuhrian realism as the *telos* toward which American Protestantism was moving.[39] Various attempts by idealists to impose the "ideal" upon social and international questions met successive obstacles until the attempt was abandoned and the whole task was either transmuted into a realist frame, or the idealists opted for political "irrelevance" and "irresponsibility" (or thus went the narrative).[40] In the pages that follow, I suggest instead that realism be seen as a critique, a qualification, emerging from within Christian internationalism— not a neat secession, but a fraught and complex realignment. "Realism" as a category was more diffuse and less stable than often portrayed.

More recent group biographies such as those by Heather Warren and Mark Edwards have done much more to embed Niebuhr in the ecumenical networks of which he was a part, placing him as one among others like John C. Bennett, Francis P. Miller, Henry Pit Van Dusen, and Georgia Harkness.[41] But a telling absence in Warren's work—which follows these realists through the 1920s to the 1940s—is the milieu of New York-based radical Christian internationalism in which most of her subjects were enmeshed. Almost the entire cast of characters played a role in the shaping of *The World Tomorrow* magazine at the heart of that milieu: Niebuhr was employed as editor from 1928 to 1934 and was lead columnist from 1932; Van Dusen was treasurer in the 1930s; Bennett served as a contributing editor and wrote regularly on socialism and religion in the 1930s; and Miller, a contributor on foreign policy as early as 1926, was a foreign correspondent into the late 1920s. On this point in particular, Mark Edwards's recent addition to the history of realism is welcome. By means of considerable archival research, Edwards "re-members" realists by casting them as they were—a network of scholar-activists who constituted an old Protestant left.[42] Building on Edwards's and Warren's work, and incorporating the insights of several fine earlier histories of the peace movement, I offer here an account of Christian thinking in which pacifists and realists are situated alongside one another—which is, for much of the time, exactly where they were.[43] At the same time, by examining the broader project of Christian internationalism, of which pacifism and realism were subsets, and by centering on empirical sites that were neither definitively pacifist nor realist, I seek to loosen the hold of that very dichotomy.

Two Sites of Collective Deliberation

This inquiry has been designed around an intensive excavation of two enter-prises in collective deliberation: a periodical and a world conference. Coher-ent enough to be considered a movement, Christian internationalism consisted of distinct but overlapping strands. While a legalist strand (to use Herman's terms, a "political" strand) had long existed in Christian internationalism, arising before World War I and continuing well into World War II, the two strands most distinctive to the interwar period, and the two to have received least at-tention in extant literature, are the radical anti-imperialist internationalism of missionaries-turned-socialists like Sherwood Eddy and the ecumenical inter-nationalism that flourished in the remarkable spate of world conferences in the 1920s and 1930s. The two sites of collective deliberation around which this study has been shaped have been chosen because they are representative of just these two strands. *The World Tomorrow* magazine was the preeminent voice of a kind of radical Christian internationalism that flourished in the decade after World War I. Edited between 1926 and 1934 by Kirby Page, Devere Al-len, and Reinhold Niebuhr—and before that by old Left stalwarts Anna Rochester, Norman Thomas, and John Nevin Sayre—the now largely for-gotten journal was home to a community of radicals who sought to develop Christian critiques of American nationalism, militarism, and imperialism. Likewise, the "Oxford 1937" world ecumenical conference—technically the Universal Christian Conference on Church, Community, and State—was, I argue, the most important event in the development of a new, distinct strand of internationalism that gave shape to ecumenical thought in America and abroad for decades.

In each case, the nature of the enterprise was related to the nature of the intellectual method. *The World Tomorrow* sought to create something of a foreign policy "counterpublic": It offered an alternative reading of foreign policy and world affairs to the mainstream, and it sought to crystallize an antiwar, anti-imperialist, and antimilitarist minority of public opinion in the wider public square. Oxford 1937 had an altogether different nature. The world conference and all it encompassed was the enterprise in itself. More than just a formal series of speeches and panels spread over a fortnight, it included the practice of vast scholarly exchanges of papers over years in the lead-up, the experience of shared living and shared prayer, the exoticism and *communitas* of travel, and elaborate follow-up campaigns. World conferences such as Oxford 1937 were in themselves seen to be important expressions of supranational Christian sol-idarity in a world ridden by nationalisms.

The advantage of focusing on sites of collective deliberation is that they were indeed collectively constituted. By nature, such enterprises were creatures of a wider movement, and as such they enable historians to enter therein. Rather than coming to the enquiry with a category already in place such as pacifism, or rather than being committed in advance to the following of one group of individuals, following each site's origins, conduct, and legacies means that new individuals emerge, new categories and unanticipated networks present themselves. *The World Tomorrow*, for example, cannot be approached with a single analytical category in mind. Participants and historians alike have found it near impossible to find a simple epithet with which to sum up *The World Tomorrow*'s project. As editors, Kirby Page, Reinhold Niebuhr, and Devere Allen resorted to various versions of the following phrase as their definition: "A Journal Looking toward a Social Order Based on the Religion of Jesus." Kirby Page later reached for a two-part definition, labeling it "a magazine of Christian pacifism and Christian socialism."[44] David Shannon, in his history of the Socialist Party of America, identified *The World Tomorrow* as the "leading journal of liberal Christianity and Christian-motivated political radicalism."[45] Robert Moats Miller's classic work dealing with interwar Christian periodicals, *American Protestantism and Social Issues, 1919–1939*, resorted to describing the journal as representing "the non-Stalinist left"—true, but a negative definition at best.[46] Peace movement historians Charles Chatfield and Charles DeBenedetti called it "the foremost exponent of the Social Gospel"—also true in a limited sense.[47] Elsewhere, describing the magazine's approach, Chatfield called it the "preeminent voice of social critique."[48]

One reason that finding a neat epithet is so difficult is that the journal, at its peak in the late 1920s and early 1930s, represented a vast coalition of organizations and interests—Christian socialists, Christian pacifists, advocates for third-party politics, black interracial activists from the NAACP and National Urban League, Quakers, YMCA and YWCA leaders, revisionist history professors, Women's International League figures, Socialist Party leaders, modernist clergy, and emerging Marxist-"realist" theologians, to name a few. Indeed, its linking of various initials and acronyms rivaled any later New Dealer's organizational chart: Here were the FOR, the FCSO, the FSC, the LID, the LIPA, the WRI, WILPF, WPP, NAACP, and NUL, among others. Little wonder that Martin Marty characterized this world as one full of numerous little "fellowships" and "leagues."[49] Since the forming of coalitions had a central place in *The World Tomorrow*'s activities, following the journal's own life lets historians make connections with networks they had not anticipated. Similarly, examining the production of international thought at ecumenical world conferences means that, in addition to observing the contributions of Americans such as Reinhold Niebuhr and John Foster Dulles, one encounters currents emanating from many other quarters—postliberal theology flowing from Switzerland, anti-imperialist analyses coming from the Philippines and Korea, arguments about racial equality emerging among Japanese students, and arguments about national distinctiveness coming from Germany and Scandinavia, to pinpoint a few.

Across both case studies, between and among their distinctive approaches to Christian reflection on international relations, certain commonalities appear. Both enterprises, as will be seen, overlapped in their constituent networks of thinkers and intellectuals. More importantly, both exemplified in themselves the three characteristic features of interwar Christian internationalism identified above—the elaboration of enterprises devoted to producing a Christian knowledge and public engagement on international relations, a structure of thinking that rendered Christian universalism as antinationalist, and a broad antipathy to racism in world affairs. As far as the former, each enterprise provided a setting beyond the state and the academy in which international thought was produced that interrelated with mainstream "secular" international relations thinking. *The World Tomorrow* provided a space in which missionary internationalism merged with the revisionist historiography of the likes of Harry Elmer Barnes and Charles Beard and the anti-imperialism of Latin Americanists such as Samuel Guy Inman. Oxford 1937 saw major figures in international thought such as Alfred Zimmern, Oxford University's first professor of international relations, and Max Huber, former president of the Permanent Court of International Justice, blend ideas with twentieth-century theologians such as Reinhold Niebuhr and Emil Brunner. And not only did Oxford 1937 organizers "import" international relations experts to contribute to their conference, ecumenism made a longer-term contribution, an "export" into wider international thought. Three major thinkers heavily represented in international relations disciplinary textbooks—Reinhold Niebuhr, Martin Wight, and Herbert Butterfield—were all shaped significantly by this ecumenical internationalist milieu. And not least, later U.S. secretary of state and Oxford 1937 attendee John Foster Dulles owed much of his impetus in campaigning for U.S. sponsorship of postwar international organization to his experience at the Oxford conference.

Both *The World Tomorrow* and Oxford 1937 also exemplified the Christian critique of nationalism. Indeed, of all the aspects of interwar Christian internationalism, this was the most significant and yet remains the least well understood. Because of its importance to the wider field of the history of religion and foreign relations, it warrants further attention.

Christians against the Idea of a Christian Nation

It has long been acknowledged that the predominant way in which American Christians have understood their country's role in the world has been through the framework that construes America as a Christian nation. At times, the idea has been the subject of overt argument, such as when Cold War apologists—whether President Eisenhower; his secretary of state, John Foster Dulles; or their contemporary Billy Graham—pitted Christian America against atheistic Communism in the 1950s. So important was the assertion of this identity that U.S. paper currency changed its imprint to remind Americans where to place their trust.[50] In other, earlier times, the idea had been simply assumed, rather than asserted. When Americans were engaging with the world through missionaries, bankers, and marines in the early twentieth century, the notion that the world was divided into "Christian nations," such as America, and pagan nations, such as those to whom missionaries were sent, was so "obvious," so given, that it formed part of a pretheoretical background, the deep basis of practice.[51]

Indeed, one of the most striking features of the League of Nations debate was the fact that Christian supporters of the League and Christian opponents of the League both assumed the Christian nation framework. For supporters of Wilson, being a Christian nation formed the basis for understanding America's providential role in fulfilling historical destiny, redeeming the world, and ushering in the Kingdom of God on earth. For the "anti-internationalists" documented in Markku Ruotsila's work, America's status as a Christian nation meant it should not join the League, lest it be "unequally yoked" with "unChristian" nations in an international organization, an interpretation of the Second Epistle to the Corinthians made by means of dubious analogy. The ubiquity and force of the Christian nation framework was such that it animated both sides of the debate.[52]

Calls to preserve America's identity as a Christian nation have pervaded culture and history wars in the twenty-first century as well. Conservative Protestants in this regard have varied little from the declension narrative articulated by Jerry Falwell in his 1981 *Listen America!*, which in turn goes back, as Sacvan Bercovitch shows, to the jeremiads of the early national era.[53] They argue that America had better return to its roots as a Christian nation or suffer the consequences. With some exceptions, it has for the most part been Christians who have supported the idea of identifying America as a "Christian nation," while opponents of the idea have tended not to be Christians.[54] Such a phenomenon is perhaps not surprising; it is part of the power dynamic inherent in positioning Christianity as a moral establishment for the nation. What is striking about interwar Christian internationalism, however, is that we find Christians themselves critiquing and abandoning the idea of America as a Christian nation. And while David Hollinger has rightly pointed to ecumenists "giving themselves hell" over that same idea in the 1940s to 1960s, their self-criticism began two decades earlier.[55]

For the community of *The World Tomorrow*, the idea of America as a Christian nation could not be reconciled with the contrast they observed between Jesus's peace-making, self-sacrificial ethic on one hand, and the evidences of hubristic militarism, imperialism, and nationalism on the other. The imagined community into which they grafted readers was not coterminous with the nation-state; it was a transnational network of radicals who placed commitment to the ethics of Jesus above the nation. But Christians in America, they urged, needed to refuse in advance to provide the easy sanction for war they had historically offered; they needed to maintain with force the distinction between the ethical demands of Jesus and Uncle Sam. Meanwhile, ecumenists at Oxford 1937 saw the idea of a Christian nation, in the words of Brunner, one of the theologians present, as a "dangerous fiction."[56] Guided by new postliberal theological emphases, their logical starting point was, however, different from that of *The World Tomorrow*. They formed a critique of nationalism not from a reading of the biography of Jesus but from a recovered theology of the "Universal Church," a community in which nation and race were to be transcended, and a community, unlike Nazi Germany, that was in principle universal. Nationalism was irreconcilable with the idea of the church as a supranational community. For ecumenists at Oxford, it was a common ploy of nations to identify themselves with the cause of Christ, an example of the perennial tendency of the nation to associate itself with divinity and make itself an idol.

But for neither of the two enterprises examined here did rejection of the idea of Christian nationhood mean withdrawal from political participation. Rather, it meant involvement in politics on a different footing: the holding of a certain critical "distance" between their identity as Christians and their identification with the host culture of America.[57] Thus, paradoxically, while *The World Tomorrow* figures rejected the idea that America was Christian, they still wanted it to behave in a more Christian manner. The former was dialectically related to the latter. Christians, they argued, needed to work against the presence of the deep forces that caused war globally—and because it was their home, this included American political culture. In the mid-1930s, as *The World Tomorrow* network promoted a neutralist agenda for America, it was not because they considered the United States too virtuous to be enmeshed in foreign entanglements, but because they saw Christians in America as needing to ensure war was not waged in their name again. To editor Kirby Page, American churches were powerful sociological and political entities that would, for better or worse, exercise a strong influence over public debate on war, peace, and international conduct; his job was to shape such influence for the better.

For ecumenists at Oxford 1937, the rejection of Christian nationhood as a category related to their assertion that no nation could set itself up as part of divine revelation in the world, as was being witnessed in Nazi Party ideology in Germany. More broadly, Oxford delegates concluded, no nation could assert the national interest or national sovereignty as an ultimate moral norm. What was needed, they argued, was some check against the idea and practice of national sovereignty in international life. Thus, while *The World Tomorrow* community tended toward advocating neutralism, ecumenists returning from Oxford 1937 tended toward the opposite. American Christians cited the findings of the Oxford conference as a basis for their advocacy—regardless of their position for or against intervention—of American sponsorship in building a new international organization.

Missionary Origins

The distinctive nature of interwar Christian internationalism begs the question of its origins. What gave rise to its distinct approach to Christianity and nationhood? To date, most explanations of interwar Christian internationalism—where any have been offered—have relied on one of two explanations. First, the movement is presented as an offshoot of the enthusiasm surrounding President Wilson's League plans. Missionary historian Dana Robert offers such an argument by way of context. American and British Christian internationalism, she argues, was set within a "moral vision of one world that . . . stemmed from the idealism of Woodrow Wilson's Fourteen Points."[58] I argue that in fact the roots of interwar Christian internationalism predated Wilson's Fourteen Points and, in the long run—with the major exception of Dulles—the movement owed little to it. Whereas Wilsonian internationalism was "statist," in that it insisted on the redemptive power of the state in international order, Christian internationalists held out no such hope by the interwar period. And whereas the Wilsonian moment represented a high point of American messianic nationalism, the same was not true for the Christian internationalists after Wilson. Wilson's views on race—centered on notions of white supremacy—were equally far from the equalitarian Christian internationalists examined here.[59] While undoubtedly Wilsonianism affected the climate in which all internationalist movements operated in the 1920s, especially League of Nations enthusiasts, there is no ground for seeing it as a sufficient cause or point of origin for the distinctive character of the interwar Christian internationalism examined here.

A second explanation identifies Christian internationalism, including that of the Wilsonian moment, as an inevitable and logical fruit of the theological liberalism and Social Gospel theology that had developed in America in the late nineteenth and early twentieth centuries. There is a certain plausibility to this claim. Shortly before he died in 1918, America's most influential advocate of the Social Gospel, New York minister Walter Rauschenbusch, predicted that international relations would be among the tasks that the "men and women who are now young must take on their mind and their conscience for life and leave their children to finish."[60] The "Christianizing of international relations" constituted the logical extension of the Social Gospel. The ethical and theological demands were the same, only writ larger. "Before the War the social gospel dealt with social classes; today it is being translated into international terms."[61] As will be seen in the next chapter, important aspects of the Social Gospel did shape the Christian internationalist project—especially its understanding of sin as structural, its emphasis on the progressive realization of community in organizational life, and its interpretation of Jesus primarily as an historical, ethical exemplar.

However, that explanation can only take us so far. There was, in fact, no inevitable development from late nineteenth-century and early twentieth-century Social Gospel thinking to the Christian internationalism of the interwar period. After all, the Social Gospel had been expressed in a variety of positions on American foreign relations. "It seems to me that God, with infinite wisdom and skill, is training the Anglo-Saxon race for an hour sure to come," wrote leading Social Gospel minister Josiah Strong, relishing the possibility of further U.S. expansion in the Western hemisphere. Anglo-Saxons had a "genius for colonizing," he enthused.[62] For Washington Gladden, next to Rauschenbusch one of the Social Gospel's leading exponents, the Social Gospel had reinforced his vision of American exceptionalism. The foreign policies of presidents McKinley, Roosevelt, and Taft made them equivalent to "great missionaries of the cross."[63] And, in early work for his German Baptist denomination, Rauschenbusch had used his pen to advertise German theological education as part of an effort to ensure white people's upper hand "against the blacks of the South and the seething yellow flocks beyond the Pacific."[64] Interwar Christian internationalists' emphases on racial equality, anti-imperialism, and anti-exceptionalism stood them in stark contrast to their Social Gospel forebears.

The origins and character of interwar Christian internationalism in fact owed more to the missionary enterprise than to Wilsonianism, the Social Gospel, or any other factor. Already in the 1910s, the writings of John Mott, Joseph Oldham, and Sidney Gulick signaled the emergence of a missionary discourse on international relations that was distinct from the legalist and institutionalist emphases of liberal internationalism. In contrast to the predominantly Eurocentric focus of the latter, these missionaries maintained a concern with the Asia Pacific region and Africa.[65] Each stressed the cultural and racial elements of the world situation—particularly the racial antipathy provoked by immigration laws, exploitative tourism practices, and assumptions of intrinsic superiority in a world that was rapidly "shrinking." With this background, it is not surprising that John R. Mott's YMCA missionary network was instrumental in forming the world's first international non-governmental organization devoted to cultural diplomacy and race relations in the Pacific in the 1920s: the Institute of Pacific Relations.[66] The exposure of missionaries to actual points of intercultural, interracial, and international relations in the Asia-Pacific, together with their relative sensitivity to the currents of the new Asian nationalisms, fostered and shaped their vocational transfer from missions to internationalism more than Wilson or Rauschenbusch did.

But interwar Christian internationalism was even more shaped by the profound and far-reaching crisis in missiology that emerged in the 1920s.[67] Such a crisis—as has been well documented by historians of missions from Charles Forman to William Hutchison and Grant Wacker—consisted of an unprecedented groundswell of criticism of the missionary enterprise so that its very validity came into question as never before in the era of modern missions.[68] As Hutchison has shown, many critics were liberal-modernists for whom the traditional evangelical claims of salvation through Christ—and hence a theological basis for traditional missions—were no longer tenable. John D. Rockefeller Jr., and the famous "Laymen's Inquiry" he funded under the leadership of William Ernest Hocking, represented the liberal-modernist critique.[69] So too did Pearl Buck, novelist and daughter of missionaries in China, who exemplified a revulsion not merely toward the association between missions and political imperialism, but also toward the cultural and spiritual "imperialism" inherent in preaching an exclusivist Gospel that called people to leave other religions in favor of Christ.[70] Meanwhile, at the other end of the spectrum, the missionary enterprise came under fire from conservative fundamentalist leaders who believed that missionary boards had been so corrupted by liberalism that they were now useless for missions traditionally understood. J. Gresham Machen's voice was among the most articulate of this camp.[71]

In between these polar positions—seeking to refashion a middle-ground consensus—were several of the major leaders of the YMCA and the Student Volunteer Movement (SVM), such as John R. Mott, Robert E. Speer (who represented Presbyterian missions as well as the SVM), and Sherwood Eddy. Many of these leaders and many others in mainline seminaries and in ecumenical forums such as the International Missionary Committee were, like Eddy, liberal evangelicals rather than modernists (Speer and Mott were more conservative in theology than Eddy) and correspondingly sought to salvage the kerygmatic aspects of the traditional missionary enterprise rather than discard them entirely. They insisted on the perennial validity of missions, but argued that only in a reconstituted mode, whereby the Gospel was shorn of its association with Western imperialism, was the enterprise viable. This left them in the position of decrying political imperialism while still, in Speer's words, retaining the "fine spiritual imperialism" of the Gospel of salvation in Christ.[72]

This middle-ground response—of defending missions while seeking to reconstitute them—was where most of the intellectual energy came from that animated Christian internationalism in the 1920s. As these missionary leaders sought to reconstruct missions on a new footing, they were compelled to engage with the efforts and demands of those in non-Western, missionary-"receiving" countries to obtain independence from relations of Western tutelage and to establish equality and mutuality. As Forman notes, in the interwar period, missionary theorists responded with "a new appreciation for the culture of the East and an emphasis on emerging churches in Asia and Africa." They sought to foster a new ethos that Forman characterizes as "ecumenical sharing"—an emphasis on "the need for churches around the world to help each other understand the Christian faith." As the process of "indigenization" occurred, they hoped, each national and cultural grouping would contribute its particular strengths and emphases to the common good of the ecumenical, supranational church.[73]

Along with the stress on ecumenical solidarity came two closely related ideas vital to the character of interwar Christian internationalism. One was that racial equality was an essential but lost Christian truth that needed to be recovered in the face of rising scientific and political racism. The other was that precisely because of failures in areas such as race relations and international relations, the locus of Christianity could no longer be seen as the West. America and other Western nations could not claim to be "Christian nations" in a sea of non-Christian nations; the term simply had no validity.

In the 1920s, an outpouring of books, lectures, and addresses from missionary leaders made the forceful case that notions of white supremacy, whatever their apparent grounding in science and anthropology, were not consonant with true, apostolic Christianity. Not only were such views sub-Christian, they argued; they were in themselves a singular cause of global unrest and injustice. The New Testament idea of trans-ethnic solidarity in the body of Christ needed to be recovered and applied to present-day race relations at large, they argued, frequently citing or alluding to Pauline passages like Ephesians 2:14 ("for he is our peace, who hath made both one") or Galatians 3:28 ("There is neither Jew nor Greek, there is neither bond nor free, there is neither male nor female: for ye are all one in Christ Jesus").[74] Senior missionary figure Joseph H. Oldham, who became the intellectual architect of Oxford 1937, used his book *Christianity and the Race Problem* (1924) to survey contemporary scientific literature on race and juxtapose it with Christian theology.[75] Robert Speer, president of the Federal Council of Churches after 1920, convened a special commission, "Church and Race Relations." With that body's and the Missionary Education Movement's support, and with input from around the world, Speer published a book entitled *Of One Blood* (an allusion to the Apostle Paul's speech in Acts 17:26), which he hoped would "bring the white world short up against the folly of the proposition laid down by Lothrop Stoddard."[76]

But it was not simply a case of missionaries and ecumenists looking *at* diversity; as will be seen in chapter 4, they voiced their views on race in partnership with nonwhite leaders in emerging ecumenical organizations. Missionary and ecumenical organizations provided vital spaces for nonwhite Christian leaders from Asia, Africa, and the United States to give voice to protests about existing race relations and to assert their demands for recognition of racial equality on an international stage. At the 1922 Peking conference of the World Student Christian Federation (an ecumenical organization essentially founded by Mott and closely connected to the YMCA), a special study section on "Christianity and International and Interracial Problems," dominated by Japanese students, produced a text known as the "Peking Resolutions." These announced their belief "in the fundamental equality of all the races and nations of mankind."[77] Another example was the landmark 1928 world conference of the International Missionary Committee in Jerusalem, which featured a study section on race relations headed by black YMCA luminary Max Yergan and others such as John Hope, president of Morehouse College in Atlanta. Through their reports and recommendations, which were stridently anti-imperialist in their analysis, the section steered the International Missionary Committee to officially resolve that "any discrimination against human beings on the ground of race or color" was a "denial of the teaching of Jesus."[78]

Closely related to criticisms of America and other imperial powers' record on race relations were deep questions over the legitimacy of calling America and other Western missionary-sending nations "Christian nations." The term, and the imperialistic relationship it helped sustain, was no longer tenable, according to missionary leaders seeking to reconstitute the enterprise. Mainline Protestant missionaries of the 1890s to the 1910s had argued confidently that Christianity needed to be adopted by countries such as China and Japan so as to ensure their modernization processes were successful and ethical in character; the implication was that America could export a model to be applied globally.[79] Christian "principles" were the key to building a happy and just social order. By the 1920s, this narrative, if not in tatters, was widely viewed with deep skepticism; instead, many missionaries and those with whom they were in contact argued that Christian nations had not demonstrated the superiority of their own social and political orders. They had failed to meet their own Christian ethical standards in intergroup relations, as seen in the mass killing of the Great War, in the race for imperialistic expansion, or in ongoing racial injustice. Leading liberal missions theorist, Daniel Johnson Fleming, in his classic 1925 work, *Whither Bound in Missions*, memorably captured this shift, with his challenge to the traditional cartography of missions, both literal and metaphorical: "It has long been the custom, when making missionary maps, to paint the sending countries white and the receiving countries black. In recent years, however, we have been startled into the realization that the West is part of the non-Christian world, and that there is no sharp division into lands that are white and those that are black unless, indeed, the West is of a deeper black because it has had access to Christ so long."[80] The old "moral mapping" of the missionary enterprise, to use Miroslav Volf's term, had lost its coherence.[81]

Organization of the Book

Proof of the importance of missionaries to interwar Christian internationalism can be seen in the very specific, immediate ties they had to the two sites of collective deliberation examined in this book. Sherwood Eddy and John R. Mott each personally influenced, respectively, *The World Tomorrow* and the Oxford 1937 conference. Eddy took on much of the cost of running *The World Tomorrow* after 1926, and acted as the main financial support of its editor—his close friend and former YMCA staffer Kirby Page. Meanwhile, John R. Mott

continued to be the most influential American in the early ecumenical movement. Having founded and led the World Student Christian Federation since
1895, he became head of the International Missionary Council in 1921 and
later the chairman at the Oxford 1937 world conference. Part 1 of this book
deals with *The World Tomorrow*, part 2 with Oxford.

Chapter 1 follows *The World Tomorrow* editor Kirby Page from his early career
as an aspiring YMCA missionary world traveler with Sherwood Eddy to his
vocation as an independent foreign policy publicist in the mid-1920s. It explores how Page's interests expanded from mere personal pacifism in 1917 to
encompass a wider concern with American imperialism, immigration, and racial politics by the mid-1920s, a matrix of concerns he took to his editorial
role at the journal. Page sought to juxtapose recent research into the historical
Jesus with the problems of nationalism and imperialism in the American twentieth century, a project in which he was not alone, but of which he was arguably the major exponent of his time.

Chapter 2 introduces a theoretical framework with which to read *The World
Tomorrow*—one that fuses an old category, "foreign policy public," and a new
term, "counterpublic." With Page as editor, the journal presented a distinctive
mix of muckraking rage and middlebrow didacticism as it sought to educate
readers about the hidden realities of American imperialism in Latin America
and American militarism everywhere, from colleges to *Cosmopolitan* magazine.
In the 1930s, as *The World Tomorrow* became interested in disrupting wider public
discourse, it amassed American clergy opinion in a series of highly publicized
surveys. The oppositional nature of the journal was at its peak when U.S. Army
chief Douglas MacArthur penned an open letter condemning the nearly trea-
sonous internationalism of the journal.

The final chapter in part 1 begins with the sudden death of the journal due
to a funding crisis in 1934. It then explores the two, seemingly contradictory,
impulses of the radical Christian internationalist coalition that had been behind
the journal—one represented by those such as Kirby Page, Dorothy Detzer,
and H. C. Engelbrecht, who went on to advocate for American neutralism in
the 1930s, and who influenced the debate surrounding the Nye Committee,
commencing in 1934, and the other, represented by those such as Reinhold
Niebuhr, who went on to advocate for American interventionism at risk of
war in the crisis of 1938–1941. Reading closely the journal's associations with
Niebuhr's Fellowship of Socialist Christians, the chapter focuses on the emergence of realism and its new "feeling rules."

Part 2 turns to ecumenical world conferences as sites of collective deliberation. Chapter 4 sets out to challenge historiographies that have seen the

ecumenical movement merely as a forum for the extension of American power, and points instead to the mutuality of influences and forces shaping the movement. It argues for interwar ecumenism's place in the history of international thought and interwar internationalism, rather than simply in the ecclesial prehistory to the World Council of Churches. Surveying the major conferences of the 1920s—Peking 1922, Stockholm 1925, and Jerusalem 1928—the chapter highlights the major themes and debates in 1920s ecumenical internationalism: namely, the stress on racial equality as a matter of theological confession as well as political activism, and the unresolved tensions between Anglo-American social Christianity and Continental theology, which both politically and philosophically was suspicious of an internationalism shaped merely by American "*aktivismus*."

Beginning with the long shadow cast by the attempted nationalization of the German evangelical church, chapter 5 explores ecumenists' newly developing theology of the nation and international life. The chapter first examines the sources of a new postliberal theological consensus that pervaded the conference, and which managed to transcend, to a significant extent, the divide between Anglo-American and Continental social Christianity that hampered 1920s ecumenical efforts. In doing so, it traces the way conference organizers like Oldham deliberately cultivated relationships with both American realist theologians (Reinhold Niebuhr and colleagues) and Continental neo-orthodox theologians such as Emil Brunner. The new postliberal theological consensus stressed afresh the importance of the Universal Church, appealed anew to the Bible, appropriated older understandings of sin, and critiqued Progressivist views of history. In specialized "sections," delegates applied these theological emphases as a kind of filter through which to vet the contribution of big-name contributors to the conference, such as Alfred Zimmern, the Marquess of Lothian, Phillip Kerr (future British ambassador to the United States), and John Foster Dulles. In their characteristically dialectical style, Oxford delegates critiqued simplistic equations between liberal internationalism and Christianity, and likewise denounced nationalism and racism as idolatry and sin.

Chapter 6 asks whether the postliberal internationalist consensus forged at Oxford was able to make an "Atlantic crossing" and take root in American soil. American delegates and organizers pursued a vigorous program of dissemination and publicity, including replica mini-conferences in American cities that discussed and digested the reports of the Oxford conference. Meanwhile, utilizing course catalogs and calendars from Union Theological Seminary, where Oxford attendees Niebuhr, John Bennett, Henry Pit Van Dusen, and other ecumenists taught, the chapter explores the way the seminary, together with the closely associated journal *Christianity and Crisis*, instantiated realists' embeddedness in global ecumenism. Niebuhr's realism preserved part of the Oxford consensus, its dialectical critique of nationalism, but saw another part, the primacy of the church, or ecclesiology, slip from prominence.

The final chapter tracks the work of one of the most politically influential instruments of 1940s Christian internationalism, the Federal Council of Churches' Commission on a Just and Durable Peace. The chapter locates the roots of the commission in the post-Oxford ecumenical network, highlighting the way ecumenical Protestants sought to base their advocacy of a new American internationalism on the norms agreed upon at the recent world conference. Focusing on Dulles's leadership of the commission, though, the chapter explores how Dulles over time reconstituted Christian internationalism—Americanizing it in the process. As Dulles instrumentalized churches in the service of the nation, his internationalism began to appear more like the messianic nationalism he and his colleagues had spent their energies opposing.

PART I

Radical Christian Internationalism
at *The World Tomorrow*

Chapter 1

Anti-imperialism for Jesus

When a regional student secretary of the YMCA asked Kirby Page if he had ever considered "getting a job with John R. Mott or Sherwood Eddy and traveling over the earth," Page recalled, "the suggestion made my mind whirl."[1] The prospect would have been dizzying indeed. Page, a young Texan graduate student at the University of Chicago, had an interest in history, skills in stenography and clerical work, and impressive tennis abilities—but nothing that would immediately suggest a career with two of America's most well-known and celebrated missionary world travelers. While he was enthusiastic about missions and had even written his Chicago master's thesis on the history of the YMCA in China, such an appointment was more than he would have dared hope for. Page had been one of tens of thousands of students to hear Mott, Eddy, and other luminaries like William Jennings Bryan speak at Student Volunteer Movement (SVM) meetings and to "pledge" his life to foreign missions in response. But Eddy and Mott's international cultural and political eminence, though perhaps difficult to imagine today, was considerable. They had forged relationships with political leaders at the highest levels in East Asia; Mott was courted by successive U.S. presidents, with President Wilson nominating him as his first choice for ambassador to China.[2] As David Hollinger puts it, such late Victorian missionaries were the "bullfighters" of American culture: the heroes whose exploits were told and retold in the press and around lantern slide projectors.[3] Standing apart even from mainline missionary colleagues, YMCA missionaries like Eddy and Mott in particular were so prominent in the 1900s to the 1910s that contemporaries overseas likened them to a geopolitical force in their own right.[4]

As it turned out, Page did indeed find himself working for Eddy in 1916, after applying for a vacancy as his personal secretary. His experience in stenography—vital for the frenetic pace of steam-driven travel and telegraphic correspondence—gave Page an entrée into a world of missionary internationalism. His work with Sherwood Eddy, however, was at once the fulfillment of long-held hopes and a radical departure from them. Page did travel the world. But rather than engage primarily in the foreign missionary enterprise, Page used his exposure to world affairs and his affiliation with Eddy to become one of mainline Protestantism's most prominent and radical analysts of world affairs, taking up the emerging Christian internationalist outlook of the missionary enterprise and, in the early to mid 1920s, directing it at the contemporary politics of American imperialism, nationalism, and militarism.

Connected to the YMCA missionary milieu of Eddy and Mott on one hand and the radicalism of *The World Tomorrow* magazine on the other, Page's career embodied the links between mainline Protestants and the new, radical, anti-imperialist strand of Christian internationalism that emerged in the 1920s. Indeed, not only did Page exemplify such links, he played a leading role in forging them. Andrew Preston has suggested that "radical" is not a designation that fits Page. "Though he was a Socialist," writes Preston, "Page was no radical; a former Student Volunteer and YMCA secretary, his was very much a mainstream, mainline vision."[5] Preston is right to note Page's pedigree. But Page's significance lay precisely in his ability to join the mainline to the radical. Through organizations such as the Fellowship for a Christian Social Order (FCSO) and *The World Tomorrow*, Page was instrumental in forging a new network and a new voice that joined elements of the liberal Protestant establishment, especially the YMCA, SVM, and Federal Council of Churches, to other, more radical and politically marginal groups such as the Quaker-based Fellowship of Reconciliation and the Socialist Party. In doing so, he knitted together a new network of radicals out of old mainline Protestant fabric. When John Nevin Sayre, the owner of the ailing *World Tomorrow*, sought Page out as editor in 1926, it was largely because he knew this about Page.

While many other American internationalists and peace activists of the 1920s gave their attention to international law or institutions—the League of Nations, the World Court, or the Outlawry of War campaigns, for example—the network closest to Page focused on what recent scholars might call "cultural forces," on what they saw as the lurking influences of militarism, imperialism, and nationalism in American life. Page made it his mission to question the religious sanction American Protestants typically gave to their nation's foreign policy. Not only did he wield the muckraker's spotlight to expose U.S. wrong-doing overseas as others did in the 1920s, he juxtaposed such contemporary phenomena with the political and ethical choices of the historical Jesus and attempted to drive a wedge between nationalism, militarism, and imperialism and Christians' contemporary profession of Jesus's name.[6] Page's career rep-resented one long argument that the politics of Jesus could not be aligned with the status quo in American foreign relations.

This chapter offers a prehistory to Page's years at *The World Tomorrow*. This background offers a vital glimpse into how an aspiring YMCA mission-ary became an anti-imperialist. Page's early revulsion to war, which crystal-lized for him while working with Sherwood Eddy in wartime Great Britain, soon developed into an internationalism that blended YMCA piety with So-cial Gospel critiques of structural sin. Page's fresh appraisal of the historical Jesus as an antimilitarist, in which he drew on then-recent New Testament scholarship on first-century politics, aligned with his simultaneous "discov-ery" of the recent and contemporary history of American imperialism. Page's conceptual mapping—which provided a basis for his *World Tomorrow* work after 1926—consisted in a distinctive joining of ethical primitivism, focused on recovering what Jesus did in his context, with a new revisionist and anti-exceptionalist understanding of America as enmeshed in universal war-making forces.

From Missionary to Antiwar Publicist

Growing up in Texas, Page had not given a thought to the ethics of war, peace, or foreign policy. He recalled no conversations about war when he attended Drake University.[7] Indeed, right through to his first overseas trip for the YMCA in 1916, it appears unlikely that such questions crossed his mind. That all changed with his first international assignment with Sherwood Eddy—although not in the way either would have anticipated. As Sherwood Eddy's personal secretary in the YMCA, Page's first job was to assist him in preaching in the training camps of British soldiers. Page recalled his "amazement at Sherwood's power over audiences," which continued to grow "as I heard him night after night." As the United States was not involved in the war yet, Eddy and Page served with the British YMCA, wearing British uniforms. Yet despite don-ning the same colors, the two soon came to adopt drastically different views of the war effort. The Allied cause was, for Eddy, a crusade worthy of Christ.

In his wartime tract entitled *The Right to Fight*, he condemned the "growing menace of Prussian militarism"—its atrocities, its ambitions for world conquest, and its violation of Belgium.[8] As a YMCA chaplain, he urged Allied soldiers in France that this war effort was "a kind of holy crusade, a half-divine crucifixion of humanity for saving the world." He was pleased that America had entered the war on Good Friday: It befitted the redemptive, sacrificial role the nation was to play in world history.[9]

But Kirby Page meanwhile began to form his own convictions about war. When off duty in London, he soon became acquainted with the Quaker pacifist Henry Hodgkin, founder of the British and International Fellowship of Reconciliation (who also assisted in the establishment of the American Fellowship in 1917), as well as Maude Royden, the female pacifist minister of City Temple. It was during conversations with Hodgkin and Royden that Page began to question the ethics of armed conflict. The end result, as he recalled it, was a personal conviction against war that remained with him the rest of his life.[10] Page's conviction was that "the religion of Jesus"—by which he primarily meant the ethical example offered by the historical Jesus—had no place for endorsing war. The primitivism of his Campbellite Disciples of Christ background (Page studied Divinity as an Undergraduate at the Disciples's own Drake University) provided an important basis for his adoption of Quaker-oriented pacifism. Just as Alexander Campbell, the antebellum founder of the Disciples denomination, had urged the modern church to strip away all historical accretions and return to the pure practice of the New Testament, so too Page argued historical Christianity had departed from the original pattern; war was an aberration from the "primitive" first ideal.[11]

Independent of his being a pacifist, Page's involvement in Eddy's global YMCA network played a vital role in the development of his approach to international affairs. During the war—and increasingly so after—Page's association with Eddy gave him opportunities for travel, exposure to world affairs, and international contacts that would have been hard to attain in other ways. For example, although, as a declared pacifist, Page was banned from travel in the war zones under YMCA policy, he still travelled with Eddy and several other missionaries through Asia in 1917–1918, meeting with and interviewing Sun Yat-sen, among others.[12] And when employment with Eddy was temporarily impossible in 1918, Page worked instead for Eddy's YMCA superior, the internationally famous John R. Mott, President Wilson's first choice for the ambassadorship to China in 1913. Indeed, with Mott's high establishment prestige and ease of access to several U.S. presidents, it was not surprising that the first letter Page wrote as Mott's secretary was addressed to Woodrow Wilson.[13] Being associated with Eddy and Mott at the high point of their influence, Page was taken into their nearly antiquated world of "religious statesmanship"—the term itself an artifact of its period, and one that connoted the influence and access Eddy and Mott enjoyed among political leaders internationally.[14] Whereas, in the 1910s, Eddy and Mott's religious statesmanship was characterized by a broad affinity with the overall direction of the foreign relations of the United States, in the 1920s, Eddy and Page's internationalism took on an increasingly oppositional and radical hue.

In the wake of the war, and around their divergent views of that conflict, Eddy and Page together articulated a new expression of the Social Gospel that stressed international and interracial justice. Back in New York, they forged a partnership that became an institution—a two-man enterprise—devoted to promoting their vision of a "Christian social order." Able to live off the interest accrued from his father's estate, Sherwood Eddy used his money in the 1920s to become an informal philanthropist supporting causes that fit with his internationalism and Social Gospel radicalism.[15] And it is likely that the largest sole beneficiary of Eddy's funding was Kirby Page. After trialing Page as a personal editorial and research assistant, Eddy eventually financed Page's move out of parish church work and into a career as author and speaker, remaining his primary financial support throughout the 1920s–1930s.[16] Much of Eddy and Page's work was done together. From their shared office space at YMCA headquarters in Manhattan, the two often acted as a publicity bureau—part of an army of "irrepressible pamphleteers," as Devere Allen later lampooned them.[17] Working through Doubleday and Doran publishers, they published hundreds of thousands of copies of pamphlets—authored by them and others—in their "World Problems" series. They crisscrossed the country on the collegiate YMCA circuit, speaking on international relations and other "danger zones of the social order." They endorsed and republished anti-imperialist texts such as Anti-Imperialist League stalwart Moorefield Storey and Marcial P. Lichauco's *The Philippines and the United States* (1926), and organized petitions addressed to the federal government for causes such as Filipino independence and recognition of Russia.[18] There was also international travel. Page embarked five times on Eddy's annual traveling seminar. Through it he made contacts with Christian Labourites and Socialists in Britain, toured the French-occupied Ruhr in 1923, and visited Russia on the seminar's first and famous visit in 1926. On these journeys, and on extra travels with Eddy, he stitched together a network of international colleagues who would write for *The World Tomorrow*.

Internationalist Theology

With Eddy's de facto institutional support, then, what kind of Christian internationalism did Page develop and promote? In the first place, Page retained the liberal evangelical emphasis on personal piety and spirituality that he and Eddy inherited from YMCA-SVM culture. His turn to radical internationalism did not imply, to him at least, that individual spiritual encounter with God mattered less. But, if anything, personal relationship with Jesus and his Spirit was reframed as a way of finding the "resources" to live as a radical—a selling point that Page thought made his Christian radicalism compare favorably to secular or materialist radical cousins. For several decades, beginning in the early 1920s, Page wrote books deliberately according to a pattern of topical balance. Each year he would write something on war and international questions, something on economics and social problems, and something on Christian discipleship and devotional spirituality. Among his first works from 1921–1922, for example, were *The Sword or the Cross,* which made his case for peace, another Federal Council of Churches "discussion manual" on the ethics of economic relations, and a book on Christian spirituality entitled *Something More.*[19] Around the *Abolition of War* (1924), *Imperialism and Nationalism* (1925), and *National Defense* (1931), he also wrote *Living Creatively* (1932), *Living Prayerfully* (1941), and several other works, deliberately alternating "between individual nurture and challenge to social action."[20]

This rhythm was also reflected in his own approach to piety and spiritual experience. With freedom to use his time as he wished, he spent half a year speaking and half a year withdrawing for study and writing: a dialectic of output and input. Like Eddy and the generation of student volunteers converted in the Dwight Moody era, Page, even in his most radical years, maintained the "morning watch," a discipline of daily private Bible study, contemplation, and prayer fostered by the pietistic-Methodist strains of evangelicalism in the YMCA. Page encouraged readers—radicals, pacifists, and socialists included— like him to seek the strength of Christ personally in their cause. If people would "saturate themselves daily in the mind of Christ" and "spend time in conscious communion with the God he so luminously reveals," then "building the new society will become more joyous and challenging. For men in every age, Jesus is the way, the truth, and the life."[21]

But while Page retained much of the piety and rhetorical styling of his YMCA liberal evangelicalism, the engine room of his Christian internationalism was the way he combined Social Gospel emphases with new concern for international affairs. One crucial aspect of the Social Gospel for Page was its stress on structural, or "solidaristic" sin. Studying the New Testament at Drake University, Page read Walter Rauschenbusch and Washington Gladden, and, as he later reflected, he learned from them the possibilities of "sinning by syndicate."[22] But the significance of Page's work lay in the way he applied such an approach not merely to the traditional Social Gospel concerns of Christian socialism and economic democracy at home in America but sought instead to elaborate with considerable specificity how structural sin manifested itself in America's relations with the world. Because of this, the negative, critical side of Page's work was always arguably stronger and more pronounced than the constructive; before it was a call to build, it was a call to repent.

Most significantly for his own work and that of *The World Tomorrow*, he tied his concern with structural sin to the growing belief among intellectuals of the 1920s, such as Walter Lippmann, that foreign relations *ought to be* subject to democratic control.[23] Public opinion mattered because it was instrumental in shaping the environment in which foreign policymakers governed and had to justify their governance. By not contributing to better public opinion, Page argued, everyday American Protestants could be engaged in sins of complicity with their country's racist and imperialist foreign policies. For example, in a major 1926 address to students on "International Relations in the Light of the Religion of Jesus," Page urged his listeners that they each had "a two-fold responsibility." As well as reforming their conduct and attitudes in actual, "personal relations with individuals of other races and nationalities," they also had to take responsibility for the "creation of the kind of public opinion which will break down the mental and emotional barriers erected by nationalism." Personal relationships were increasingly mediated and affected by impersonal institutions and thus, "much of our present day sinning," Page argued, "is done at long range."[24]

At the heart of Page's internationalism was the Social Gospel's emphasis on the historical Jesus as an exemplar of ethical principles. Like many of his fellow Protestants with liberal and modernist tendencies in the 1920s, Page downplayed what he saw as useless bickering over doctrine. In his major 1929 work, *Jesus or Christianity*—billed by its publishers as offering "foundations for the *World Tomorrow*"—Page argued organized religion was archaic and irrelevant. Jesus cared more about "social ethics" than contemporary church leaders who displayed an "excessive emphasis upon theological beliefs." Page expressed surprise and bemusement that many churches in America still cared about theological documents such as the Westminster Confession or the Nicene Creed— an attitude well at odds with the neo-orthodox and postliberal currents that emerged in ecumenical circles in the 1930s, as will be discussed in part 2.[25]

While not alone in his attitude to orthodox doctrine, Page stood out in the way he developed a historical-biographical reading of Jesus as an anti-imperialist and internationalist. He drew on recent biblical scholarship to make his arguments, especially that of Columbia University's New Testament scholar Vladimir G. Simkhovitch who, by reading Josephus's *Antiquities* afresh, had placed Jesus of Nazareth in a political-military context.[26] For Page, Simkhovitch revealed how Jesus's life could be read in the terms of the "human problems" of nationalism, militarism, and imperialism—which were the categories of his own internationalist analysis. Just as Jesus refused to take up the nationalist and militarist proposals in his day, so Christians in the 1920s needed to refuse the same. "It is impossible to believe," Page wrote, "that Jesus could have failed to consider seriously the proposal of the zealots and others of his followers that he should lead them against Rome." With the masses at his disposal, Page asked, why did Jesus not do as a typical messianic king should? Why did he not use military means to defend national honor and drive out the imperial oppressor, thus establishing the Kingdom of God? Page answered that Jesus had seen "the futility of the military method" and had "recognized in it a fundamental contradiction of the way of life which he had chosen as his own."[27]

To build an ethic or politics on the answer to "What would Jesus do?" was neither new nor unique in American Protestantism, but it was Kirby Page who, arguably more than any other, employed the method in reflection on international affairs. Progressives and urban reformers in the late nineteenth and early twentieth centuries had put the formula to frequent work, wondering what Christ would do if he came to violent Chicago, for example.[28] Nor was such speculation restricted to Progressives. Bruce Barton's 1925 book, *The Man Nobody Knows: A Discovery of the Real Jesus,* cast Jesus as "the great advertiser of his own day."[29] The biographical approach was eminently flexible. Page took the method in a different direction again. A typical pamphlet of Page's, entitled *Was Jesus a Patriot?*, exemplified his approach. Jesus was a *true* patriot, Page argued, in that he believed in the universal solidarity of mankind and the idea that "above all nations is humanity." Page felt contemporary Christians needed to reclaim the meaning of patriotism from "arch militarists," who stressed national loyalty and interest.[30] Later, as editor at *The World Tomorrow*, Page advertised a series of articles premised on the same logic of contrast. Entitled "Would Jesus Be a Christian Today?," the series included pieces on whether Jesus "would be an imperialist," whether he would "uphold capitalism," and whether he would "discriminate against other races." And in a nod to Barton, the series also included a piece questioning whether Jesus in fact "would be a success."[31]

Juxtaposing events in first-century Palestine with twentieth-century America begged the question of what happened in between. Here Page answered with a critique of church history and a call for a pre-Constantinian ethic. In *Jesus or Christianity*, he argued that the early Christians had maintained a rightful distance from war and imperialism so long as they remained a persecuted minority. As the church became more powerful, drawing closer to the forces of empire, it had betrayed the example and teachings of Jesus. Since then, organized Christianity had not only been forced into compromises, it consistently offered divine sanction to warfare, nationalism, imperialism, and other atrocities. Nothing short of a new departure was needed for the true religion of Jesus to have effect, according to Page.[32]

Decrying doctrine and theology, Page in fact made a theology of his own out of his historical method. For Page, Jesus provided an ethical template that could be transplanted and applied to the democratic control American Christians theoretically exercised over their country's foreign policy. But the absences in Page's theology produced new presences. His eschewal of the eschatological and apocalyptic notes in the Gospels left him open to a Progressivist postmillennial view of history: an almost unspoken assumption in his work that made it easier for erstwhile "realists" to dismiss what sounded like "optimism" in the critical atmosphere of the late 1930s. His disavowal of organized religion and ecclesiology led him at times to imply that America, the nation, rather than the church, was the agent that should—but alas, did not—apply Jesus's values. His rendering of Jesus's views on economic and social life sounded, at points, more like Eugene Debs or Walter Rauschenbusch's vision of fraternal socialism than anything from first-century Palestine. Naturally enough, Page's present filtered his historical retrieval of the primitive Jesus.

But if Page's work was all about juxtaposing the historical Jesus with contemporary American foreign relations, his greatest contribution lay in naming and analyzing the nature of the latter. As with his theology, he approached his analysis of American world affairs by means of history. Although he lacked training in the field of diplomatic history or the emerging discipline of international relations (but did have a master's degree in history from the University of Chicago), Page managed to ride the crest of the new wave of revisionist historiography on U.S. foreign relations and war by reframing the United States as one imperial, war-making power among others. Indeed, in his framing and argumentation he actually went ahead of and anticipated the revisionists of the period: This was a case of the middlebrow popularizer outpacing the scholars whose work he would later diffuse.[33] Harry Elmer Barnes, one of the most important revisionist historians of the period, acknowledged Page's role in this regard: "In recent years no other American has been more active in his efforts to promote intelligence in thought and action in the United States with respect to international affairs than Kirby Page," he wrote in a scholarly review in 1926.[34] As Page developed his anti-exceptionalist view of American history and began to stress what he saw as the hidden realities of American commercial expansion, race relations, and imperialism, he developed the analytical orientation that characterized radical Christian internationalism in the 1920s. His approach not only shaped the career of *The World Tomorrow* magazine when he assumed its editorship in 1926, it permeated the movement for which the periodical spoke.

Discovering American Imperialism

In the first half of the 1920s, Page's concerns quickly and notably widened from a basic pacifist renunciation of war to a wider analysis of "international relations" that encompassed imperialism, racism, and nationalism. But it was his intellectual encounter with the history of American imperialism that formed the leading edge of this wider application of revisionist logic. Discovering American imperialism compelled Page to dispense with an exceptionalist frame for interpreting the history of American foreign relations and to look at his country with newly critical eyes. His gradual development from part revisionist to full revisionist, from pacifist to anti-imperialist and anti-exceptionalist, can be traced in his writings between 1923 and 1926, in the same publications that cemented his vocation as one of American Protestantism's most outspoken and radical interpreters of world affairs in the 1920s.

Page's first major work on war, *War: Its Causes, Consequences and Cure* (1923), signaled his place in the mainline, mainstream Protestant vision Preston notes was characteristic of Page. Tightly organized and edited, the book received instant praise from high places in the liberal Protestant establishment. John R. Mott ensured the book was supplied to all YMCA secretaries. The Federal Council of Churches' Sidney Gulick circulated it to fifty-three thousand clergy, with a letter of recommendation enclosed. Even Mohandas Gandhi published the work serially in twenty parts in his magazine *Young Men of India*. Within three months of is publication, sales of *War* reached one hundred thousand.[35] The Federal Council of Churches' longtime ecumenist, Samuel McCrea Cavert, claimed the book had "probably done more than any other single publication to bring the ministers and other Christian leaders sharply face-to-face with the question as to what they are going to say about war."[36]

The book also showed Page at the beginning of a trajectory. There were signs of his revisionist reading of the war, but the implications were not fully developed. Part 1, on causes, was entitled "Why Was the World War Fought?" Here Page made the bold assertion that Britain and France had been enmeshed in the same underlying causes of war as Germany: All were at fault for starting the war. Page identified what he saw as the deeper patterns of systemic behavior common to all the powers: "economic imperialism," "militarism," "alliances," "secret diplomacy," and "fear." The publication of this view by a former YMCA staffer in 1923—less than five years since the armistice—was bold enough. Although it echoed views of the war's opponents from the 1910s, its interpretation nonetheless ran directly against the rationale of redemptive war that apologists from President Wilson to Sherwood Eddy had offered for the war. And it ran counter to the war guilt clause inscribed into the peace treaty.[37]

Importantly, though, at this stage, Page did not portray these forces as more than a European problem. Only the section on economic imperialism offered a tiny hint that the United States was part of the system. A table copied from the *Encyclopedia Britannica* showing colonial possessions as of 1910 revealed that the United States controlled 114,370 square miles in Asia—ranking just below Russia, Britain, Turkey, Holland, France, and Japan, but above Germany. Page did not take the trouble to explore this; the significance appeared not to have struck him. Written over several years, from 1919 to its publication in 1923, Page's *War* marked just the beginning of his transition.

The first sign that Page was exploring the implications for a more universal conception of the causes of war—one that included the New World as well as the Old—came in a high-profile book, coauthored with Sherwood Eddy the following year. While the first half of the book featured Eddy's coming out as a pacifist in a "personal testimony," Page's half, the second half, simply offered short answers to a series of fifty questions arranged thematically. But strewn among the short answers was the idea that the United States was enmeshed in the global problems of contemporary imperialism. For example, question eleven of fifty asked, "In what way is economic imperialism a cause of war?" Page answered by exploring the competition over raw materials and markets, which led to the practice of securing control of economic assets through annexation, the forming of spheres of influence, or the taking of concessions.[38] Here Page included the United States as a new player in the drama:

> During the past decade the United States has become increasingly involved in world affairs by reason of heavy investments in various parts of the earth and because of the great importance of foreign markets in maintaining our prosperity.

> Our custom of protecting our traders and investors in Latin America by threats
> of force and by actual armed intervention is creating much suspicion and ill will
> against us. Out of such situations in the past many wars have arisen.[39]

Importantly for Page, his questioning of U.S. imperialism was not restricted to, nor even focused on, colonialism following the 1898 Spanish–American War. For him, the contemporary "informal" imperialism in Latin America provided evidence of U.S. participation in the war-making forces typically attributed to Europe. To drive the point home, Page resorted to a technique he began to use often on matters of imperialism: He sought to evoke empathy by posing an imaginary scenario in which the United States was on the receiving end of interventionism. Granting Japan, for argument's sake, the same prerogatives as the United States and other imperial powers, he posed the question: "Has another nation a right to send armed troops into the United States in order to protect the lives and property of the citizens who reside here? . . . Suppose the feeling against the Japanese grows more intense on the Pacific Coast and the lives and property of Japanese citizens are constantly menaced, would we allow any interference from Japan?" How can the United States "claim rights," asked Page, "which we are not willing that other nations should possess?"[40]

U.S. insistence on its right to protect citizens in Latin America related to its larger problem of claiming "police power" in the region. Theodore Roosevelt's 1904 corollary to the Monroe Doctrine was both imperialistic and erroneous, Page argued in *The Abolition of War*. When the president had stated that the United States ought to exercise "international police power" in the Western hemisphere in cases of "chronic wrongdoing" or "impotence," he had shown the United States was acting exactly like any other imperial power.[41] Roosevelt's rationale was "exactly the way the British talk of their fleet and Poincare referred to the French army in the Ruhr." Page argued, "No nation has a right to arrogate to itself the duties of international police." Noting the Latin American countries' deep resentment of "our self-appointed guardianship," Page called for abandonment of discretionary military intervention and for U.S. participation in the multilateral creation of "effective international agencies of justice and security."[42]

While interventionism in Latin America remained a primary focus of Page's anti–imperialist campaigns in *The World Tomorrow* and elsewhere, his 1925 work, *Imperialism and Nationalism,* showed a wider conceptual development in that he related recent happenings in Latin America to the wider history of American expansion. The book was, admittedly, poorly structured and barely edited (perhaps bearing the marks of a quick assembly of facts and quotes at the New York Public Library, a practice of which Page later wrote nostalgically),[43] but it was striking for the way it marked Page's intellectual encounter with U.S. imperialism. Oddly, from a literary point of view, the first three chapters offered a history of the former Turkish Empire and the Near East, discussing European imperialism and the new nationalisms. Then, the final two chapters turned, without warning, to a descriptive narrative of U.S. history. This section of the book was revealing for its logic, however. Page's narrative of U.S. expansion and imperialism showed clearly his rejection of any kind of exceptionalist framework. One figure from whom he was able to draw some guidance—albeit backhandedly—was Theodore Roosevelt, who frankly acknowledged in 1914 that Germany's rationale in occupying Belgium out of "necessity" was the same rationale used earlier by the British Empire in relation to the Danish, and by the Americans in relation to Spain in Florida in 1813.[44]

Page then moved through the nineteenth century, cataloguing the gains of the United States in the Mexican-American war, the purchase of Alaska and the annexation of Hawaii, and the executive order providing for the possession of American Samoa. He did not interrupt the narrative at 1898 in order to point out that postwar colonialism was an aberrant process, a special foray into imperialism.[45] Nor did he cast as a separate chapter incursions into Latin America—the Panama Canal, Haiti, Santo Domingo, Nicaragua; he merely catalogued them in sequence.[46] For Page, these events amounted to the "steady territorial and economic expansion of the United States."[47] It was not a new behavior for the United States; the nation's very history was a continuous development of this pattern. Importantly, this argument set Page apart from the anti-imperialists at the turn of the century who had argued that American colonialism in the Philippines was a diversion from the true mission of the United States—a position Paul Kramer terms "Jeremiadic" anti-imperialism.[48] Following the "self-liquidating" logic of the Jeremiad, such anti-imperialists argued that the nation needed to repent and return to its true anti-imperialist foundations. This kind of argument was not possible for Page; he did not distinguish the mythical, true America from the historical record he uncovered.

While Page painted imperialism as more or less universal and permanent, he did not wish it to continue. Because it flourished in the shadows of public ignorance, Page argued, it needed to be exposed to the light of public scrutiny. One mark of his anti-exceptionalism was the way Page cited British scholar John A. Hobson's classic work to show the moral difficulty inherent in recognizing one's own imperialism. "Each nation, as it watches from outside the Imperialism of its neighbors, is not deceived . . . [but] no nation sees its own shortcomings."[49] Part of Page's own vocational task, as he saw it, was simply to present the facts to Americans who were unaware of their own nation's behavior. There were historical aspects to this process of public enlightenment: "the territorial and economic expansion of the United States has taken place so gradually that its significance has not been recognized by most people." But the past flowed into the present: "it is highly important that citizens of the United States should recognize the elements of grave danger in American imperialism and nationalism."[50] Page saw a gulf, a disproportion, between the importance of the issues and the public's actual awareness of them. "The foreign policy of the United States is of enormous significance to the peace of the world. And yet very few citizens are informed as to what is going on in the State Department."[51]

Publishing his anti-imperialist arguments in 1924–1925, Page anticipated much of what was eventually accepted as official policy by the Hoover and Roosevelt administrations. Responding in part to rising criticism of interventionism in political debate, Hoover signaled a shift away from interventionism by accepting the findings of the Clark Memorandum, which argued Roosevelt's Corollary was not a legitimate construal of the Monroe Doctrine.[52] Franklin Roosevelt's Good Neighbor policy, under which the United States, among other things, renounced its right to intervene in Latin American countries to protect its citizens, took such policy shifts further. While a range of international as well as domestic factors explain this change—not least Japan's claims of the right to Monroe Doctrine-style intervention in Manchuria—the importance of anti-imperialist activism in U.S. politics around the 1928 and 1932 elections needs to be seen as a factor, albeit one still to be sufficiently explored.

Robert David Johnson's leading work—one of the few to address the question of anti-imperialism in the 1920s—has demonstrated that around 1924–1927, U.S. imperialism was fast becoming *the* new issue for the mainline peace movement, a rival to the Outlawry of War campaign in its prominence. In 1924–1925, for example, a new generation of leaders, such as Dorothy Detzer, were climbing the ranks of the Women's International League for Peace and Freedom (WILPF), arguing that American intervention in Latin America should become the central concern of the peace movement.[53] For Johnson, activists such as Detzer formed a public lobby group who supported the work of "Peace Progressive" senators such as William Borah.

Historians of missions and historians of anti-imperialism alike have tended to miss the way Christian internationalists such as Page provided a vital anti-imperialist voice in the 1920s—one connected to the wider currents and networks of debate. Not coincidentally, for example, Detzer became secretary of *The World Tomorrow* during Page's editorship—a fact Johnson misses. And the case of Samuel Guy Inman illustrates the point even further. A former missionary to Mexico, Inman became a Latin Americanist at Columbia University in the 1920s, with a strong interest in cultural diplomacy. For Inman, who toured many U.S.-occupied areas, including Haiti, the United States was the latest in a series of "conquistadores" in Latin America.[54] But, in 1924, he drew great attention to himself (including from the State Department) with an explosive article of his own in the *Atlantic Monthly* entitled "Imperialistic America." Inman explored piece-by-piece how it had come to be that "out of twenty Latin-American republics, eleven of them now have their financial policies directed by North Americans officially appointed," with "six of these ten hav[ing] the financial agents backed by American military forces on the ground."[55] Inman triggered a response from Sumner Welles in the *Atlantic*, having already been grilled earlier by a hostile Senate Foreign Relations subcommittee over his views on U.S. intervention in Mexico.[56] Like Detzer, Inman also became a regular contributor to *The World Tomorrow* during Page's editorship. Yet in two substantive accounts of anti-imperialist thought in the 1920s, both of which examine Inman's individual career at length, the wider missionary anti-imperialist milieu around Page and *The World Tomorrow* is entirely missing.[57]

Inman and Page are but two examples of missionary-grounded Christian internationalists who formed a distinct and important constituency in the rising current of 1920s anti-imperialism. While it is difficult to isolate specific links between policy changes and domestic political stimuli, the missionary presence in the Progressive anti-imperialist lobby, and that lobby's influence in helping shape the normative and discursive shifts from Republican-era interventionism to the Good Neighbor policy, seems significant. As will be discussed in part 2 of this volume, across the missionary-ecumenical axis of the SVM, YMCA, World Student Christian Federation (WSCF), and the International Missionary Committee (IMC), criticism of imperialism and racism on the part of Western powers became "standard parts of most analyses of the missionary task."[58] But Kirby Page stood out for combining Social Gospel critique with revisionist investigation into the history and character of U.S. imperialism that went beyond generalized denunciation. Not only this, he did so ahead of most of his cohort of mainline Protestants and provided leadership in shaping the analytical orientation of Christian internationalism. As we will see in the next chapter, the greatest vehicle by which his anti-imperialist ideas engaged the public—indeed fostered a counterpublic—was *The World Tomorrow* magazine.

Defining "International Relations"

Page's critique of American imperialism was only one facet of his widening analysis of international relations. By the time Page assumed the editorship of *The World Tomorrow* in 1926, the scope of his project had grown to encompass not only imperialism but also race relations, militarism, and nationalism. In his booklet *International Relations in the Light of Jesus*, a reprint of a speech he gave to 2,500 students at the highly publicized National Student Convention in Milwaukee in 1926—just one sign of his ongoing prominence in mainline YMCA–SVM circles—Page laid out the interlocking concerns that made up his radical Christian internationalist agenda. First, immigration policies and race relations were for Page, as for other Christian internationalists, a constitutive part of international relations. Informed by his travels with Eddy on the old YMCA circuits, Page told the students at Milwaukee that American exclusion laws had "deeply wounded" the Japanese people. Congress had inflicted a "burning insult."[59] Students questioning Page after his speech drew more from him on this issue:

"Do you advocate unrestricted immigration?" they asked.

"Other nations ought to have some voice," he replied.

"Is there any menace to world peace in our effort to maintain a high standard of living?"

"It is high time we began to think."[60]

Page also drew attention to the Supreme Court's position on the ineligibility for citizenship of Hindus in America. Indians, Page reported, felt the court's decision "stamps them as an inferior race."

However, the weight of Page's analysis of international relations fell on domestic political culture, particularly on what he saw as the deeper, subterranean causes of war: namely, nationalism and militarism. Both forces were present in Europe in 1914, and both were present, he argued, in revisionist terms, in 1920s America. The issue of military training in colleges became a rallying point from which Page and colleagues mounted larger arguments about the rising tide of militarism in America. In 1925, Page, Eddy, and several other radical Christian internationalist figures established the Committee on Militarism in Education to oppose compulsory training in schools.[61] Leading figures on the committee such as Sherwood Eddy, who were once well-respected itinerant speakers at campus Christian associations, now frequently found themselves banned from speaking to YMCA groups because of their opposition to compulsory Reserve Officer Training Corps units.[62] Page warned his student audience of the alarming growth in American military training programs. While in 1912 only 96 institutions had offered courses in military training, in 1926 there were 225 institutions doing so—with a corresponding 400 percent rise in enrollments.[63] Such entrenchment in the education system, endorsed by all levels of government, amounted, Page argued, to a dangerous elevation of the "military virtues" in the national culture: the very definition of militarism, according to Page.

Even more than militarism, however, Page saw nationalism as the principal cause of conflict. Nationalism, he argued, was a modern and artificial form of group identification. Because it was artificial, it could be changed; because it was harmful and caused war, it *should* be changed. In *Imperialism and Nationalism*, he drew upon British nationalism scholars such as G. P. Gooch and Ramsay Muir, agreeing with their assessment of nationalism as a distinctly modern form of consciousness, one that was a "sentiment" and "subjective."[64] Continuing this analysis, Page explained to his student audience in Milwaukee that nationalism is "an emotion, a state of mind, a psychological experience." Contrary to what nationalisms claimed, nations were not built on historical or empirical realties such as "race, language, geography, common economic interests, religion or culture." Nations were bound by "sentiment" that could be constructive at times, but which most often became "divisive and destructive." According to Page, nationalism "often binds people together in such a way as to make them antagonistic to other groups. Each nation emphasizes the points at which it differs from other peoples, exaggerates its own virtues and underestimates its own faults, while depreciating the good qualities of other nations and grossly distorting their vices."[65]

Nationalism reinforced two political commitments according to Page. One was the principle of "national sovereignty"; the other was a commitment to the preservation of "national honor." Even though nations were artificial units, it was "almost universally believed that a nation is an ultimate political unit, that there is not and should not be any higher law than the law of a nation." Moreover, it was a basic assumption that "the primary duty of a nation is to safeguard its own people and advance their welfare, without being obliged to consider the rights and interests of other nations."[66] Thus, nationalism could shape other forms of international behavior, such as imperialism. In his most developed work on international politics and foreign policy, *National Defense* (1931), Page argued nationalism was ultimately behind other subordinate causes. To nationalism "must be attributed chief responsibility . . . [it] created or accentuated other dangerous factors. Imperialism and militarism in their modern forms are products of nationalism."[67]

The critique of nationalism, had, of course, a positive corollary. He often articulated it in vague and untheorized terms, but Page pointed to a belief in the solidarity of humankind that transcended national divides. Although such an assertion had the marks of Kantian liberal cosmopolitanism, Page did not cite enlightenment authorities and instead used the fraternal language of the Social Gospel's stress on the universal brotherhood of man, tinged with a Quaker emphasis on the divine element in individual personality. Whereas ecumenical internationalists in the 1920s to 1930s increasingly tied the assertion of universal, supranational solidarity to a theology of the Universal Church—sidestepping the question of religious pluralism—Page by and large did not. He offered, consciously or not, a relatively threadbare articulation of the positive component of his internationalism. More important than the "yes" in his work was the "no" to imperialism, militarism, and nationalism.

Conclusion

It was "just before lunch" one Friday in April 1926 when it occurred to John Nevin Sayre, president of *The World Tomorrow* magazine, that there was a "bare possibility" that Kirby Page might wish to be editor. He had "tried to get Kirby and the F.C.S.O. crowd into partnership as far back as 1921," but to no avail.[68] A deeply committed pacifist, a founding member of the Fellowship of Reconciliation, and a liberal Protestant clergyman, Sayre had been with the journal since its inception with Norman Thomas (later a Socialist Party leader) as editor in 1918. But problems of legality, financial viability, and fidelity to the Christian-radical vision had plagued the journal from the start. Being an independent Christian radical periodical and staying afloat financially was not easy. After yet another financial crisis in 1926, the end of the journal looked imminent; readers were advised as such in a circular letter. Sayre's last-ditch effort to rescue the magazine from extinction consisted in re-establishing it on a new footing: a "a new deal . . . a clean sweep all the way around."[69] The plan centered on two people in particular: Kirby Page as editor and Sherwood Eddy as financier.

When Sayre managed to secure Page and Eddy for his ailing periodical, he brought in two figures who were at the center of a new current of radical Christian internationalism. As seen in the next chapter, the collective enterprise of the journal became an extension of much of what Page in particular had already foreshadowed in his own work. It also became an instantiation of the network of Christian internationalists Page and Eddy had helped forge.

The "F.C.S.O. crowd" to which Sayre referred was the Fellowship for a Christian Social Order, founded in 1921 with Eddy and Page in the key positions of leadership—Eddy as chairman and Page as executive secretary. The rationale for the new fellowship was to seek reform of all areas of "arrogance and antagonism" in the relationship of "classes, nations and races"—the big three concerns of Page, and later of *The World Tomorrow*.[70]

In establishing the National Committee for the Fellowship, Eddy and Page linked high-profile figures in mainline Protestantism on the one hand with leaders in the peace movement on the other. This was one example of the way they pushed mainline Protestants leftward while seeking to draw the peace movement into the mainstream. The committee included figures in theological education, such as Dean Charles Reynolds Brown of Yale Divinity School and Charles W. Gilkey of the University of Chicago, as well as Rufus Jones, who was among the leaders of the American Friends Service Committee and the Fellowship of Reconciliation, which many FCSO members also joined, and into which the FCSO merged in 1928. Also on the committee was A. J. Muste—arguably America's most prominent and long-term peace activist of the twentieth century, a figure linking the peace movement of the 1930s to the movement of the 1960s. Bromley Oxnam and Samuel McCrea Cavert, respectively the future president and the general secretary of the Federal Council of Churches, were also instrumental in the National Committee of the FCSO. Cavert would later play a major role in the American engagement in the ecumenical movement—as we will see in part 2. A young Reinhold Niebuhr, still working in Detroit, served as a regional secretary to the new fellowship. Arguably no other single group provided such a cross-section of those who would become leaders of Christian internationalism in the decades to come.[71] While the FCSO was to "bind together for mutual counsel," and would not, as a fellowship, "go on record as endorsing or disapproving any special program or practice," its constituents were free to do so as individuals.[72] And being brought into *The World Tomorrow* in 1926, that's exactly what Kirby Page and the FCSO crowd did.

Following Kirby Page's trajectory from World War I, when he was an aspiring YMCA missionary, to his assumption of the editorship at *The World Tomorrow* does more than merely provide the backstory for the biography of a periodical, as important as that is. Page's development sheds light on the distinctive characteristics of Christian internationalism that have not been captured in conventional historical narratives—whether of missionaries' complicity in American cultural expansionism, of the travail of liberal Wilsonian internationalism, or of the conflict between pacifism and realism. Neither one of these narratives squarely fits or serves to explain Page's story. Page was at the leading edge of a current of missionary-connected criticism of U.S. imperialism that has barely figured in scholarship at all. Wilsonian liberal internationalism, while it had noble democratic ideas sewn into it, did not come close to addressing the problems of militarism, imperialism, and nationalism that concerned Page. As seen in the next chapter, while Page and *The World Tomorrow* supported the League of Nations, Wilsonian internationalism operated almost entirely on a parallel track to their brand of Christian internationalism. And while Page was later the subject of realist criticism, realists shared more with Page's Christian internationalist outlook than they acknowledged. One of the most important things they shared as a central frame of reference was the argument that American Protestants needed to read against the grain of national self-image. Rather than seeing the thirst for empire as an Old World foible, they needed to identify American imperialism for what it was. American Christians needed to renounce and work against nationalism, repenting of their historical tendency to grant the nation-state divine sanction for its claims of greatness and paramount interest.

Chapter 2

The World Tomorrow as a
Foreign Policy Counterpublic

A letter arrived on Kirby Page's desk in May 1931 that was signed "General Douglas MacArthur, Chief of Staff, United States Army." MacArthur was disgusted by the mix of religion and internationalism on display at *The World Tomorrow*—particularly in the journal's recent mass survey of twenty thousand clergymen. "Any organization which opposes the defense of homeland and the principles hallowed by the blood of our ancestors, which sets up internationalism in the place of patriotism . . . cannot prevail against the demonstrated staunchness of our population," he warned. Assembling biological and geometric metaphors, he let Page know what he thought was a truly Christian position on world affairs: "I confidently believe that a red-blooded and virile humanity which loves peace devotedly, but is willing to die in the defense of the right, is Christian from center to circumference, and will continue to be dominant in the future as in the past."[1] Page, for his part, relished the response from MacArthur and the wider publicity it brought, and he published the letter in full in the next edition of *The World Tomorrow*. His interchange with MacArthur was but one marker of what he and others at *The World Tomorrow* had been consciously crafting: a community of discourse that stood in opposition to—*counter* to—the state, the military, and much of mainstream public opinion on U.S. foreign policy. This chapter charts the operation of *The World Tomorrow* as a "foreign policy counterpublic" from 1926, when Page assumed editorship, to the early 1930s, when the oppositionality of the journal crested.

In 1926, John Nevin Sayre's hopes for "a clean sweep" for *The World Tomorrow* were largely realized.[2] Eddy's financial support and Page's editorship meant new headquarters for the journal at 52 Vanderbilt Avenue, in the heart of mid-town Manhattan. Their new business constitution for "World Tomorrow Inc." took the paper out of the hands of the "Fellowship Press," the printing arm of the Fellowship of Reconciliation. The budget was expanded, the paper stock improved, new artists were commissioned, and larger honorariums were used to entice big-name contributors like John Dewey, Charles Beard, Henry Noel Brailsford, and British Prime Minister Ramsay MacDonald, to name a few. There were also changes in staffing. Page and Eddy had agreed to take over *The World Tomorrow* on the condition that all editors and staff who stayed on would only do so "enthusiastically," or otherwise resign. But little enthusi-asm was forthcoming from some. Two key editorial figures of the early 1920s, Anna Rochester and Grace Hutchins, both of whom were increasingly tend-ing toward Communist radicalism, felt the magazine had been sold off behind their backs, and they resented the incursion of Kirby Page, so "fresh and full of zest."[3] Devere Allen, the zealous young pacifist and editor under Roches-ter, was also suspicious, wondering if the journal would become so "Chris-tian" as to alienate youthful readers and make it impossible for him, a self-confessed adherent to non-denominational "mysticism," to stay on.[4] Rochester and Hutchins resigned, and Allen stayed on only after some coaxing and a European holiday. The vacancies left by Rochester and Hutchins were even-tually filled by Reinhold Niebuhr and economist (and later New Dealer) Paul H. Douglas.

Despite the clean sweep, there were continuities. As editor, Page inherited a journal whose positioning in the world of periodical literature had long been characterized by the attempt to articulate a simultaneously Christian and "rad-ical" position on political, social, and, to an extent, international issues. The stress on being distinctively Christian *and* radical pervaded the internal memo-randa and policy statements of the early 1920s. John Nevin Sayre had pictured the intended audience of the journal in diasporic terms: *The World Tomorrow* would reach "dissatisfied Christians who desire interpretation of current prob-lems from the viewpoint of Christians who are social radicals and pacifists . . . scattered radicals who have a Christian background and have dropped all church connections; radicals within the churches; [and] open-minded Chris-tians of all ages."[5] According to Sayre, the journal's Christian radical ethos, together with its relative financial and institutional independence, would also set it apart from existing religious and secular periodicals. On one hand it would offer a "frankly Christian" viewpoint on the same social and political prob-lems covered by liberal weeklies and monthlies such as *The Nation,* the *New Republic,* and the *Atlantic Monthly*. On the other hand, he hoped it would offer a more self-consciously radical position and tone than other liberal Protestant periodicals. Here Sayre singled out the *Christian Century*, the twentieth century's most significant mainline Protestant publication—a close cousin within the wider network of socially concerned mainline Protestant outlets. *The World Tomorrow* contributors and editors frequently wrote for *Christian Century* and other religious enterprises such as the *Churchman* and the Federal Council of Churches. But while such connections were to remain, *The World Tomorrow* would be different, argued Sayre, in that its "policy would be less that of a detached liberal . . . than that of an evangelical radical who is frankly trying to persuade his readers of the necessity of change."[6]

But what did it actually mean to be "radical?" Were Kirby Page, Sayre, and others seeking the overthrow of the existing order? At times, they came close. In the early Depression years of the mid-1930s, the question of whether to welcome the seemingly imminent downfall of the existing order did indeed become a real one. Some of the Christian Socialists at *The World Tomorrow* did indeed see hope, for a while, in the prospect of an apocalyptic class war that would usher in a new, more just economic and international order—not the least of these was Reinhold Niebuhr, as we will discuss in the next chapter. But *The World Tomorrow*'s radicalism is not best seen in its predictions of class war so much as in the way it fostered "counterness"—studied oppositionality— toward the state and the wider foreign policy public.

In offering a reading of *The World Tomorrow* as a foreign policy counterpub- lic, I am deploying a phrase unknown to those working at *The World Tomorrow* in the interwar years. I use it here as a composite of two terms developed by historians and social scientists much later. Yet, it captures succinctly the role the journal played. The term "foreign policy public" (not counterpublic) was originally developed by figures such as Ernest May more than forty years ago. Its function was to describe the limited group of persons in the wider public sphere who were sufficiently informed on matters of foreign policy to engage in public discourse, and who, in turn, may have influenced foreign policy outcomes.[7] The emphasis was on *delimiting* the foreign policy public from the public at large, separating those who were really influential from those who were not.[8] The term "counterpublic," on the other hand, has its own history. Existing outside the worlds of diplomatic history and foreign policy analysis, "counterpublic" belongs to communications theory and political philoso- phy. Developed in recent decades by thinkers such as Nancy Fraser, Michael Warner, and Robert Asen, it is an effort to emphasize the multiplicity of publics constituting the public sphere, in direct contrast to the kind of singular public sphere described by Jürgen Habermas in his famous *Structural Transformation of the Public Sphere* (1989).[9] The "counter" part of counterpublic most often refers to the actual social exclusion or marginality of members of a group from the wider public sphere and the means of publicity they employ to address this exclusion. Yet the term "counter" can also denote the oppositional quality of a public—a definition that better fits *The World Tomorrow*. Communications theorist Robert Asen argues that counterpublics are "constituted neither necessarily nor exclusively by actually or potentially excluded individuals." Instead, Asen suggests we see counterpublics as "discursive entities," which, though situated within the wider public sphere, "set themselves against wider publics."[10] Within this framework, *The World Tomorrow* could clearly be seen as fostering a foreign policy counterpublic, even though the majority of is constituents—white elite liberal Protestant males—did not fit the classic demographic profile. In fact, the very significance of *The World Tomorrow* lay precisely in this fact. As a radical magazine it was constituted by and addressed elements of the socially powerful liberal Protestant "establishment." Like the YMCA-SVM leaders Page and Eddy themselves, the journal was distinctively mainline-radical.

Although *The World Tomorrow*'s aims and methods as a counterpublic were clearly connected to Kirby Page's own work and belief in the causality of public opinion, the periodical was a collective enterprise. Reading the journal collectively—in its full fabric—means reading beyond one individual and his intentions. Until recently in American intellectual and religious history, periodicals were most often read with a view to extract and report the editorial line of the paper, or as an archive from which to retrieve the views of particular authors.[11] As two recent theorists of periodical studies point out, such an approach meant often being "too quick to see magazines merely as containers of discrete bits of information rather than autonomous objects of study."[12] In reading the journal as a collective enterprise, in this chapter I look at more than editorials and articles: correspondence, advertisements, reviews, discussion questions, opinion surveys, and other lesser-known parts of the periodical are all part of the formation of the counterpublic. The full fabric of the journal needs to be read as instrumental in the forging of an oppositional community of discourse.

In this chapter, then, I explore three modes of counterpublicity operative in *The World Tomorrow*. First, I explore the journal's use of didactic, middlebrow forms of communication in service of anti-imperialism. Reviewing the best and latest in anti-imperialist scholarship, and providing supplementary features such as maps and study guides, *The World Tomorrow* positioned itself as educating readers against American imperialism. Second, I take into view the evocation of suspicion and the mode of exposé by which the journal linked its staunchly revisionist stance on the causes of the past war with a hunt for the evil effects of American militarism in the present. Third, and finally, I examine *The World Tomorrow*'s most idiosyncratic mode of counterpublicity: its use of the survey technique to crystallize an oppositional viewpoint and intervene in the wider public sphere on questions such as U.S. imperialism in Latin America, military training in colleges, and whether the church should ever sanction and support a war again.

Educating against Empire

In contrast to its urgent, angular tone in the 1930s, *The World Tomorrow* of the mid to late 1920s was often characterized by something resembling polite crusading—oppositional politics expressed in didactic, middlebrow modes of communication. This was clearly seen in its approach to U.S. imperialism. Soon after Page's assumption of editorship, two special themed editions appeared on the topic—one on the Caribbean and one on the Philippines—in February and May 1927. In striking similarity to the emergence of that paragon of middlebrow publishing, the Book of the Month Club, in 1926, Page and *The World Tomorrow*'s contributors used the journal to disseminate elite scholarship to a wider audience of students and educated generalists, mediating the "high" to the middle. Their agenda was to foster an anti-imperialist public by means of education. Ignorance, argued Page, legitimated American imperialism. As he editorialized in the Caribbean issue, "only . . . as the people know the truth . . . can they exert a positive influence for a policy of enlightened sympathy as against a policy of greed; for a policy of non-interference as against a policy of increasing intervention; for a policy of friendly cooperation as against a policy of rule or ruin." *The World Tomorrow* would do its bit to cast the "light of truth" and help throw "the balance of public opinion toward a future in the Caribbean of which those citizens who come after us need not be ashamed."[13]

To "enlighten" *The World Tomorrow* readers, Page marshaled the input of a range of professional scholars of a revisionist and Progressive stripe. Historian Herbert Adams Gibbons took readers through the events of 1898–1899 in his article "How We Got the Philippines." Sounding more like a turn-of-the-century anti-imperialist, he suggested America had been drawn by its policy of retention into problematic and unwanted entanglements in great power politics—an activity from which it was presumably separate beforehand. Imperialism led to a whole cycle of interventions, military build-ups, and complicity in racial hubris, unwelcome to Gibbons.[14] In the Caribbean issue, historian

Leland Jenks recapped the history of policy surrounding the Panama Canal and, like Gibbons, remarked that "the manner of our taking the Canal Zone in Panama was strikingly similar to the behavior of other imperialistic nations."[15] Edwin Borchard of Yale—one of the most renowned international law specialists of the period—laid out the legal history of the Monroe Doctrine in "From Monroe to Coolidge." He argued that U.S. expansion southward, which, unlike Page, he did not see as entirely unjustified, would have occurred with or without the doctrine.[16] Paul H. Douglas, then an academic in economics at the University of Chicago, later an editor for *The World Tomorrow*, reflected on the fact-finding mission in Haiti in which he had recently participated with the Women's League for International Peace and Freedom. Douglas's rationale for his article aligned with Page's for the edition: "The nature of our military control over the Republic of Haiti is but little understood by even intelligent Americans who have been confused by the conflicting reports concerning our administration."[17] The didacticism of the imperialism editions was furthered with maps, tables of statistics, and reprints of news media.[18] Bibliographies recommended books widely circulated and cited by *World Tomorrow* figures—including Carleton Beals's *Mexico: An Interpretation*; Raymond Leslie Buell's *International Relations*; Parker Moon's recent *Imperialism and World Politics*; and, perhaps most widely cited of all, Scott Nearing and Joseph Freeman's *Dollar Diplomacy*—many of which could be purchased by mail order from *The World Tomorrow*'s bookstore.

The point at which the educational aspect of the magazine reached its zenith was its provision of discussion-group questions. Sayre had proposed as early as 1921 that each monthly issue of *The World Tomorrow* contain a study course. A group could meet weekly and use the prescribed questions and the bibliography as stimulus. Such a technique tapped into the emerging trend of "democratic methods" in modern adult education. Youth organizations—in particular the YMCA and YWCA—were in the 1920s beginning to emphasize the role of group discussion in Christian education, rapidly developing syllabi around which groups could talk about issues such as world affairs and foreign missions.[19] With its close links to the YMCA, group discussion became a lasting feature of *The World Tomorrow* too. In 1927, under Page's editorship, Grace Loucks of the National Student Staff of the YWCA was brought in to write discussion questions. Her specialized expertise from "the Y" resulted in a considerable improvement in the quality of questions from Kirby Page's early efforts. The editors soon advertised the benefits of the questions, suggesting the magazine was "peculiarly fitted to discussion clubs on the campus and in churches as a source of reliable and adequate information."[20] Some evidence of the magazine being used for group discussions appeared in the form of a telegram from an "enthusiastic group of students" in Evanston, Illinois. It was reprinted in full in the magazine: "met today at noon at Northwestern University to organize discussion group . . . proposal made that organization be known as World Tomorrow club."[21] The discussion questions were particularly useful, wrote the students, when used in conjunction with the book lists and reviews supplied by the magazine—the latter, as scholar Joan S. Rubin notes, being a characteristic aspect of 1920s middlebrow print enterprises.[22]

The questions in the Caribbean imperialism edition encouraged readers to become aware of the varied rationales for intervention employed by the U.S. government. They were asked:

> For which of the following reasons would you be willing to hold intervention or exercise of control by the United States in the Caribbean countries justified?
> To protect investments?
> To protect lives of American citizens?
> To insure the production of necessary raw materials?
> To provide naval or military security?
> To keep order in the country?

They were then asked to match the rationale to the site of intervention—Haiti, Puerto Rico, Nicaragua, and Mexico, testing their knowledge of recent foreign policy. In a characteristic *World Tomorrow* move, the questions then offered a twist that appealed to empathy and the Golden Rule ("do unto others . . .") in the third and fourth questions: "Of what other interests would you be conscious if you were looking at the question of America's policy in the Caribbean from Mexico City? Haiti? London? Moscow?" And "what would be your attitude towards the same policy were you a citizen of Haiti? Nicaragua?"[23]

Despite their didacticism, the imperialism editions were nonetheless a conscious engagement in the culture conflict raging in print media during the 1920s over America's role in the world. Demonstrating that he had one eye on the wider periodical press, Page framed his Caribbean edition deliberately in opposition to the noted pro-expansionist weekly, *Liberty*, and in agreement with the anti-imperialist *New York World*. He opened with a citation from *Liberty*: "Always the eagle has been taking a wider flight, never a narrower one. Timorous Americans who have been afraid of our destiny have always been swept aside. So may it ever be!" Page appreciated the frankness of *Liberty*. It illustrated clearly where American policy was going to go if the "advocates of imperialistic dominance by the U.S.A. win out." But he resented the invocation of Manifest Destiny to support expansion. "If we have a Destiny, that Destiny is in the hands of human beings—in the hands of the American people."[24] On the other hand, Page shared the *New York World*'s suspicion of the State Department's motives in the Nicaraguan and Mexican crises of 1927. He agreed that Secretary Kellogg's claim that Bolsheviks were controlling both countries was no more than a legitimizing strategy, a cloak for American imperialism. *The World Tomorrow* reprinted the *World*'s warning: "if the American people want peace, they will have to begin to fight for it now. They cannot trust either to the good intentions or to the wisdom of the State Department. For the State Department is clearly and unmistakably looking for trouble."[25]

Cultivating a Counterpublic

Beyond its scrutiny of the State Department's policies in Latin America, *The World Tomorrow*'s promotion of suspicion toward the state in general—and the military establishment in particular—was an important corollary to its revisionist interpretation of war. The October 1926 edition on "Militarism in the U.S.A."—Page's first issue as editor—revealed just how foundational such revisionist suspicion was. From front to back, the entire issue sought to expose the allegedly hidden presence of war-making causes in domestic political culture. If the deeper causes of the Great War in Europe belonged not to Prussian barbarism but to more universal tendencies in socio-psychology and public sentiment, then there was potential, the edition implied, for those same forces to be breeding war today. The cover illustration, a sketch drawn by Lynd Ward and made available courtesy of the Committee on Militarism in Education (one of *The World Tomorrow*'s key related counterpublicity agencies), featured an American military officer marching in the foreground. But in the background, his larger shadow bore the unmistakable features of the Prussian soldier depicted in propaganda cartoons of 1917–1918, with stooped shoulders, sloped brow, and spiked helmet. American and German militarism were cut from the same cloth, the picture suggested.[26] Reinforcing the parallel—in a move unthinkable for YMCA-connected internationalists years earlier—Page published a German contribution on the question. Ludwig Quidde of the German Peace Society explored the prestige of officer training in Germany before the war, the militarism of state officials, the build-up of armaments, and the "narrow national outlook" that coalesced with militarism. And he concluded with a present-day warning: "Out of the World War has come a new and dangerous militarism, a militarism of the mind in all nations participating in the war."[27] In his editorial, Page agreed. A new militarism of the mind was propagating itself in the United States. Referring to his copy of *Webster's* dictionary to define militarism, Page editorialized that his mission was to oppose "the spirit and temper which exalts the military virtues and ideals, and minimizes the defects of military training and the cost of war and preparation for it."[28]

While they saw militarism as a matter of the mind, those in *The World Tomorrow* network were particularly concerned with the concrete institutional bases that promoted it. Reinhold Niebuhr—then still a pastor in Detroit—contributed a piece using figures collated by the Committee on Militarism in Education to expose the "baneful psychological effect upon the average member of the R.O.T.C." Sixty thousand students were enrolled in such courses on compulsory terms—a measure that Niebuhr argued congressional measures should oppose.[29] Longtime Social Gospeller and educational theorist Professor George A. Coe offered an exposé of Citizen's Military Training Camps. These camps, designed for the education of citizens (not soldiers), were administered federally by the War Department. Fifty-two such camps ran annually at a cost of $2.8 million in public money, Coe reported. Attendance in 1925 had tripled from four years earlier, now peaking at 33,000. Coe questioned the kind of "citizenship" being promoted at these citizens' camps. With something approaching an ethnographic method, he analyzed in detail the practices of the camps and the training manuals issued through them by the U.S. Army. His conclusion: The notion of citizenship forwarded at the camps was premised on "militaristic nationalism."[30] Students came through the camps absorbing an "unexpressed assumption that we are to work vigorously for industrial and military strength, and that if anybody gets into our way we are to fight."[31] The militaristic outlook problematically placed the nation above humanity, argued Coe.

As a counterpublic, part of the business of *The World Tomorrow* was not just to educate and expose but to critique opposing publicity sources. In exposing the "interlocking directorates" of their opponents, they employed a tactic regularly used against them. In the militarism issue, for example, New York's renowned psychologist-philosopher and adult educator Harry A. Overstreet essayed on the publicity forces involved in "militarizing" the "minds" of Americans. He identified a network of organizations that linked the Military Intelligence Association, the Reserve Officers Association, the American Legion, the *Army and Navy Journal* and *Army and Navy Register*, and other civic organizations devoted to preserving "traditional" institutions. Such groups were

all engaged in spreading "scepticism [sic] as to any save a warlike means of set-
tling international disputes; and . . . admiration for the warlike virtues."[32] But
most frightening of all for Overstreet was the increased peacetime role the
military were arrogating to themselves in shaping the "public mind." Eager to
build suspicion, Overstreet urged the "ordinary, easy-going American," who
was unlikely to believe such claims, to go see the new publicity bureau of the
War Department firsthand. The visitor ought to "look over the scores of releases and future releases of speeches and articles, all earnestly, sometimes truc-
ulently concerned with shaping the future policy of America, and he will
realize that the War Department, both in its army and navy branches, has assumed unto itself, in an astounding and unprecedented way, the business of
educating the social and political mind of America."[33]

But, beyond military institutions such as the R.O.T.C. and the War Department, *World Tomorrow* editors and writers sought to counter militarism anywhere they saw it—in the cinema, the press, and culture at large. One of *The
World Tomorrow*'s most characteristic counterpublicity techniques was to collate
and reprint media, framing them in such a way that positioned readers against
them. For example, the November 1927 edition included a one-page collage
of clippings taken entirely from a single issue of *Cosmopolitan* magazine—then
the leading "youth" magazine for men and women. According to *The World Tomorrow*'s count, in one single edition there were sixty-two separate advertisements for private military schools. Institutions such as Illinois Military School,
Western Military Academy, or Staunton Military Academy appealed to boys
and their parents with promises of discipline, prestige, tradition, and salubrious
surroundings, while the reality, argued *The World Tomorrow*'s captioning, was that
students were being "saturated" with ideas about military preparedness. The
heading above the collage stated that it all amounted to a process of "Militarizing
Our Youth."[34]

Just as the journal positioned readers against some publicity sources, it
related readers favorably to others. A distinctive counterpublicity feature of
The World Tomorrow was the regular column entitled "Not in the Headlines."
As early as 1921, Sayre had proposed bringing in a column called "NEWS
THAT IS NEWS." This would be a regular department "filled with brief,
live paragraphs setting forth the most important happenings from the W.T's
viewpoint"—bite-sized "news" items that were not within the scope of the
mainstream press.[35] The feature was one of the most enduring and successful
of the journal's existence. It was doubled in size to a full two-page spread under
Kirby Page's editorship in 1926, and produced primarily by Agnes Sharp, one
of *The World Tomorrow* staff. The very acquisition of news items relied on and

helped establish networks and relationships with other alternative publicity organizations. Sayre initially proposed to use releases from the Church League
for Industrial Democracy and the Methodist Federation for Social Service.
Over time the column grew to include a wider variety of radical and reform
organizations for news. Throughout the 1920s, "Not in the Headlines" became a regular outlet for reports and releases from the NAACP, the Women's
International League for Peace and Freedom, and War Resisters' International,
to name a few—each of which also had personnel connected to *The World Tomorrow* in some capacity.

Importantly, reading a news page that was outside of the mainstream news
was a participatory act that aligned readers with the counterpublic. Whereas
Sayre had hoped the column would highlight "happenings from the W.T's
viewpoint," the column can better be seen as helping *create* a viewpoint for
the paper into which readers were grafted. More than just an alternative information source, the column related readers to a new world of concern. The
November 1926 column, for example, ran paragraph-sized reports on the
scheduling of a conference to discuss Filipino independence, the undermin-
ing of the British labor strike by American coal supplies, the lack of reporting
given to black victims after a storm in Miami (from NAACP and Federal
Council of Churches reports), the formation of a Mexican Federation of Labor,
and the American Legion's resolve to support military training in schools, just
to list a handful.[36] Purveying and consuming alternative news stories further
created the sense of being at odds with the wider public ignorance. And, the
column was popular among readers. When the Harlem-based black literary
periodical *Opportunity* wrote to congratulate the editors of *The World Tomorrow*, they cited it: "Of especial interest to us is its calm but effective column
Not In The Headlines. Truth gets a hearing in *The World Tomorrow*, and we are
thankful for it."[37]

Intervening in the Wider Public: The Surveys of Opinion

It is a characteristic element of counterpublics that they oscillate between gathering and sending, speaking inward and outward.[38] In the famous—to some,
notorious—surveys of opinion that Kirby Page developed through *The World
Tomorrow* between 1928 and 1934, these two dynamics were joined, the con-
nective becoming the declarative. Page's initial technique in 1928, of circulating
questionnaires among academics, clergy, and leaders of peace organizations,
reflected an older, Progressive-era trend of gathering petitions of "leading" or

"distinguished" citizens in order to make a public statement on an issue. Generating publicity by gathering high-profile names was part of his tool kit as a "publicist"—a self-designation that accurately reflected his concern with crafting cause and effect in public discourse. But, strikingly, the purpose of Page's initial questionnaire in *The World Tomorrow* was to illustrate a lack of consensus rather than a coherent body of opinion. The highlighting of difference was in itself the story aimed for consumption in the wider public.

The theme of the first survey, unsurprisingly, was U.S. imperialism; the issue was what the Monroe Doctrine actually allowed for in U.S.–Latin American relations—a live question in public debate with the hundred-year anniversary of the doctrine just passed. Page introduced the questionnaire, pointing out how the doctrine had developed a "sacred" aura in American political culture, and yet nobody seemed to know its precise meaning. Such confusion allowed it to provide a justification for just about any policy a president wished for. There were versions for every administration since the Civil War. It was, Page said, quoting William R. Shepherd, "elusive in meaning and vociferous in utterance. . . . Neither a principle nor a law, nor even, in a strict sense, a policy, it is instead a sentiment long cherished."[39] Page sent out 950 questionnaires to lawyers, judges, academics, peace leaders, bishops, clergymen, and editors. Three hundred and one people from around forty states completed and returned the surveys.

Asked to assume that the Monroe Doctrine was authoritative, the subjects were to state what they thought it provided for in certain situations. For example, they were asked "Do you favor the continuance of the policy of armed intervention in Latin America by the United States in order to protect the life and property of our own citizens, as, for example, in Nicaragua at the present time?" To this, 134 respondents answered "yes," and 154 answered "no," with 13 unsure. Similar questions were asked about the doctrine's conferring of an obligation on the United States to protect European nationals in Latin America—again the numbers were split, with slightly more weight on the negative.[40] This was an amusing, but serious matter for Page. The answers did not follow party, ideological, or demographic lines. Indeed, the confusion brought "Greek against Greek," as he said—Progressive against Progressive, radical against radical. "A certain question is answered in one way by Philip Marshall Brown, Herbert Adams Gibbons, Alain Locke, H. L. Mencken, President Ray Lyman Wilbur and Rabbi Stephen Wise; while the opposite reply is given by Charles A. Beard, Raymond L. Buell, Sidney B. Fay, John H. Latane, Parker T. Moon and Norman Thomas."[41] If many of the major international relations theorists and historians of the country could not agree on the meaning of the doctrine, what hope had the rest of the country? The confusion, argued Page, allowed Coolidge to justify his interventionist Caribbean policy by invoking in reverent tones the name of Monroe.

What Page called for, then, was a sharp distinction to be made in public debate—and here he had in mind the larger public, not just his counterpublic—between the original Monroe Doctrine and its new derivatives. The older notion of maintaining the integrity of Latin American nations against European colonization and monarchism needed to be distinguished sharply from "the Roosevelt Doctrine" of international police power and the later "Coolidge doctrine" of arbitrary armed intervention. But as well as definitional precision, Page argued there should be developed a "Pan-American Doctrine" in which the United States would cooperate with Canada and Latin American countries in "strengthening pacific means of maintaining security, perhaps by the Pan-American Union, or, if this seems unwise, by creating new Pan-American agencies of justice."[42] As discussed in chapter 1, Page was arguing for many of the changes that *did* occur, at least formally, in U.S.–Latin American policy under the soon-to-be-elected Hoover and, later, Franklin Roosevelt. Indeed, his call to disaggregate the Coolidge and Roosevelt versions of the original Monroe Doctrine was almost in exact accord—but two months ahead—of the findings of an internal Memorandum in the State Department in December of the same year (the Clark Memorandum was made public in 1930).[43] As a mark of how timely his intervention was, Page managed to publish his *World Tomorrow* survey results, shorn of some of his anti-imperialist imperatives, in a leading scholarly journal, the *Annals of the American Academy of Political and Social Science*—the middlebrow activist and popularizer again interacting with the academy.[44]

Page soon employed another questionnaire in service of his other most dearly held theme: war guilt and revisionism. As discussed in chapter 1, Page's major book *War,* which he had written between 1918 and 1923, had come out strongly against the argument that Germany was solely responsible for World War I. Back then, Page had been at odds with American public opinion at large, and historians were still to promote the idea of universal war guilt in coming years. As such, throughout the 1920s and 1930s, Page managed to court a relationship of mutual appreciation with revisionist scholars. Harry Elmer Barnes's *Genesis of the World War*, one of the major works of 1920s historical revisionism, praised Page, among others, in checking the tendency toward a "Pollyanna" view of American history.[45] Barnes wrote reviews and comments for *The World Tomorrow*—as did future revisionist celebrity-scholars Charles A. Beard and Mary Ritter Beard, whose work in the mid-1930s popularized the view that munitions makers and industrialists caused war. Sidney B. Fay, another pre-eminent revisionist historian of the 1920s, also contributed to *The World Tomorrow*, calling for the deletion of the "morally monstrous" war guilt clause in the Treaty of Versailles.[46] *The World Tomorrow* was a gathering point for revisionists, and its 1930s survey on the question of German war guilt only cemented its status in this regard. Distributing around 1,200 surveys, *The World Tomorrow* received 429 back, including responses from 205 professors, 36 college presidents, 58 editors, and 13 military and naval officers. Out of the results, Page managed to crystallize and publicize the view he had long promoted. As he wrote in the October 1930 edition of *The World Tomorrow*, which was reported, in turn, in the *New York Times*, there was now a greater revisionist consensus than at any other time since the last war. Of the 429 respondents, only 48 still attributed "sole guilt" to Germany. In a sign of a rising tide of neutralist sentiment, around one-third of respondents now questioned the wisdom of U.S. entry into the previous world war.[47]

Despite the relatively favorable response to their surveys of elite opinion, Page and *The World Tomorrow* changed tactics in 1931. Instead of surveying and reporting the views of individual experts, they opted decisively for an approach that crystallized a new conception of the counterpublic as a "mass" whose opinion could be articulated as data. In part, the change reflected the emerging prolabor political currents of the early Depression years. Rather than focusing on workers, Page refigured American Protestant clergymen—unlikely candidates—as the "mass" in question. As Sarah Igo has so effectively shown, there were broader intellectual currents afoot too: This was the dawn of the age of the "averaged American." In these very years, social scientists were attempting for the first time to capture the intimate personal lives of Americans, abstract their views, combine them with that of others', and then feed the total result back to the public as data. "By proclaiming the necessity of their impersonal techniques, by presenting collections of facts as more authoritative than individuals' perceptions . . . and by fostering communion with abstract others, surveyors helped to manufacture the idea and perhaps even the experience of 'the mass.'"[48] When Page and *The World Tomorrow* sent out survey questionnaires to 53,000 clergy in 1931, they were among the first in American political life to deploy a technique that later became ubiquitous. It was not until Franklin Roosevelt's 1932 presidential campaign that electoral races used modern polling. And it was not until the 1936 and 1940 elections that the Gallup polls gained prominence as a neutral mediator of "the public."[49] In the world of print media, the *Literary Digest* stood out for using the survey technique around election campaigns and issues such as Prohibition.[50]

But Page and *The World Tomorrow* were significant for employing the technique on matters of war and foreign policy and for doing so with oppositional intent.

The change to a mass survey technique also had reasons that were particular to Page and *The World Tomorrow*'s peace activism. Page had long been interested in challenging and countering the historical tendency of the churches to provide religious sanction to warfare on the part of the state. *War* (1923) had sought specifically to establish the antithesis between war and the imitation of Jesus. It had included a pledge—the so-called "slacker's oath"—by which Christians could individually renounce war and, en masse, utilize the social power of their numbers against war. There were also new elements and actors stressing a quantitative approach. *The World Tomorrow* had been developing a close relationship with the War Resisters' International movement, which heavily promoted the idea of a transnational network of individuals who would renounce war and resist it by the weight of their numbers.[51] Then there was Gandhi—a darling of *The World Tomorrow*—who inspired the counterpublic by his leadership in campaigns of mass resistance against British rule. The final catalyst for the mass survey approach seemed to come from an individual devoted to numbers: physicist and erstwhile peace activist Albert Einstein. In a speech in New York in late 1930, Einstein had given the War Resisters' movement a compelling statistic: He suggested it would only take 2 percent of a population resisting war in order to create a kind of pacifistic critical mass. With that number of citizens refusing to take up arms, the state would be prevented from waging war. "So small a proportion as two per cent will accomplish the desired result," he told a gathering in New York City, "for . . . [t]here are not enough jails in the world to accommodate them!" *The World Tomorrow* published Einstein's "two per cent" address in January 1930, and returned to the theme repeatedly.[52] The survey was their contribution to building the 2 percent.

In 1931, *The World Tomorrow* sent out 53,000 surveys to American clergy and received a total of 19,372 returns by the closing date. Mass responses meant tabulation had to be done by machine and the calculations checked and authorized by a certified accountant. Like the war guilt questionnaire, Page interpreted the responses as showing a growing and pleasing consensus. He admitted it would be foolish to question the perennial relationship between the churches and war too quickly, but was hopeful that the survey seemed to reveal signs of a "revolution" in "churchmen's thinking."[53] Of those who replied, over 53 percent—that is, 10,427 ministers—replied "yes" when asked, "Are you personally prepared to state that it is your present purpose not to sanction any future war or participate as an armed combatant?" A greater proportion, a total of 12,076, answered "yes" to the question, "Do you believe that the churches of America should now go on record as refusing to sanction or support any future war?" Not to be overlooked was the overwhelming consensus that had formed around the other issues championed by *The World Tomorrow* in the 1920s—namely military training in schools and American interventionism in Latin America. When asked, "Do you believe that the policy of armed intervention in other lands by our Government to protect the lives and property of American citizens should be abandoned?," 12,017 said "yes," and only 3,899 said "no"—a big shift even since the 1928 Monroe Doctrine questionnaire and a sign of the rising tide of anti-imperialist opinion. The issue of military training in schools received the most unanimous response. Only 2,574 supported military training in public high schools and colleges or universities, while 16,018, around 83 percent, opposed it.[54] The 1,101 responses from students at theological seminaries showed the same majorities, only with even higher margins. "Opposition to the war system appears to be even more vigorous in theological seminaries than among clergymen generally," remarked Page.[55]

For Page, and for the press that covered the survey, the biggest story was the amassed "no" to war being articulated by a group considered vital to the nation's moral establishment. The lede Page offered was that 10 percent of all clergy in America had foresworn war. His figure had a simple—if amateur—mathematical logic to it. In constructing the survey, Page had estimated there were around 100,000 clergy in America at the time of the survey; his roughly 10,000 responses against war corresponded to 10 percent of all American clergy. The sample of 53,000, he said, was chosen for the pragmatic reason of managing the expense and time of the project.[56] It left out Jews, Catholics, Lutherans, Southern Baptists, and Southern Methodists. The absence of the theologically and politically conservative southern denominations likely accentuated the trend toward radicalism that Page was seeking to demonstrate. Of those who did send replies, almost one-third were from the Methodist Episcopal denomination, already overrepresented among the ranks of Social Gospel and peace campaigners. Presbyterians, Congregationalists, Protestant Episcopalians, Baptists, and Disciples of Christ ministers all contributed close to 2,000 responses each. The Reformed Church and Reinhold Niebuhr's denomination, the Evangelical Synod, as well as the Unitarians, were responsible for several hundred responses.[57] Notwithstanding the limits of these surveys, Page's aim was not to measure opinion for its own sake but to mobilize the data for the purpose of intervening in wider public debate.

In seeking wider publicity, Page and *The World Tomorrow* were quickly rewarded. Bertrand Russell again chipped in with a commendation for the "valuable work" the journal had done.[58] *The Nation* editorialized favorably that the survey was a sign of a gradual weakening in the traditional alliance between churches and the war system.[59] Historian Harry Elmer Barnes tipped his hat to the courage of the clergy (a "fine thing") in the radical *New York World-Telegram*, and he let them know he was no "slavish eulogist of the ministerial group."[60] But, most prominent of all the commendations—and one framed in a special inset in *The World Tomorrow*—was from Albert Einstein.[61] It was a "gratifying revelation" for Einstein to read of the 54 percent of respondents ready to declare their unwillingness to participate in war. "Only such a radical position can be of any help to the world," he wrote. The originator of the 2 percent plan liked what he saw, and *The World Tomorrow* cherished the endorsement.

The journal found a surprising friend in Bruce Barton, the author made famous by his portrayal of Jesus as an example of successful business advertising in *The Man Nobody Knows*. *The World Tomorrow* had never been sympathetic to Barton's implicit sanctification of big business. Yet, precisely because of Page's growing acumen as a publicist, Barton was interested in the journal's work. He agreed too that modern war was morally different in kind from older wars, and, like Page, he believed that the forces of advertising and publicity could be utilized to prevent another war. Agitation for peace, he argued, "ought to be a part of the educational program for every nation, supported by continuous advertising." He offered an idea Page had expressed five years earlier (while Barton was likely still busy with *The Man Nobody Knows*): "If the nations of the world would appropriate the cost of one battleship each year to be expended in international advertising it would go a long way toward persuading people that another war must never happen."[62]

But because the surveys were a self-conscious act of counterpublicity, *The World Tomorrow* relished negative coverage as much—perhaps more than—the positive. In the June 1931 edition (following the release of the results in May), pride of place was given to the lengthy letter from General Douglas MacArthur, discussed above. Page had personally mailed the survey results to MacArthur, and the general had written back to express his surprise and dismay at so many clergy willing to flout constitutional obligations. At the heart of MacArthur's rather emotional response lay a sense of what was robust, right, and "Christian." In his letter, published in full, MacArthur argued Jesus had come not to bring peace but "a sword," citing the Gospel of Matthew. When military men fought, they sacrificed, like Jesus, in service of freedom, liberty, love of country, and love of God. Drawing on the metaphor of a sacred national "altar"— made popular by Abraham Lincoln almost seventy years earlier—MacArthur said, "I can think of no principles more high and holy than those for which our national sacrifices have been made in the past." Moreover, he accused Page of messing with the fabric of the national story, which rested on a fundamental dualism: "History teaches us that religion and patriotism have always gone hand in hand, while atheism has invariably been accompanied by radicalism, communism, bolshevism, and other enemies of free government." So who was really Christian? It was the muscular patriot, argued the general.[63] MacArthur's response generated further publicity in itself. The *Chicago Tribune*, reporting from Washington, summarized MacArthur's reaction thus: "Such an attitude on the part of clergymen was unchristian, a menace to law and order and an unauthorized invasion of the political field by the church."[64] From New York, no less a personage than publishing magnate William Randolph Hearst took time to applaud MacArthur—"It was high time for someone in authority to voice the contempt of the nation for the sapping expedition against the national defense."[65]

Criticisms echoing MacArthur's response followed from others too. Rear Admiral Fiske, whom Page had opposed in a high-profile radio debate on the tenth anniversary of the armistice, wrote to the magazine dismissing the survey's significance as having about the same importance as the replies of clergymen answering questions on proposed cures of cancer.[66] Only students of war should discuss the causes of war, he argued, neglecting the counterargument that cancerous cells did not benefit from the sanction and support of churches for the flourishing of their cause. In contrast to Page's anti-imperialist critiques of Theodore Roosevelt's diplomacy, Fiske suggested peace was best kept by following the late president's mantra, "speak softly, but carry a big stick."[67]

Through the 1920s, some of the most vocal opposition to Page, Eddy, and *The World Tomorrow* had come from the American Legion. Sherwood Eddy had had public lectures shut down due to Legion pressure only years earlier.[68] Edward Spafford, previously National Commander of the American Legion, and a figure responsible for the anti-Eddy campaign, wrote to the journal to say that he liked peace as much as anyone else, but that no less than the integrity and legitimacy of patriotism was at stake. Like MacArthur, he aligned atheism with pacifism and religion with nationalism, warning, "he who takes from the child his love of country is as guilty as he who takes from a person the consolation of his God."[69] The survey had hit a raw nerve for anxious defenders of civil religion in the 1920s.

Rather than retreating from criticism, then, the editors of *The World Tomorrow* sought to use it for their own ends. They took pains not only to reprint correspondence from well-known public figures, but also to trawl for vituperative responses in the smaller periodical press that they could collate and frame for readers. Such deliberate sourcing and foregrounding of opposition—from outlets that were almost a caricature of themselves—provided the reader with another act of participation in the counterpublic. *The World Tomorrow's* June 1931 issue included a piece from the *Iowa Legionnaire*, which condemned the "treason" from the "communists, hyphenates, peace-at-any-price pacifists" at *The World Tomorrow*.[70] A few pages later, space was given to the *Pennsylvania Manufacturer's Journal*, whose editors looked forward to the next war, when the "traitors" would provide everyone with a "brand new national sport: gunning for clergymen."[71] The laughter and foreboding evoked in facing such opposition only further established and reinforced the journal's "counterness."

Conclusion

On one level, *The World Tomorrow* can be read as becoming increasingly oppositional and "counter" in the early 1930s. Their deployment of the mass survey technique managed to present and frame mainline Protestant clergy as opponents of the state and as dissenters and critics of U.S. foreign policy in Latin America. Such counterpublicity efforts bred criticism from opponents, which in turn fueled the fires of counterpublicity, in an escalating cycle. *The World Tomorrow's* culture-war skirmishes took place in other settings than the periodical press too, such as the radio waves and the public speaking circuit. *World Tomorrow* figures had, by 1932, developed their own "World Tomorrow Radio Hour" on the safe and sympathetic WEVD Eugene V. Debs memorial station. But, in one instance in a long and conflicted relationship, Page's fellow editor Devere Allen found himself barred from speaking on NBC's radio network in 1933. NBC's censors labeled Allen's manuscript "offensive" (where he quoted statistics on arms spending) and blocked him from speaking on the grounds that he would undermine public "confidence" and "faith." "Faith in whom?" fumed a full-page editorial days later entitled "Radical Truth Goes off the Air."[72]

Meanwhile, ahead of a planned trip south to offer the 1932 commencement address at Baylor University in Texas, Page was the subject of a scathing attack in the *Fundamentalist of Texas*, whose entire front cover, as he recalled in his autobiography, was covered in orange ink, with the headline reading: "International Red Communist and Atheist to Deliver Commencement Address at Baylor University." The headline was accompanied by a half-page photo of Rev. Ethelred Brown, an African American pastor who worked in the offices of *The World Tomorrow*. "The whole country is stirred," wrote editor Frank Norris, "over Baylor University having, Kirby Page, editor of *The World Tomorrow*, which is the official mouthpiece of the Communist organization in America, to deliver the commencement address next Wednesday, June 1, 1932." Referring to *The World Tomorrow*'s evident practice of employing black office staff and publishing black authors, Norris argued that Page "carries his communism into practical application by repeatedly advocating social equality with the Negroes."[73] Page was no Communist, but the latter charge he would happily have accepted. Students sympathized with Page and reacted against Norris's extremes. Yet, as Page recalled it, the controversy was enough for the Board of Trustees to change their mind and withdraw the honorary doctorate they had reportedly intended to bestow on him.[74]

While the sense of oppositionality reached a fever pitch in the early 1930s, paradoxically *The World Tomorrow* was becoming more closely aligned with the wider foreign policy public. The journal was becoming closer to mainstream opinion and policymaking, and the movement was mutual. Politically, the three distinctive planks of *The World Tomorrow*'s foreign policy counterpublicity in the 1920s—its opposition to U.S. interventionism in Latin America; its adoption of a revisionist, antimilitarist interpretation of the past and present; and its emphasis on foreswearing future involvement in war—became increasingly shared by sections of the wider American public, including policymakers and members of Congress. All three planks were compatible with the rising tide of "neutralist" opinion—a more precise category than, and a subset of, "isolationism."[75] As will be seen in chapter 3, *The World Tomorrow*'s connection to the rise of neutralism was one of its key legacies. Yet it was not its only legacy. Beneath the surface of the mass antiwar publicity generated by the surveys, another school of thought was being nurtured in *World Tomorrow* circles—one that would have its own contribution to make to religious interpretation of American foreign relations: Reinhold Niebuhr's Christian realism. The contrasting legacies of *The World Tomorrow* are the subject of the next chapter.

Chapter 3

A Funeral and Two Legacies

Throughout the 1920s, *The World Tomorrow* editorial team had, on the whole, expressed a consensus, consciously conceived, that a "Christian feeling" ought to be positive. Promoting the religion of Jesus meant holding out the attractiveness of His disposition. An advertising leaflet for *The World Tomorrow* from 1921 related Jesus to the problems of modern life through the category of "temper." "Today we face a world so torn by doubts and fears, so much at war with its own best impulses, that more than ever we must turn for hope to the warm and living spirit of Jesus whose life and love stand in contrast to the appalling temper of our times." It remained an emphasis in the mid-1920s as well. Planning papers from 1925 reveal the journal's policy on the emotional tenor of editorials: "The tone should avoid cynicism altogether and employ skepticism with caution. While optimism would be equally foolish we should bring all the zest and enthusiasm into our pages that we can—a warmth and faith and religious reliance on the power of good to conquer when used rightly."[1] Letters from readers such as Mrs. Post (widow of the late Louis F. Post, the Progressive reformer, who as assistant secretary of Labor under Wilson opposed the Justice Department's Red Scare deportations) congratulated the journal on its "constructive work." Post stated her admiration of the "fine temper of the editors. They haven't time to get angry with their fellows."[2]

But, by the early 1930s, the temper of the journal had changed. The very aesthetics of the magazine's production—produced in weekly editions from 1932—reflected a more critical, urgent, and sober editorial tone. Cover designs were starker, less ornate, more consciously angular and modern. Headlines offered less appeal to deliberative reason and more jagged, newsy phrases and predictions. Woodcut illustrations, where they were included, became increasingly modernist in style, emphasizing the impersonal bleakness of industrial and military landscapes, instead of the portraits and rural scenes of the 1920s. And, on the editorial pages, one figure in particular was singlehandedly doing his best to transgress the policy about positive feelings. From December 1932, Reinhold Niebuhr was assigned a special opening editorial page entitled "Ex Cathedra." Here he had no room for warmth or upbeat good cheer and called for the opposite. He attacked Democratic Party mantras to "banish fear" and "live on optimism and goodwill." Churches had contributed to a culture of sentimentality, and Niebuhr wondered whether pulpits would "preach more repentance and less hope," they might have a message that politicians could not "imitate so unctuously."[3] Niebuhr's columns dripped with sarcasm and did not hold back from labeling the moderate American Federation of Labor meetings as "pathetic," and Republican politicians as "stupid little children."[4]

The noises coming from Niebuhr in the 1930s *World Tomorrow* were one marker of the way the magazine fostered in its pages the growth of "Christian realism" in the early Depression years. As a qualification from within Christian internationalism, realism was characterized as much by its challenge to reigning affective norms (or "feeling rules," in the terminology of social movement theorists[5]) as it was by its analyses of social change and new theological emphases. In this chapter, I position Niebuhr's realism as one of two legacies left by *The World Tomorrow*—one of two ways, seemingly opposite, that the radical Christian internationalism nurtured in the community of *The World Tomorrow* engaged with wider American foreign policy public in the 1930s–1940s. Avoiding the somewhat misleading terms "isolationist" and "internationalist"—for they were both internationalist—I here trace the way *World Tomorrow* figures took the lead on both sides of the debate over American neutralism and interventionism. I argue that despite the observable differences between these groups—often characterized as "pacifists" and "realists"—they shared common analyses of imperialism, race, and, especially, nationalism. Both groups can be seen as having roots in *The World Tomorrow*.

With little warning, in early August 1934, *The World Tomorrow*'s Manhattan offices closed, and the journal ceased to operate. "The W.T. is dead. Long live socialism, pacifism and religion!," Page wrote to Devere Allen. "Am sad at the funeral," he scrawled in handwriting, "but rejoice in seed sown and now growing vigorously." He and "Reinie" were now going to spread the message of *The World Tomorrow* through the pages of *Christian Century*. Niebuhr was already a contributing editor there, and Page was to join as well. In fact, Page had just closed a deal with the *Christian Century* to purchase the bankrupt weekly for a grand total of $352 cash, plus a commitment to take on subscriptions not yet fulfilled.[6] The sustained financial vulnerability of *The World Tomorrow* had taken its toll. The revenue stream from advertising and subscriptions was not enough to meet costs, and last-ditch efforts to secure additional donations from a wealthy Socialist had failed.[7] As *Time* magazine had remarked of the journal in 1932, it was rare for a monthly to go weekly at the height of the financial and economic crisis that was the Depression.[8] And, indeed, over time, the financial strain proved too much. As Page recalled, "I was always too optimistic, and the 1932 change to a weekly proved to be the final blunder."[9] But Page's metaphor of seed being sown was apt. *The World Tomorrow*'s particular brand of Christian internationalism did indeed grow vigorously in many corners of American debate over foreign relations in the 1930s–1940s. But he was only half right; the growth was not all in one direction.

The World Tomorrow's Neutralist Legacy

Historian George Herring has suggested that if 1920s "isolationism" was characterized by "engagement without commitment"—with America laying claim to isolation and normalcy on one hand, while engaging in peace treaties, interventionism, and cultural exports on the other—then 1930s isolationism was characterized, by contrast, with an overriding commitment to guaranteeing American neutrality.[10] Old rhetoric about remaining free from "foreign entanglements" became attached to new agendas, such as Congress's succession of Neutrality Acts passed from 1935, the proposed Ludlow amendment to introduce popular referenda on declarations of war, and the highly publicized investigations of the Senate's Special Committee on Investigation of the Munitions Industry headed by Gerald P. Nye (R–ND).

Several factors combined in the early to mid-1930s to bring peace activists in general—and notably those at *The World Tomorrow*—to the fore of such neutralist agitation. Disillusionment following the much-anticipated Geneva Disarmament Conference in early 1932, along with the inability of the League of Nations to do anything effective about the Japanese occupation of Manchuria, made internationalist peace activists like Kirby Page look to domestic legislation as a priority. It was the only aspect of international peace over which they felt they could exercise any control. And, with the furthering of anti-capitalist sentiment in mainstream politics in the mid-1930s—with criticism of "organized money" even appearing in President Roosevelt's speeches near the end of his first term—opposition to war and militarism became tied to suspicion of financiers and industrialists.[11] Not only were "bankers" out of favor, but "munitions makers," allegedly in cahoots with high finance, also became the target of public disdain. Such a combination of anticapitalism and antimilitarism, themes dear to *The World Tomorrow*, allowed its coalition of writers and activists to play an increasingly central and less "counter" role in public debate. In addition to those international and domestic political factors, the very dynamics of Roosevelt's presidency also made room for activists to take leadership in public debate. Unlike Woodrow Wilson in 1917–1919, the newly incumbent president was quiet on foreign policy in the early 1930s, and, as a result, as Robert David Johnson notes, he left a vacuum that peace movements sought to fill.[12]

The logic of *The World Tomorrow*'s anti-imperialism extended naturally into support for neutralism. Although the journal could never get behind Roosevelt's domestic agenda—to their Socialist eyes the New Deal was an attempt to save the already damned system of private enterprise—they did offer quiet approval of the changes the president wrought in America's relations with Latin America, welcoming, if doubting, his pledge that the United States would now be a "Good Neighbor."[13] Secretary Hull had reversed the position of Coolidge and Kellogg, stating to the Montevideo conference in December 1933 that "no state has the right to intervene in the internal or external affairs of another." The president himself confirmed the new stance: "The definite policy of the United States from now on is one opposed to armed intervention."[14] The year 1934 also saw Roosevelt rescind the Platt Amendment in relation to Cuba and promise the Philippines independence—although *The World Tomorrow* thought the way arguments for independence had been made was disgraceful, neither side "caring hardly one whit about the fulfillment of our long-standing pledge . . . and thinking of turning the Islands loose primarily in order that certain American agricultural interests might benefit."[15] Thus, with the question of U.S. imperialism seemingly annulled for the moment, Page and other radical Christian internationalists began to reroute the concern they once had with interventionism in Latin America into an advocacy against all kinds of U.S. interventionism anywhere. This caused them now to look at American entry into the Great War as caused primarily by its basic commitment to mercantile interventionism. The real factor in the war, Page now reckoned, was not "democracy," or even just the abstract forces of competitive imperialisms, but the American commitment to protect life and property on the high seas. This attitude had been the trip wire that caused entry into the war, and it was the trigger that needed to be avoided in the future—buffered and sealed off by legislation safeguarding America against the impulses of the executive branch.[16] With all these factors converging, Page and *The World Tomorrow* had reached a far greater congruency with public discourse and with the contours of Congress's foreign relations agenda than at any time before.

A clear sign of *The World Tomorrow*'s move from a marginal to a central position in foreign policy discourse—an indicator of its riding the crest of surging neutralist sentiment—came in the reception afforded to their 1934 survey of clergy. While the survey was largely a repeat of the 1931 effort—more surveys sent out, but still around twenty thousand returned—shrill opposition had given way to tempered appreciation and applause from mainstream media outlets. The antiwar position of the clergy still made news, but not as treason, nor as an oddity, but rather as one facet of a wider tide of popular antiwar revulsion. The National Broadcasting Company, which had earlier censored Devere Allen, cooperated with *The World Tomorrow* to allow an interpretation of their survey data to be broadcast on the national network. Page was pleased too, with how the survey had been "treated generously by editors around the nation." Not only had the survey been given prominence on front pages and editorials of major dailies, the tone of the commentary was "more appreciative and less critical of radical tendencies than many observers had expected."[17] *Time* favorably covered Harry Emerson Fosdick's public and dramatic renunciation of war at a *World Tomorrow* meeting convened to discuss the survey results in New York, and Fosdick reported to Page that he had never received so much positive correspondence in his career.[18]

With such momentum building, then, what happened to *The World Tomorrow*'s contributions to neutralist politics after mid-1934, after the journal's sudden demise? The short answer is that several figures with close ties to the journal—not just Page, but also Charles Beard, Dorothy Detzer, A. J. Muste, and H. C. Engelbrecht—went on to play major roles in shaping American public opinion in favor of neutralism. Through its relationship with H. C. Engelbrecht, *The World Tomorrow* served as the incubator for one of the most influential books in the public discussion around the high-profile investigations of the Nye Committee. As a young, multilingual history PhD student, Engelbrecht had been in and out of *The World Tomorrow* for years. He worked in the office as assistant editor in 1927 and 1928 before taking a job editing *Social Science Abstracts*.[19] He returned to the journal in the early 1930s as a contributor and as one of four specially appointed associate editors who were given much page space in the journal for their own work. In that capacity Engelbrecht began to publish exposés of the international munitions industry. Articles such as "The Bloody International" and "The Traffic in Death" began to reveal research into the workings of Krups, Vickers, and their allied American interests.[20] Despite the impression one might get from the reception of his books, though, Engelbrecht was always cautious about attributing too much causality to the military-industrial complex. He shared *The World Tomorrow*'s more holistic view of the cultural causes of war. "Let us have all the exposés of the arms industry we can get; focus a searchlight on its devious paths; curb its activities wherever possible," he wrote. "But let us not be drawn away by this sensational subject from the more prosaic task of fighting the more important war-makers." Those targets included the whole pantheon of *World Tomorrow* foes: "the chauvinistic press, especially the Hearst papers, the *Chicago Tribune*, *Liberty* . . . the army and navy departments and their militarist allies, including the American Legion, the Navy League, the D.A.R., and the *Army and Navy Journal* . . . imperialism practiced by governments and powerful bankers . . . military training in the R.O.T.C. and narrow chauvinistic education." There would be no arms industry without these allied publicity forces.[21]

Nonetheless, Engelbrecht kept on with his exposés of arms production and found a public ready for his insights. His research, conducted and written up with another writer, F. C. Hanighen, became published as *Merchants of Death*— one of the most iconic book-length exposés of arms manufacturers in the mid-1930s, circulating the corridors of power when Senator Nye convened his special Senate investigation into the same issue. It was the *New York Times* "Book of the Month" in May 1934, and the same year was translated and sold in France, Holland, and Sweden.[22] The *New York Times* was right in predicting that *Merchants of Death* would be one book to provide the Nye Committee with "plenty of points for inquisitorial departure" as it commenced its work.[23] So much so did the title "Merchants of Death" become associated with the Nye Committee that later works of history, such as that presented on the U.S. Senate's website, often use the names interchangeably.[24]

Dorothy Detzer, a fellow *World Tomorrow* executive, and leader of the Women's International League for Peace and Freedom, strengthened *The World Tomorrow*'s connection to the Nye Committee even further. A longtime anti-imperialist and pacifist, with broad experience overseas, Detzer was "secretary" of *The World Tomorrow* (in the executive sense) from August 1932 until the journal's end. She shared the platform with Kirby Page and other *World Tomorrow* figures at antiwar events and reviewed works for the journal, such as Benjamin Williams's critique of the "Doctrine of [Alfred Thayer] Mahan."[25] Detzer was one link among many between WILPF and *The World Tomorrow*—

others such as Jane Addams, Emily Greene Balch, and Carrie Chapman Catt had long been involved as contributors. Although other *World Tomorrow* editors often found WILPF antiwar arguments to be too centered on legal machinery and too moderate at times, WILPF's leadership in 1920s anti-imperialism made them a vital part of the *World Tomorrow* network. Moreover, Detzer's suspicion of the munitions industry made her voice a forceful counterpart to Engelbrecht's—one made all the more effective by her personal access to Senator Nye in 1934.[26]

Beyond the sensation caused by the eventually discredited Nye Committee, Page and *The World Tomorrow*'s long-held commitment to promoting revisionism can be connected to the rising importance of history in public debate in the late 1930s. Not only did Page find greater reception for his own views, so too did other major figures in professional history. Both Charles and Mary Beard had long been involved in the journal's community—reviewing, commenting, and participating in symposia, such as the one on the Monroe Doctrine. Further, both had, along with John Dewey, Kirby Page, and several others, contributed essays to *Recent Gains in American Civilization*, one of many books consisting of published *World Tomorrow* articles.[27] The Beards, with their histories of America and their public commentary, became two of the most influential figures providing an intellectual rationale for neutralism. Charles Beard, like Detzer and Engelbrecht, helped popularize the link between finance and war, implying that the horror of the Great War had been caused and exacerbated by capitalist-industrialist interests seeking to profit from munitions manufacturing. The vindictive Treaty of Versailles made a mockery of fighting for an ideal like democracy. And now, he said in 1936, in the light of these costly lies, America did not want to get "badly burned again."[28]

Like the Beards, Page linked his analysis of the last war to political agitation designed to keep America out of the next one. His role as a foreign policy publicist had not begun with *The World Tomorrow*; neither did it end with the journal's demise. In 1935, Ray Newton of the American Friends Service Committee, a colleague of Page's, convened a group that became the basis for the Emergency Peace Campaign—an organization aimed at mobilizing an antiwar public through mass publicity and persuasion. Page, long used to managing campaigns on foreign policy issues, became chair of the speakers' bureau of the Emergency Peace Campaign, overseeing the 643 men and women volunteering to speak around the country. Harry Emerson Fosdick—fresh from his role in the 1934 *World Tomorrow* meetings—lent his services as a speaker, as did the celebrity aviator-explorer Admiral Richard E. Byrd. Page's connections from *The World Tomorrow* and the Eddy Seminar enabled him to bring to

America several British peace campaigners, including George Lansbury, the recent leader of British Labour who had resigned due to his pacifist principles, and Maude Royden, the longtime *World Tomorrow* contributor who had encouraged Page's conversion to pacifism twenty years earlier.[29] Significantly, it was Eleanor Roosevelt who launched the Emergency Peace Campaign. Though Page was not, of course, the only progressive or radical to associate with Eleanor, he was nevertheless working alongside the First Lady. The arrangement was emblematic of his move—in relative terms—from the margins to the center of popular foreign policy discourse in the mid-1930s.[30]

Page's role as a foreign policy publicist climaxed with his work on the Keep America Out of War committee. There he authored the influential booklet *How to Keep America out of War*, of which 330,000 copies were distributed under the imprint of seven peace organizations.[31] Writing in 1939, Page brought themes and categories developed through the last two decades to bear on the present European war. As he did for U.S. imperialism in the 1920s, he evoked moral equivalence and empathy. "What would Frenchmen or Englishmen or Americans have done if they had stood in German shoes during those years [of the Versailles settlement]?"[32] Americans needed to understand that the causes of the present war lay in the three forces of nationalism, imperialism, and militarism, and that on these counts, the British, French, and Americans were just as bad, if not worse, than the Germans. Britain led the world in imperial possessions, and Germany's longing for imperial expansion was merely the hunger of a "have not" who envied the satisfied and smug "haves." American territorial expansion highlighted the common heritage of imperialism in the United States: "aggression is written all over" this U.S. "map."[33] Page seemed to avoid discussion of the persecution of Jewish people; Jews appeared in his text only as part of his historical analysis of the first-century antiwar ethics of Jesus, who had refused to distinguish between good and bad empires in his nonviolent submission. Concerns over fascism overseas were subordinated to worry about fascism at home, which Page thought would inevitably result from a U.S. war effort. Such moral and analytical weaknesses in Page's argument were not unique to him and plagued the sprawling antiwar coalition that united Far Right and Far Left in 1939–1941. Page's predictions were more prescient on the totalizing nature of the war that would ensue. War was to be avoided because, unlike the scenarios imagined in just war theories, "modern war is an armed conflict between entire populations waged with all the diabolical weapons forged by science."[34]

While Page was providing leadership to neutralists and peace activists of all stripes, one other remnant of *The World Tomorrow* community focused on maintaining the Fellowship of Reconciliation's (FOR) uncompromising commitment to nonviolence. With the demise of their quasi-official publication, the FOR took the opportunity to start a new journal, entitled *Fellowship*, which became arguably the most important periodical representing Christian pacifism in the late 1930s–1940s. Edited by Harold Fey, a *World Tomorrow* writer—later *Christian Century* editor—and close colleague of Page, *Fellowship* emphasized the rejection of all war, the promotion of racial equality, and, as the name suggested, the practice of "fellowship" as a way of living. Crucial to *Fellowship*'s ongoing importance was the newly focused energy of A. J. Muste. The pastor turned pacifist had been a part of *The World Tomorrow* community since its inception but in the Page years had receded from central focus. *The World Tomorrow* had supported Muste's "labor education" programs but provided only cautious support of his forging of a militant labor party in 1934. As his biographers have written, though, Muste, already disillusioned with Trotskyist infiltrators in the workers movement, underwent a profound second conversion to Christian mysticism and pacifism in 1936 while traveling in Europe.[35] This transformation—in which he sensed a divine call to return to church work—saw him take leadership in fellowship circles by 1940 and maintain an unflinching commitment to Christian nonviolence and peace activism for the next three decades. In the longer term, *Fellowship* and its editors formed a vital—perhaps unrivaled—link between Old Left and New Left. When groups such as the National Committee for a Sane Nuclear Policy (SANE) and the Congress on Racial Equality (CORE, formed in 1942 by Muste and FOR colleagues) emerged in the 1950s, one common denominator was the Fellowship of Reconciliation and A. J. Muste. As Martin Luther King Jr. was reported to have remarked in the 1950s, "the current emphasis on nonviolent direct action in the race relations field is due more to A. J. than to anyone else in the country."[36]

The Interventionist Legacy: Niebuhrian Realism

With former *World Tomorrow* figures forming an all-star cast in the neutralist and pacifist case *against* war, it was striking that an equal and opposite contribution came from other former counterpublicists at the journal. Reinhold Niebuhr's attacks on Page-style notions of moral equivalence, together with his arguments that New Testament injunctions to nonviolence could *not* be applied to nations' foreign policies earned him equal doses of notoriety and fame—and increasingly the latter. If Muste became a "mentor to the New

Left," as Dan McKanan labels him, Niebuhr, in the eyes of many others, became a "father" to Cold War liberalism and realism.[37] How, then, did *The World Tomorrow* serve as an incubator not only for 1930s antiwar neutralism but also for Niebuhrian realism?

Examining Niebuhr's place in the coalition of *The World Tomorrow* highlights Christian realism's emergence as a reaction to, or rather a qualification from within, Christian internationalism. As will be seen in part 2 of this volume, realism owed much of its theological treatment of international life to the ecumenical internationalism articulated at the Oxford 1937 world conference, in which Niebuhr and fellow realists played a major—indeed, disproportionate—role. The following account of the Fellowship of Socialist Christians associated with *The World Tomorrow* should also be placed alongside the account of the Theological Discussion Group in chapter 5. But Christian realism also owed much of its origins to the radical Christian internationalism of *The World Tomorrow*.

The World Tomorrow as a Gathering Point for Realists

The World Tomorrow acted as a gathering point for the cadre of theologians who would make up Christian realism in the 1940s—namely Niebuhr, John C. Bennett, Henry Pit Van Dusen, and Francis Pickens Miller. While the Depression provided the climatic conditions for their reformulation of Christian ethics, *The World Tomorrow* provided a specific medium for its articulation. Not only was each of the realists connected to production of *The World Tomorrow*, the journal itself was institutionally aligned with the organizations in which they met and forged their new ideas.

Tracing connections between *The World Tomorrow* and its surrounding world of little "leagues" and "fellowships," provides a strategy for reading the journal in its own right.[38] Naturally, from its beginning, *The World Tomorrow* was aligned with the Fellowship of Reconciliation, the organization that officially published it from 1918 to 1926, and with which it remained closely tied. When John Nevin Sayre brought in Kirby Page as editor, as discussed in chapter 1, he also brought in the "F.C.S.O. crowd," the network around the Fellowship for a Christian Social Order. This move also eventually linked Niebuhr to the journal.[39] But, there were also several other organizations tied to the magazine. From 1929 *The World Tomorrow* became a chief outlet for the new organization chaired by John Dewey, called the League for Independent Political Action (LIPA). Dewey's group was devoted to promoting the "desirability of a new political alignment," outside of the two-party framework, "based upon the realities of American life." The platform for their liberal-Progressive alliance resembled much of what finally became policy in the Second New Deal: social insurance, taxation of "unearned" income, and protection of workers. *World Tomorrow* editors and contributing editors such as Reinhold Niebuhr, Kirby Page, Norman Thomas, and George Coe held places on the league's executive committee. Editorial space in the journal was given over to "welcoming" enthusiastically the league's cause. Indeed, so close were the two organizations that *The World Tomorrow* housed LIPA's offices within its own at 52 Vanderbilt Ave.[40] As the league began to dwindle, however, and as Niebuhr became less enamored with Dewey's liberalism and more inspired by Norman Thomas's socialism in the lead-up to the 1932 election—Niebuhr joining the Socialist ticket himself—LIPA's importance to *The World Tomorrow* was eclipsed by a new organization called the Fellowship of Socialist Christians.

The Fellowship of Socialist Christians

While the Socialist Party itself was an important institutional forum for Niebuhr, Thomas, Allen, Page, and others to articulate a common antiwar position in anti-imperialist and anticapitalist terms in the mid-1930s—and while membership doubtless furthered their sense of being counter to the mainstream— the smaller, frankly religious Fellowship of Socialist Christians was arguably more important to Christian realism's development. Despite its small size (around five hundred members met in small cell groups in 1934), the fellowship provided the site in which Niebuhr and his colleagues began to lay out the programmatic elements of what "realist" meant. For members, and especially for Niebuhr, the answer was defined in opposition to "liberal religion" and its apparent failures.

The first mention of the Fellowship of Socialist Christians (FSC) in *The World Tomorrow* was a small note in November 1931 used to support the argument, made in an editorial, that church ministers and rabbis were responding to the current economic crisis by becoming Socialists in rapid numbers. "In New York City a group of clergymen and seminary students meets regularly as a fellowship of Socialist Christians for the mutual exploration of social problems."[41] The group was much closer to *The World Tomorrow* than the editorial acknowledged. Initially populated by a wave of younger, radically minded collegiate YMCA figures and seminarians—such as Francis Henson, Buell Gallagher, and the YWCA's Winnifred Wygal—the fellowship came to be increasingly influenced by Niebuhr and his theological colleagues John Bennett and Henry Pit Van Dusen. Editorials, articles, and announcements about fellowship retreats and meetings appeared frequently in *The World Tomorrow* over the next three years.[42] Indeed, for the remainder of the journal's life, *The World Tomorrow* was the primary outlet of the fellowship. Soon after *The World Tomorrow*'s death, with the FOR having commenced publishing *Fellowship*, the FSC started an alternative periodical entitled *Radical Religion*. Later renamed *Christianity and Society*, it was, throughout the 1930s, one place where Niebuhr and company were able to develop the realist analyses they had begun to espouse in *The World Tomorrow*; like the latter, it was a space for a rougher-edged, angrier radicalism than that on offer at the mainline *Christian Century*.[43]

The Fellowship of Socialist Christians, according to its founding statement, gathered members in the belief that a "Christian ethic is most adequately expressed . . . in our society in socialist terms." The Christian Church, they argued, needed to recognize the "essential conflict between Christianity and the ethics of capitalistic individualism."[44] The fellowship not only made abstract declarations, it focused on its members' behavior and outlook. The group mandated its own form of progressive income tax (given to a charity of the member's choice), with rates increasing sharply from a minimum income of $1,400, as part of a program of "rigid discipline" designed to "encourage rigorous living standards." Not everyone liked being taxed, and the practice "reduced the membership of the Fellowship considerably."[45]

In their statements, the Socialist Christians defined themselves against what they called "Liberal Christianity." The latter, they argued, was blinded by its "evolutionary optimism," was "unrealistic," and did not have the necessary "ethical vigor" to generate real social change. The Fellowship of Socialist Christians would thus "strive to reduce the moral pretensions" that obscured "social realities," and would encourage "privileged groups," especially churches, to "recognize the extent of covert and overt violence inherent in the present order."[46] Such a critique of liberal religion, together with calls for more "realistic," Marxian political analyses, spilled over into the pages of *The World Tomorrow*, not only in features on the fellowship, but also in essays written by its members. During 1931 and 1932—while still working alongside those who would later campaign for neutralism—Niebuhr, Van Dusen, Bennett, and other members of the FSC began to use the pages of *The World Tomorrow* to reflect on the "resources" that Christianity might provide for realistic, and hence, radical, ethical action. The consensus they formed was that the way forward lay not in the rejection of organized Christianity, as others like Niebuhr's radical Union Seminary colleague Harry Ward were arguing, but rather in its revitalization through the joining of a deeper theology on one hand with a more radical politics on the other.[47] As Niebuhr put it, "adequate spiritual guidance can only come through a more radical political orientation and more conservative religious convictions than are comprehended in the culture of our era."[48]

Henry Pit Van Dusen, a colleague of Niebuhr's at Union Seminary, a member of the FSC, and treasurer of *The World Tomorrow*, wrote in the journal on what he called the "sickness" of contemporary liberal religion. If liberalism were to survive, it had to reject the Kantian presupposition that religion flowed from ethics, and instead recognize that the reverse relationship was true: "Vital religion by its very nature fecund, germinative, creative, can and should give birth to ethics."[49] Agreeing, Niebuhr argued that the "drive toward the absolute" inherent in all "vital religion" should provide the basis for social radicalism, even though historically it had typically buttressed conservatism.[50] Bennett argued that the presence of an "absolute ethic" in the Gospel was relevant to every age and condition, as it "creates a restlessness towards things as they are." Religion properly understood could and should act as a "stimulant" for social radicalism, and not an "opiate."[51]

Alongside emphasizing "vital religion," the self-dubbed realists offered new analyses of the role of power in social change. Here too they criticized the weakness of what they saw as modern liberalism. *The World Tomorrow* offered Niebuhr a space in which to rehearse and refine the arguments published in his landmark realist books of the period. One of his earliest essays calling for "realistic" religion in *The World Tomorrow* was modestly titled "Property and the Ethical Life" and was published in January 1931.[52] It offered an early version of the Christian-Marxian synthesis he famously argued for in *Moral Man and Immoral Society*, which was published the next year. A mere increase in social "intelligence" or religious "inspiration"—without changes to the actual structures of property ownership—would never produce social change, Niebuhr argued, because the real driver of behavior was self-interest. "Men of great power never divest themselves of their privileges in large numbers, no matter how intelligent they are."[53] It was too easy "to use intelligence for the purpose of rationalizing your desires and advantages."[54] To avoid the kinds of backlashes being witnessed in Russia and Germany, Americans had to be wary of the "peril" of letting radical change founder on the sand of mere "liberal reform."[55]

While Niebuhr's Marxian analysis would grow in subtlety and sophistication— becoming less simply focused on property rights and more about historical catastrophism and the dynamics of economic injustice in general—his division of people into two camps, that of realists and misled liberals, remained the same.[56] Realists acknowledged that forces of self-interest and structures of privilege and power were the real shapers of behavior, and even influenced reason. Liberals were well meaning but essentially deluded "idealists" who, naively trusting in reason, tried to create a better world through inspiration and education. Such was the picture offered, for example, in *Moral Man and Immoral Society* (1932). The same "good people in education and religion," whom he pitied in his 1931 *World Tomorrow* article, were castigated in the book—this time by name. Fellow LIPA member John Dewey was taken to task for promoting the view that with "a generally higher development of human intelligence, our social problems will approach solution."[57] Religious idealists, Niebuhr argued, such as his Union Seminary colleague William Adams Brown, had blindly swallowed the claims of liberalism in their heralding of the emergence of a "brotherly" society.[58] All such optimism amounted to "moral confusion." Proponents of such views neglected "the power of self-interest and collective egoism in intergroup relations" and the fact that "social conflict" as a result was "an inevitability in human history, probably to its very end."[59]

Realists' Feeling Rules

Insisting on the permanence of social conflict and the futility of schemes for its mitigation brought with it two implications for Niebuhr, both of which were manifest clearly in *The World Tomorrow*. The first was that Niebuhrian realism was received not only as an idea but also as a sensibility, an affective alignment. Recent sociological literature on social movements has pointed to the way that as "challengers to the status quo, social movements re-interpret specific aspects of social reality, call for new, obligatory emotions and feeling rules and wish to draw on these to mobilize individuals for collective action whose aim is to achieve social change."[60] Christian realism called for "new, obligatory emotions": it was as much defined by the adoption of a new temper and feeling as it was by a new interpretation of social and political reality.

The clearest example of the conflict over realism's new feeling rules emerged in the reaction to Niebuhr's *Moral Man and Immoral Society*. In *The World Tomorrow*, some such as Norman Thomas saw it as a salutary "epistle to the sentimentalists" and "the romanticists."[61] Many others found its tone defeatist—unchristian in feeling. One contributor referred to the typical reader being "depressed by *Moral Man and Immoral Society*."[62] Another writer, E. G. Homrighausen of Indiana, wrote to the journal to remark upon the way responses to Niebuhr's work focused, in his words, on the book's tendency "to sound the minor note."[63] Ralph H. Read, a minister and reader of *The World Tomorrow*, brought the themes of tone and temper to the fore with a provocative feature article entitled "Who Are the Defeatists?" Read recounted his attendance at a recent planning meeting for a church conference. As he recalled it, "Certain men were instantly written off the list as possible speakers because they would not inspire with hope and optimism the church people who would listen, and others were given favorable attention because they probably would speak the encouraging word." Read continued his analysis with a defense and recapitulation of Niebuhrian realism: it was simply a matter of facing the facts about social change. "The defeatist is not the man who looks at the evil in the world and then passes a distasteful or dark verdict, for such a verdict may be required. The defeatist is the man who sickens you by his promptness in blinding himself to reality so that he may hear himself sing."[64] The furor surrounding Niebuhr's work divided those who were for the new "feeling rules" from those who preferred the old ones.

The conflict over the realist temper reflected a growing split in ethical and political commitments among *The World Tomorrow* coalition—the second implication of Niebuhr's dampened forecast for social change. Niebuhr and Bennett, in particular, began to articulate a critique of Christian-motivated neutralism in social conflict that would later shape their approach to international conflict. As the Fellowship of Socialist Christians' founding principles had stated, churches needed to better recognize "the extent of covert and overt violence inherent in the present order."[65] If violence was already the hidden reality, then radicals had to start seeing justice, rather than peace, as the real goal to aim for. If they did not recognize that the "contemporary peace of any society is full of both injustice and coercion," they would tend to side with things as they were. They would constantly find themselves "in the position of preferring peace to justice" and having their "preference for peace transmuted into support of the *status quo*."[66] The responsibility to strive for justice in the present system meant that nonviolence could not always be equated with the most Christian response.

The apparent dilemma between choosing peace or justice came to a climax in a debate that rocked *The World Tomorrow* and the Socialist Party and eventually split the Fellowship of Reconciliation down the middle. The growing tension between members such as Niebuhr who were self-dubbed "realists" and those who were uncompromising in their pacifism crystallized in a debate over whether members could rightly endorse, and possibly participate in, violent revolutionary action that might occur in the seemingly inevitable class war. While it was mostly hypothetical, the question was not entirely unreasonable, given the contemporary implosion of liberal capitalist orders in Europe and the desperate violence occurring at strikes, pickets, and labor disputes around the United States. Late in 1933, the FOR sent a questionnaire to members asking their opinion on the matter.[67]

The results crystallized the gap that had emerged between "realists," who saw coercion and violence as inevitable ingredients to be factored into the calculus of social change, and those others in the fellowship who insisted—as they always had, but now even more so with the inspiration of Gandhi on their side—on the paramount importance of nonviolence. The result was a devastating split in the organization, marked by Niebuhr's resigning as chairman of the FOR and rescinding his membership.[68] So closely did the questionnaire precede the closure of *The World Tomorrow* that it seems likely to have been part of the cause of the magazine's decline. If nothing else, the unity of the broad, interlocking coalition of radical Christian internationalists that had constituted the journal's community of readers and writers was severely damaged. Whereas as late as 1931 or 1932 most members of the coalition would happily have claimed to be *both* pacifist and socialist, now in 1934 many felt compelled to define one or the other as their controlling commitment. Those who, like Niebuhr, stressed Marxian realism and the justice of structural change gave way on pacifism. Those like Sayre, Page, and (later) Muste remained convinced that violence in all individual or social forms was antithetical to the teachings and way of life of Jesus, and hence nonnegotiable.

The Common DNA of Antinationalism

Niebuhr and the realists' critique of neutralism and pacifism in class conflict became the conceptual basis of their opposition to American neutralism in international life. International justice, they argued, would not be secured by American neutralism in the face of German and Japanese militarism and expansionism; nor was the most Christian response necessarily the one that avoided violent conflict. Niebuhr had already hinted at such an approach in his response to the Manchurian crisis, in which he debated his brother, theologian H. Richard Niebuhr, in a high-profile series of articles in the *Christian Century*. There he questioned the ethics of toothless inaction on the part of the international community in responding to Japan.[69] Further international crises such as the Spanish Civil War and the Italian invasion of Ethiopia were interpreted by Niebuhr to mean that pacifism was "against the wall," incapable of providing meaningful guidance on foreign policy. Neutralist and pacifist campaigns were an example of the futility of applying "moral absolutism" in politics, he argued; "the political order must be satisfied with relative peace and relative justice."[70] By the time of his stinging 1940 tract, "Why the Christian Church Is not Pacifist," written with the Nazi conquest of Europe in view, Niebuhr had rounded out his realist critique of the pacifism he had earlier espoused. For Niebuhr, the very attempt to shape a nation's approach to international conflict based on New Testament pacifist norms was in fact "heretical." Such an approach produced a politics incapable of making relative decisions over relative goods, and thus led to a perverse preference for tyranny over war. That is, it would prefer peace to conflict even if that peace involved Hitler's subjugation of Europe. At base, argued Niebuhr, the issue was pacifists' failure to account for power, evil, and coercion in all realms of human existence, thus resulting in their liberal and idealistic overestimation of human virtue and (in language developed by the late 1930s) their underestimation of the impact of original sin in political life.[71]

The development of Niebuhr's all-too-successful critiques of pacifism in the 1930s and 1940s is well known and well established in scholarship.[72] Yet historians should be wary of Niebuhr's capacity to narrate his own journey. As explored in the introduction to this volume, Niebuhr's critiques were so powerful because he often overstated the degree to which he departed from a previous position and oversimplified the nature of the two positions he now saw as antithetical. What is often missed when historians reify the terms of Niebuhr's narration is the way he retained much that was characteristic of the milieu he claimed to reject. Both realists and nonrealists shared, from their origins, a common and important "no" toward nationalism—and with it imperialism and racism—that pervaded and defined their internationalism. The issue for realists such as Niebuhr was how to reconcile such antinationalism with their increasing support for U.S. foreign policy and their growing proximity to the state during the 1940s—when they were, in a sense, more "public" than counter. Such a tension was fundamental to the realist project. Far from drifting from their radical roots in this regard, Niebuhr and other realists retained and developed the critique of Christian nationalism developed by Page and other pacifist colleagues at *The World Tomorrow* as they came to the fore of the ecumenical movement in the mid to late 1930s.

Opposition to nationalism—especially to Christian-supported nationalism—had been a distinctive and definitive component of the radical Christian internationalist outlook at *The World Tomorrow*, and likely would have arisen even without new scholarly theories of nationalism. But, as with their revisionist analyses of the causes of World War I, their engagement with contemporary scholarship strengthened and sharpened their claims and positioned them at the leading edge of another historiographical turn. There were two themes in contemporary scholarship that especially engaged the attention of Page and others at *The World Tomorrow*. One was the new presentation of nationalism as something historically contingent—as *artificial* rather than natural. British scholars such as A. D. Lindsay and G. P. Gooch were promoting the view that nationalism was a "psychological" and emotional phenomenon, rather than a natural outworking of some empirical reality such as the biological or territorial basis of a group of people.[73] Similarly, America's Carlton Hayes, a historian at Columbia University and later ambassador to Spain, wrote about nationalism's artificiality and its unrivaled emotional significance in public life. Hayes anticipated Hans Kohn's depiction of nationalism in the 1940s as "a state of mind" and Benedict Anderson's classic formulation of nations as "imagined communities" in the 1980s.[74]

Engaging with such scholarship, *World Tomorrow* writers argued nationalism played a role in modern culture that was functionally equivalent to religion. Although Carleton Hayes published the idea in his 1926 *Essays on Nationalism*—and although he was reviewed favourably in *The World Tomorrow*—Christian internationalists did not need Hayes to tell them that nationalism was a new kind of secular faith.[75] Such an argument was already a well-developed part of their arsenal. A memorable and typical passage from *The World Tomorrow* in this respect came from the Virginian Francis Pickens Miller, who was a student of international relations at Oxford, a colleague of Page and Niebuhr's on the American student lecture scene, and a rising star in student ecumenism internationally.[76] Looking at domestic culture, Miller was concerned about the religion of nationalism taking hold in American political culture in everyday forms—even at the level of schools. Every day, he noted, "hundreds of thousands of school children stand at attention . . . before the national emblem and hymn its spangled stars." For Miller, this was "the cult of the National Being." Referring to Jesus's famous separation of that which is owed to Caesar and that which is owed to God, Miller offered a memorable quip that summed up the thinking of *The World Tomorrow* cohort well: "It isn't any longer a question of God or Caesar, for in the schools Uncle Sam is two in one."[77]

For his part, Kirby Page was relentless in his attempts to force American Protestants to distinguish between God and Caesar, Christianity and nationalism. His 1931 and 1934 surveys of clergy had sought to do precisely that. And, in his 1931 book *National Defense* (published with the biographical note "Editor, *The World Tomorrow*"), he added ammunition to his efforts by portraying American nationalism's co-opting of religion as part of a global problem. Page cataloged scores of examples of nationalistic rhetoric, assembling Japanese varieties alongside French, German, British, and American. It was no trouble for Page, for example, having cited reports on the influence of *kami* worship on Japanese nationalism, to turn by way of further illustration to Woodrow Wilson speaking of America as an "instrument in the hands of God."[78] All such appeals to divinity, according to Page, were a universal feature of national boasting and self-praise. To conclude his case, he appealed to one of the highest liberal Protestants in the land—one with whom he had closely worked on *The World Tomorrow*'s 1934 antiwar campaign—Harry Emerson Fosdick. "The gist of the matter," wrote Fosdick, "lies in the fact that the dogma of nationalism, as it has developed over the last two centuries, has become a competing religion." The most "crucial conflict today," he argued, was "Christianity versus nationalism, and until one has clearly envisaged that fact one does not understand the crux of our situation."[79]

Niebuhr's *Moral Man and Immoral Society*—the book that ostensibly marked his realist departure from idealist colleagues—revealed the profound continuity between his views on nationalism and his earlier community of discourse. At a surface level, the indebtedness was clear even in the list of references. Of the thirty-two footnotes given in his chapter on the "Morality of Nations," six were from Kirby Page's recent work, *National Defense*, others were from Charles and Mary Beard's work, others from Nathaniel Peffer, who had contributed a major feature article in the 1927 edition on the Caribbean, and others from Parker Moon, whose work on *Imperialism and World Politics* was widely read and cited among *World Tomorrow* circles. And, like his colleagues, Niebuhr argued nationalism was functionally religious. He gave it a characteristically Niebuhrian twist, however, by linking its religious qualities to the nation's tendency to claim universal validity for the pursuit of its narrow interests. Nations faced the awkward dilemma of claiming to be especially unique on one hand and to be the "incarnation of universal values" on the other. They typically resolved the conflict by resorting to false absolutes, so that "in the mind of the simple patriot the nation is not a society but Society. Though its values are relative, they appear, from his naïve perspective, to be absolute."[80] Hence nationalism both mimicked and absorbed religion. "The religious instinct for the absolute is no less potent in patriotic religion than any other. The nation is always endowed with an aura of the sacred, which is one reason why religions, which claim universality, are so easily captured and tamed by national sentiment, religion and patriotism merging in the process."[81] Niebuhr and Page, then, shared the same descriptive outlook toward nationalism: It was a global phenomenon, it involved falsely religious claims, and it was to be opposed.

Importantly, Niebuhr's and the other realists' opposition to nationalism strengthened in the mid to late 1930s as they became increasingly involved in the ecumenical movement in the lead up to the Oxford 1937 conference. In part 2 of this volume I explore further their theological critique of nationalism. As ecumenists, their early protests about nationalism as artificial and falsely religious—arguments based on engagement with contemporary history and historiography—were increasingly expressed in the register of dialectical Protestant theology. And, while they never lost sight of American nationalism as one nationalism among others, the emergence of the new German nationalism of the 1930s—where the cross and swastika became two in one—saw them develop their reflections with greater depth and urgency.

Conclusion

There were, to be sure, clear differences in the way the alternate legacies of *The World Tomorrow* network sought to relate Christianity to world affairs. While Page and the neutralists took opposition to war as their controlling ethical commitment, Niebuhr and the realists took structural justice to be theirs. Each group stressed different religious and biblical frameworks in explaining their position: the exemplary nonviolence of the historical Jesus on one hand, and the limits on pursuing justice in a sin-ridden world on the other. But the common thread of antinationalism that emerged among missionary internationalists in the 1920s and had been extended in the oppositional analyses of *The World Tomorrow* continued to shape the orientation of both the neutralists and the interventionists. It is important to recognize the way such a basal, critical posture helped distinguish their internationalism from other internationalisms on offer in the interwar period.

In the decade following World War I, American peace activists and internationalists tended to crystallize around one of two political programs: the League of Nations or the Outlawry of War. Wilsonian collective security advocates like Raymond Fosdick and Clark Eichelberger as well as internationalist groups like the League of Nations Association gave leadership to the former. They sought, and eventually found, their "second chance" at a League of Nations with the emergence of the United Nations Organization in the mid-1940s.[82] Others, like Salmon Levinson, a Chicago lawyer, and C. C. Morrison, editor of the *Christian Century*, drove the Outlawry of War campaign in the mid-1920s. They aimed at using international law and treaty arrangements to have nations "renounce" war as an instrument of national policy—the language of renunciation reflecting their links to the Temperance and Prohibition campaigns. Nations needed to get on the wagon and kick the war habit once and for all by sheer, voluntary, legal fiat. The Outlawry moment—for what it was—came with the signing of the Kellogg-Briand Pact in 1928, eventually signed by sixty-two nations.[83]

Leaders of each viewpoint often felt they shared little in common with the other. Outlawry of War advocates argued that the League of Nations was fundamentally corrupt and that an international treaty that renounced war as an instrument of national policy would render the league (which presupposed the possibility of war) obsolete.[84] League of Nations advocates like Fosdick felt the gradual, incremental progress made by the league was the best possible avenue toward peace available; it built habits of international cooperation that would further the cause of peace. Going further, some league enthusiasts developed a religion of Geneva, seeing in the institution transcendent—if not mystical—qualities.[85]

World Tomorrow Christian internationalists fit with neither program squarely or wholeheartedly. Indeed, their ill fit raises the question of whether the league and the Kellogg-Briand Pact can continue to operate as the shorthand metonyms for interwar internationalism that they often have. *The World Tomorrow* did give qualified support to the league *and* to the Outlawry program right up and through the signing of the Kellogg-Briand Pact in 1928. But an important exchange published in *The World Tomorrow* in 1927 highlighted the underlying gulf between the internationalism of that journal and the legalism of Outlawry especially. Charles Clayton Morrison, editor of *Christian Century*, was also author of the landmark work *The Outlawry of War* (1927) and a key figure in the campaign that had originated in his home city of Chicago. Page published an extended review of Morrison's work as a feature article in 1927, and, in response, Morrison provided a two-page rebuttal, which Page also published.[86] Page criticized what he saw as Morrison's emphasis on the juridical over the political aspects of international life and, most of all, his lack of attention to the causes of war. Most concerning was Morrison's lack of attention to the importance of nationalism. "Nations simply will not abandon the war system until drastic changes are made in the prevailing conception of national interest, national sovereignty, national honor, and national patriotism."[87] The problem was in the public consciousness; nationalism caused people to lend legitimacy to the state to wage war even when it was against the law. Morrison responded with evasive syllogisms. "How can a book which set itself the task of elaborating a technique of world peace be held responsible for a treatment of these questions [of causes of war]. . . . The nations will handle that after they have renounced war."[88] Morrison's fiery but somewhat vacuous reply revealed a subtle but significant gulf.

In a larger sense, the League of Nations strand and the Outlawry strand were both variants of legalism and institutionalism. They differed on their preferred mechanism—and Outlawry was arguably more "perfectionist"— but they shared a basically rationalistic view of people and of international life. Both saw international relations as improvable through the rational implementation of better laws, practices, and structures. Christian internationalists at *The World Tomorrow* like Page and Niebuhr could offer qualified support for both forms of rationalism but could not fundamentally rest their hopes with them. The various peace proposals were, in a sense, produced as a "yes"—the answer, the way out—to the problems of international conflict. Where *The World Tomorrow* differed, though, was in the "no"—the deeper, descriptive mapping of the world against which the peace proposals were to make sense. Unlike legalists, *World Tomorrow* internationalists gave primary emphasis to imperialism, racism, militarism, and nationalism as cultural, political, and indeed religious phenomena. Rather than aiming their speech at Geneva and Washington, D.C., asking for better policies, they pleaded for American Protestants to renounce their country's civil religion and, using their social influence, to join in the fight against these forces. Rather than spending their energies primarily on drumming up support for Briand's and Kellogg's diplomatic maneuvering, they agitated against the Coolidge administration's dropping of bombs on Sandinistas in Nicaragua. Rather than looking to Geneva to permeate the world with the habits of cooperation, both realist and pacifist Christian internationalists led subversive efforts to promote racial equality in the rural Jim Crow South—whether in the Mississippi Delta Farm Cooperative organized by Sherwood Eddy, Reinhold Niebuhr, and colleagues in 1934, or the Tennessee Highlander Folk School run by Christian socialists, Myles Horton and James Dombrowski.[89]

With its focus on countering Christian nationalism and civil religion, the radical Christian internationalism of *The World Tomorrow* also stood in stark relief against much else of what characterized Protestant engagement with American foreign relations in the twentieth century. As reams of scholarship have served to highlight, the 1890s–1910s, 1940s–1950s, 1980s, and early 2000s represent moments when Protestants in foreign policy debate have overwhelmingly asserted and reasserted the idea of Christian America, with its notes of America's divine "chosen-ness."[90] It is fair to see this as the dominant outlook by which Protestants have interpreted foreign relations. As Ernest Lee Tuveson's classic work, *Redeemer Nation*, argued, the notion of "Chosen race; chosen nation; millennial-utopian destiny for mankind; a continuing war between good (progress) and evil (reaction) in which the United States is to play a starring role as world redeemer," has enjoyed a long history and a hegemonic presence in U.S. political culture.[91] But it is not accurate to see it as the only way Protestants have approached foreign relations. Not only did this vision *not* characterize the outlook of Christian internationalists at *The World Tomorrow*, it was the very thing to which they themselves devoted energy to understanding, critiquing, and opposing. In this sense, the differences between pacifists and realists can be reframed as internal divisions—as fissures within a group that shared an orientation that set them apart from Christian nationalists. With much work already done on the realist versus pacifist divide, this other, larger variable of nationalism versus antinationalism is the one warranting fresh analysis in the history of religion and American foreign relations.

PART II

Ecumenical Christian Internationalism at Oxford

Chapter 4

All God's Household

What is needed is "supra-national Christianity," urged Cosmo Lang, the archbishop of Canterbury, speaking to the audience crammed into Oxford's Sheldonian Theatre. It was the opening night of a two-week conference on "Church, Community, and State" in July 1937. More than eight hundred delegates and hundreds more guests had assembled, drawn from every region in the world. Plans for worldwide representation had been hindered at the last moment, though, by the National Socialist government's denial of passports to certain members of the German delegation. Pastor Martin Niemöller of Berlin, originally scheduled to speak at Oxford, was now residing in prison.[1] He and the others restricted from traveling were all members of the German Evangelical Church, outspoken in their criticism of Nazi policies.[2] For those at the Oxford conference, the passport ban was symptomatic of a wider crisis: Nation-states around the world were making increasingly totalizing claims upon their citizens. Planners and delegates saw the task of the conference as one of reestablishing in word, and in practice, the supranational character of the universal church, and to redress the inflated, indeed "demonic," claims of the modern sovereign nation-state.[3]

The Oxford 1937 conference, held between July 12 and July 26, was the result of more than three years of intensive planning by the Universal Christian Council for Life and Work, an ecumenical Christian organization established in 1929. More than 250 papers had been translated, mimeographed, and circulated among delegates via central offices in Geneva, London, and New York. Each preparatory paper had received comments from up to thirty or forty readers.[4] As historian Keith Clements argues, this was "the most ambitious international programme of ecumenical study ever envisaged hitherto."[5] The event was technically a sequel of an earlier ecumenical world conference: the "Universal Christian Conference on Life and Work" held in Stockholm in 1925 on the instigation of then Lutheran Primate Nathan Söderblom. Building on what had begun at Stockholm, the Oxford conference went further in bringing together an unprecedented number and range of church leaders (Protestant, Anglican, and Eastern Orthodox), missionary figures, and youth organizers. Representatives came from 110 separate church communions and forty-three different nations: Scandinavian Lutherans, Russian Orthodox Christians in exile, French Protestants, and Australian Anglicans, to name but a few. Oxford 1937 also saw an unprecedented gathering of nonclerical experts in international affairs, education, and politics. Americans such as future Secretary of State John Foster Dulles debated theology and politics with figures as diverse as poet T. S. Eliot and historian R. H. Tawney. The section devoted to the study of international relations included Alfred Zimmern, founder of the Royal Institute of International Affairs and the world's first professor of international relations; the marquess of Lothian, Philip Kerr, who was later appointed British ambassador to Washington; and Swiss jurist Professor Max Huber, who was also president of the International Red Cross Committee and a former justice of the Permanent Court of International Justice at the Hague. Moreover, a new generation of theologians brought their dialectical approach to politics to the proceedings. Several leading names in mid-twentieth-century theology were present: New York City's Reinhold Niebuhr; German émigré to America Paul Tillich; and Switzerland's Emil Brunner. The intermixing of such theological currents with the international relations expertise of lay experts was one reason that Oxford 1937 was so significant in the development of interwar Christian internationalism.

Focusing on the Oxford 1937 conference, this chapter and the next three concern ecumenical internationalism—how it developed, why it mattered, and the influence it had on Americans. This first chapter, chapter 4, explores what ecumenical world conferences entailed as a practice, what the possibilities and limitations are of "reading" and reconstructing such events, and how they served as a crucial and constitutive site for the development of a distinct strand of interwar Christian internationalism. Chapter 5 focuses on the substantive ideas generated at Oxford 1937 and traces the emergence of a consensus that critiqued nationalism and racism in theological terms, while also expressing dissatisfaction with the high, almost religious, hopes associated with the League of Nations in earlier years. I there argue that the distinctive markers of Oxford

1937's internationalism were participants' dialectical critique of nationalism and their qualified support for a revived league, which could be realized through an international "ethos" (in their terms) that would emanate from the supranational social base of the Protestant ecumenical church. The two subsequent and final chapters, 6 and 7, then trace the reception of the Oxford 1937 consensus in the United States. Focusing on the international relations thinking of Reinhold Niebuhr and John Foster Dulles and the historic nationwide conferences of American Protestant churches from 1940 to 1945, these chapters together ask whether ecumenical thinking survived its "Atlantic crossing."[6]

Interwar Ecumenism and U.S. Foreign Relations

Despite its significance, the Oxford 1937 conference has been little studied by historians of internationalism and international thought. If readers today were to consult Warren F. Kuehl's *Biographical Dictionary of Internationalists*, for example, they could find entries on Zimmern, Huber, Dulles, and on missionary internationalists John R. Mott and Joseph H. Oldham. Yet they would not come away with any inkling that each of them spent two weeks of the summer of 1937 at the Oxford conference; nor would they grasp why such an event mattered.[7] The way the Oxford 1937 conference falls between the cracks of the *Biographical Dictionary*'s organizational logic is emblematic of its marginal place in other histories more generally. Detailed accounts of the ecumenical world conferences as collective events are mainly to be found in ecumenical church history scholarship—a body of literature that for the most part exists in historiographical isolation from other fields. While helpful on various organizational aspects, such works tend not to engage with the political or international thought of the conferences. Often the primary narrative concern is, instead, to map the evolution of ecumenism (defined as a quest for the reunification of churches) leading up to the founding of the World Council of Churches in 1938. Such a trend was set by numerous participant-historians within the ecumenical movement, such as George Bell, Visser 't Hooft, Ruth Rouse, and Stephen Neill, and has been carried on since.[8]

The most substantive contribution to have arisen from such ecumenical church history scholarship is Graeme Smith's recent work. Smith offers an intensive examination of the contours of theological debate at the Oxford conference and argues, rightly, that Oxford represented a paradigm shift in missionary thinking from the previous Stockholm 1925 conference: The early framework of "social ethics" at Stockholm became subsumed by a more rigorously theological discourse that was generated in response to the challenges of secularism and totalitarianism.[9] Smith's overriding concern, however, like that of previous ecumenical historians, is to debate the true legacy and meaning of Oxford in relation to the succession of ecumenical world conferences that came before and after. Within this framework, little consideration is given to the broader history of Christian internationalism or international thought.

The polar opposite methodologically, Darril Hudson's 1969 work *The Ecumenical Movement in World Affairs* is an institutional history of ecumenical engagement with international politics. Hudson helpfully canvasses ecumenical involvement in campaigns over particular issues, such as missionary extraterritoriality laws, disarmament, and international trafficking. He helpfully documents the many organizational links between ecumenical organizations such as the Geneva-based Institute for Social Research and League of Nations entities such as the International Labor Organization.[10] Yet in his work the broader conceptual relationship between ecumenism, nationalism, and internationalism remains relatively unexamined. The treatment of international thought is cursory, and, unlike Smith, Hudson pays little attention to theological complexity and as a result misses the uniqueness of Oxford 1937.[11]

The approach of this inquiry can be understood as situated between Smith and Hudson while differing from them both. Like Hudson, my focus is on the engagement of the ecumenical movement with international affairs. Like Smith, however, the methodological emphasis is on the intellectual and theological contours of this relationship rather than the organizational and institutional aspects. Historians of American religion such as Heather Warren and Mark Edwards have offered very helpful work on the particular contribution of American realist theologians to the ecumenical movement; Edwards in particular offers probing assessments of the way realists at times implicitly positioned the two-thirds world under Anglo-American headship in the 1940s.[12] My work again differs from theirs in that it situates realism as one among other American contributions and, in turn, seeks to reframe American contributions as one strand—not always the dominant one—within an enterprise that was essentially international and transnational in scale.[13]

How, then, can the relationship between the wider ecumenical movement and American Christian internationalism be conceptualized? Giving attention to this large-scale question provides an important framework in which to situate the more detailed enquiries that follow. There were three major, interrelated ways that the ecumenical world conferences were important to the development of Christian internationalism in America: First, they provided a space for American engagement with a wider transnational movement; second, they spurred the production of new kinds of international relations thinking in which the work of prominent Americans such as Reinhold Niebuhr was central; and third, they fostered the development of a distinctive ecumenical critique of nationalism that complemented and extended that of Carleton Hayes, Kirby Page, and Reinhold Niebuhr. Each point and its implications for the overall argument of this project will be considered in turn.

Ecumenical world conferences were a locus in which American Christian internationalists engaged with their international counterparts and became part of a wider transnational movement. The dynamic of this relationship was thus not merely reducible to American "cultural expansion." Contrary to the pattern implied in much scholarship on American cultural and religious nonstate actors in this period, the ecumenical movement was not a function of Americans "Americanizing" the world, or spreading American power and culture.[14] Such a model misses the *non*-American origins of the movement, as arguably more impetus for the movement came from Sweden and Britain than America. It misses also the anti-imperial currents coursing through the student and missionary branches of the ecumenical movement and the way that such conferences provided a unique site in which the empire could "speak back," as it were. It also neglects the consistent and effective critique of American social Christianity that issued from Continental theologians between the 1920s and the 1940s—critiques that issued in a new synthesis between Anglo-American and Continental political theology at Oxford 1937.

Understandably, but problematically, biographies of American Oxford participants portray their subjects often as influencing ecumenical forums without regard for these more complex dynamics. Ronald Pruessen, in his biography of John Foster Dulles, for example, alleges that the report of the international relations study section at the Oxford conference read exactly like one of Dulles's prior works, and that the panel who authored it merely reflected back his influence.[15] In contrast, I show in subsequent chapters how far Dulles actually was from the Oxford consensus all along. Richard W. Fox's biography of Reinhold Niebuhr gives a better sense of the flavor of the Oxford conference and of the British connections that Americans such as Niebuhr formed. Yet the imperatives of biographical writing again skew the account toward a recollection of Niebuhr's great influence at Oxford 1937, rather than a consideration of how he related to the currents of thinking being developed there.[16] As I will show in chapter 6, Niebuhr actually channeled—at times, wholesale adopted—the language of the Oxford conference reports in his later works. The tendency of biographers to set their influential protagonists against a seemingly neutral and passive backdrop highlights the need for a better account of the conferences in order to apply a collective counterpressure to narratives of one-way influence.

To be sure, Americans were heavily involved throughout the development of the ecumenical movement and often brought with them distinctive emphases. At Oxford 1937, for example, Reinhold Niebuhr, as plenary speaker and general contributor, performed, as one British delegate recalled, like "a volcano in perpetual eruption."[17] Henry Pit Van Dusen, former *World Tomorrow* treasurer, and colleague of Niebuhr's at Union Seminary in New York, injected a little American styling into the long sessions by calling the dignified audience out of their chairs for a "seventh-inning stretch." "Very American, and very sensible," was the retort from one British delegate.[18] Yet as well as finding their voice and exercising their influence, American Christian internationalists also found the ecumenical conferences to be a setting in which they discovered their own accent and had to reckon with difference. They came into contact with Swiss theologians insisting on the priority of Reformed biblical theology, British thinkers advocating a return to the glory of the *Respublica Christiana*, Filipino advocates urging national independence, Japanese delegates insisting on racial equality, and German thinkers propagating romantic, historicist ideas of racial and national destiny. With such currents circulating, the conferences were far from passive backdrops; they bred a character and atmosphere of their own, not reducible to the influence of any person, any country, or any network alone. Indeed, the ecumenical meetings often exercised an influence upon Americans, rather than the other way around. John Foster Dulles confessed to being deeply marked by his time at Oxford: The conference "enlightened" him as to the importance of churches in political life, a fact upon which he would draw heavily in coming years.[19] Benjamin Mays, the African American intellectual and dean of the School of Religion at Howard University, was impressed by his experience of racial equality at Oxford, and found in it a critical lever to be used against segregation and racism in the United States.[20] Daniel Johnson Fleming was prompted to rethink his "Christian nation" paradigm of missionary work after the earlier Peking 1922 conference of the World's Student Christian Federation.[21] Rather than unilateral American influence, then, the ecumenical world conferences were a unique site in which we can observe American Christian internationalism in dialogue and mutual influence with other Christian internationalisms.

The second reason ecumenical world conferences are important to understanding American interwar Christian internationalism is that they acted as a site for the development of international relations thinking. Outside the realm of the university or the state, yet with ties to both, the ecumenical conferences were a vital part of the extradisciplinary development of international thought, in which Americans played a vital role. As I argued in the introduction, a constitutive aspect of Christian internationalism was the production of a Christian knowledge of the ethics of international relations—an enterprise that transcended the divide between so-called realists and pacifists or idealists. A concern with international relations had been part of the ecumenical movement from its beginnings. The World Alliance for International Friendship through the Churches, one of the earliest ecumenical organizations with American connections, founded in 1914, had such an aim in view. Its focus was taken up in the Life and Work movement, with which the World Alliance cooperated, and which, in turn, convened the Oxford 1937 conference. Yet, over the course of the decades from the 1920s to the 1940s, ecumenical thinking on world affairs significantly deepened and grew in caliber, losing its prewar legalist and liberal inheritances, and developing its own distinctive forms of internationalism.

Oxford 1937 was a key point of transition in that longer process. At the time of the conference, the ecumenical movement was still *importing* international relations expertise. Organizers such as J. H. Oldham deliberately sought the inclusion of nonclerical lay experts on international affairs: hence the presence of Zimmern, Huber, Dulles, and many others such as the U.S. State Department's Francis B. Sayre and the special envoy from the League of Nations, J. V. Wilson. But in the years after Oxford, the ecumenical movement began *exporting* its own approach to international relations knowledge and becoming increasingly entwined with the mainstream conduct of international relations. Examples of the increasing interpenetration of ecumenical organizations with state-based international apparatus were plentiful. In the mid-1940s, John Foster Dulles was simultaneously involved with the U.S. State Department, the U.S. Federal Council of Churches, and the World Council of Churches. Several ecumenists such as Niebuhr accepted assignments and speaking engagements for the new UNESCO organization. Other World Council of Churches figures maintained a permanent lobby at the deliberations on the drafting of a UN Declaration of Universal Human Rights.[22] During World War II and in its immediate aftermath, ecumenists moved to the fore of the great wave of reconstruction and peace-planning discourse. As I argue in chapters 6 and 7, however, there were tensions between becoming officially influential and maintaining the theological emphases that characterized ecumenical thinking. This was a problem, especially for Americans such as John Foster Dulles and Reinhold Niebuhr. In becoming increasingly establishment—consulting to the government, interpreting foreign affairs to readers of *Time* and *Life*—they had to reconcile the imperatives of a new "American century" with the ecumenical critique of false universalisms. They did not always succeed in doing so.

The third reason that ecumenical world conferences such as Oxford 1937 were important to American Christian internationalism in the interwar period arises from the previous two reasons. Ecumenical world conferences fostered a distinct kind of thinking that, like *The World Tomorrow*, does not fit the glib clichés often used to explain the character of interwar internationalism. To be sure, the conferences did see elements of Anglo-American Wilsonianism and enthusiasm for the League of Nations take hold briefly. But to reduce ecumenical work to a function of mere liberal internationalism would overlook several factors: the conscious theological and political critique of liberalism at Oxford 1937, the German critique of Anglo-American social Christianity throughout the interwar period, and the importance of racial equalitarianism arising out of the student and missionary branches of the ecumenical movement. Such a focus would also detract from the definitive element of ecumenical Christian internationalism: its extended critique of nationalism based on theological, and specifically ecclesiological, reasoning.

As I argued in the introduction, a core aspect of interwar Christian internationalism was the yoking of Christian universalism to international life in such a way that it served as a check on nationalism rather than a boon to it. The ecumenical conferences fostered a critique of nationalism that can be seen as operating alongside the radical Christian internationalist critique of nationalism circulating among *The World Tomorrow* community. Yet, despite their common object of critique, and despite several points of overlap, the intellectual method behind the ecumenical and radical approach to nationalism differed. The approach of Kirby Page and other *World Tomorrow* figures had been pragmatically to highlight the harmfulness of nationalism in causing war. Their method was to juxtapose the observations of revisionist history—that nationalism had caused the Great War—with a reading of the historical Jesus. Jesus had been resistant to first-century variants of nationalism and interested instead in promoting the way of sacrifice and the brotherhood of *all* men. By contrast, in the ecumenical movement, the primary mode of critiquing nationalism was neither pragmatic and historical, nor reliant on a reading of the historical Jesus. Instead it was focused on the supranational character of the "Universal Church," as they saw it. God was building a community of people around the world, united in Christ, in which there was "neither Jew nor Greek, bond nor free" (Galatians 3:28 was a favorite text cited throughout the ecumenical movement). To conform to the New Testament vision of the church,

Christians were to see their solidarity with Christians around the world as trumping national and racial solidarities. This analysis flowed into a constructivist critique of nationalism and racism: Nations and racial groups engaged in a false "deification" of their own existence; the loyalty and identification with which they were invested was "idolatrous."

Ecumenical conferences thus fostered a specifically ecclesiological internationalism—one founded in a conception of the church itself. The word "ecumenical" actually carried the freight of this wider meaning in the late 1930s. In Ancient Greek the term *oikumene* had literally meant "household," but it was also used to refer to the whole known, non-Barbarian, world and contained within it a sense of universality. The Apostle Paul used the term to refer to the Christian Church as the "household of faith" in the New Testament.[23] Although later used to describe the "ecumenical councils" of the fourth century, it was not until the 1888 and 1900 "ecumenical missionary conferences" in London and New York that the term appears to have first been used in the modern sense to refer to interdenominational Protestant cooperation.[24] In the interwar period, and through to the post-1945 World Council of Churches era, "ecumenical" came to refer to church-unity movements. Since the late twentieth century, it has come to include even interfaith efforts. David Hollinger uses it, for justifiable historiographical reasons, interchangeably with "mainline" and "liberal."[25] Yet, at the time of Oxford 1937 and through the Second World War, the idea of the *ecumene* had distinct political and theological dimensions. In a world marked by the development of nationalisms and totalitarianisms—whether in Germany, Italy, Japan, Russia, or America—the *ecumene* as both idea and praxis was intended as a counterweight to the claim of the nation and state to be the final and ultimate arbiter of the good. Ecumenism implied a theologically rooted internationalism rather than a mere church-unity movement, although the latter was seen as the basis of the former.

Whether this specifically ecclesiological critique of nationalism could take hold in American soil was one issue hanging over the relationship between American Christian internationalism and the ecumenical movement. Undoubtedly the critique influenced a generation of American theologians and church leaders while they were engaged in the great conferences such as Oxford 1937. Perhaps it helped shape the more "cautious" patriotism issuing from American churches during World War II—as opposed to the jingoistic nationalism of World War I.[26] John Foster Dulles's mass mobilization of churches giving electoral support to American internationalism (see chapter 7) was also due, to an extent, to the influence of ecumenism. The larger question remains, however, as to whether a religious and political culture characterized by an overall "ecclesiological deficit," in Richard John Neuhaus's terms—a tendency to minimize or ignore theologies of the church—could actually support the long-term growth of an idea that was ecclesiological in essence.[27] This is a question I address in chapters 6 and 7.

Ecumenical World Conferences as a Practice

The distinctive character of the ecumenical critique of nationalism was deeply connected to the practice of the world conference. Meetings such as Oxford 1937 provided the practice and experience out of which ideas about ecumenism's role in international life arose. Just as the oppositional discursive practices of publishing a periodical such as *The World Tomorrow* were a constitutive part of radical Christian internationalism, the practice of ecumenical world conferencing and all it entailed—travel, meeting, exchange of papers, the experience of shared prayers, sacraments, and hymns—was a constitutive part of the ecumenical strand of interwar Christian internationalism. In their seminal work on pilgrimage, anthropologists Victor and Edith Turner explored the way in which, for pilgrims, travel is a "liminoid" experience in which hierarchies and rules governing social relations in normal mundane life could be partially and temporarily suspended. Pilgrims, they argued, often spontaneously experience *communitas*, "commonness of feeling," described as "a liminal phenomenon which combines the qualities of lowliness, sacredness, homogeneity, and comradeship."[28] At pilgrimage centers, the significant emotional impact of devotional activities partly derives "from the union of separate but similar emotional dispositions of the pilgrims converging from all parts of a huge socio-geographical catchment area."[29] Ecumenical conferences in the interwar period appear to have functioned like pilgrimages in this respect. Although lacking a sacred monument or locus like that to which pilgrims journeyed, travel to conferences often involved a profound sense of anticipation and an awareness of a seemingly sacred purpose at hand. Combined with the experience of transracial, transnational, and translinguistic prayer, silence, singing, and dialogue, there arose for many delegates, according to their accounts, a sense of what the Turners identify as *communitas*. Such experiential aspects should be borne in mind when exploring the way ecumenical unity itself became a basis for critiquing nationalism and racism at Oxford 1937.

Expressing the cause of international relations and peace through the practice of conferencing was not unique to ecumenists, of course. As Akira Iriye and others have shown, the 1920s were characterized by a rise in the number of international conferences connected to varieties of "cultural internationalism." The regular meetings of the Institute of Pacific Relations in Honolulu from 1925 (themselves a derivation of YMCA internationalism by origin) happened alongside myriad other efforts such as the League of Nations' committee on international cooperation, a forerunner of UNESCO, and numerous professional, scientific, and artistic international conferences.[30] Indeed, the connection between conferencing and internationalism went back at least to the Hague Peace conferences of 1899 and 1907 and became embodied in the League of Nations ethos. The league's council had declared, for example, in 1921 that "no association of nations can hope to exist without the spirit of reciprocal intellectual activity between its members."[31] International conferences were a primary means to that end.

But when delegates lodged in the colleges and met in the town hall of Oxford in July 1937 they were also following a specific and well-established pattern of ecumenical world conferencing. Such meetings had a history of their own—parallel to the broader trend of international conferences. Although there were other antecedents, the most important event to shape the patterns and practices of twentieth-century ecumenical conferences was the World Missionary Conference held in Edinburgh in 1910. Indeed, John R. Mott's remarkable service in chairing both the Edinburgh 1910 and Oxford 1937 conferences twenty-seven years apart underlines the continuity between the two events. So too did the instrumental work of Mott's counterpart in the International Missionary Council, Joseph H. Oldham, who, having served as the general secretary of Edinburgh 1910, went on to play a more decisive role than any other individual at Oxford 1937 in his capacity as director of research and preparations.

At Edinburgh 1910, organizers established several of the standard practices that characterized ecumenical conferences for subsequent decades. First, the Edinburgh conference was a summer event, with 1,200 delegates gathering by means of steamship from around the world, though mainly from America and Northern Europe. Its length of ten days was typical, as was the format for each day. Opening night featured the reading of greetings sent from dignitaries, and plenary addresses following on subsequent evenings. One of the most important patterns Edinburgh established was the allocation of daytime hours to the deliberation of special study "commissions" working on topics chosen years before the actual meeting. Each commission had the task of conducting research (in Edinburgh's case through a mass questionnaire mailed to missionaries) on an assigned question and collating that research into a report to be debated by the whole conference. The report was then subject to final revision and, pending revision and adoption by the conference as a whole, was then published and disseminated internationally.[32] At Edinburgh, there were eight commissions, each comprising around twenty people. At Oxford 1937, there were five study "sections," as they were termed, each including around eighty people, with smaller drafting committees assigned the work of finalizing reports.[33]

But whereas at Edinburgh delegates almost solely discussed aspects of the missionary enterprise and only indirectly addressed international affairs, ecumenical conferences in the 1920s to 1930s featured special commissions on "international relations," "international and interracial relations," or "the Universal Church and the World of Nations" as standard fare. The only exception to this pattern came at the conferences of the Faith and Order movement, which deliberately left ethical reflection to other parts of the ecumenical movement in order to focus on the liturgical and doctrinal aspects of church union.[34] At the conferences of the World Student Christian Federation, the Life and Work movement and the International Missionary Council—that is, all the other major interwar ecumenical organizations aside from Faith and Order—international relations became a category for group research and study.

Because of the standard pattern of study commissions, plenary meetings, and divine worship, each ecumenical conference produced and left behind a considerable array of sources for the historian. In this sense, the "conference" encompassed more than the two weeks of meetings that constituted the event itself. Exchanges of correspondence and papers for peer review occurred years in advance. Subsequent publicity, reporting, and dissemination of the conference's findings continued for months and years afterward. This makes "reading" the conference both difficult and rewarding.[35] Conference sources typically capture the process of dialogue and debate that encompassed but extended beyond the meeting itself. Ecumenical conferences were by definition aimed at producing consensus. In theory, the years of research and deliberation were to crystallize in a series of short reports and statements. Yet despite, or because of, the drive toward consensus, disagreement occurred frequently, and more often than not, was captured in the assiduous process of conference reporting. Tracing international thought at the ecumenical world conferences thus provides a unique way not only to trace a univocal "official line" but also to reenter a world of debate over the nature of international organization, the status of nationalism, and the problems of racism and imperialism in the Protestant view.

Tracing the emergence of international relations thinking at these 1920s conferences provides a vital backdrop against which to appreciate how Oxford 1937 both continued and altered ecumenical thinking. Some parts of the

ecumenical movement, especially those connected to the missionary enterprise, stressed the importance of race relations to international relations. Their
conferences were also the site of overlap with the anti-imperialist analyses of
the *World Tomorrow* community. Other parts of the ecumenical movement—
specifically the Life and Work network—had their own history and ethos, and
focused more on European questions such as Germany's relation to the League
of Nations, and the relative merit of Anglo-American rationalist or German
historicist understandings of nationhood. Oxford 1937 should be seen as encompassing and enfolding these vast and disparate backdrops. The character
of these distinct ecumenical endeavors is best understood by exploring three
major meetings: Peking 1922, Jerusalem 1928, and Stockholm 1925.

Peking 1922

The first ecumenical world conference in which reflection on international
relations was a specifically assigned part of the program was the 1922 meeting
of the World Student Christian Federation (WSCF) in Peking. Despite the
youth of its student constituents, the federation itself was one of the oldest
ecumenical organizations operating in the twentieth century. Founded in
1895 in a meeting of international YMCA leaders in Sweden, its global reach
was a product of the missionary tours among students undertaken by John R.
Mott between 1895 and 1897. Mott's travels resulted in groups of Christian
students being established and incorporated into the federation from Switzerland, Budapest, Athens, Constantinople, Beirut, Ceylon, India, Australia,
New Zealand, China, and Japan, to name a few.[36] Importantly for its approach
to understanding international relations as a category, the federation afforded
representation to nonwhite members, particularly those from East Asian
countries, decades before other ecumenical organizations. At the first convention of the WSCF in Northfield, Massachusetts, in 1897, Mott noted that,
as well as six hundred Americans, "there were present students and Christian
workers representing twenty-five other nations or races."[37] Mott noted that
the nomination of Kajinosuke Ibuka of Japan to the position of vice president
of the federation created "probably the first world's Christian gathering at
which an oriental has presided, but it will not be the last."[38]

Reflecting its relatively equalitarian approach to representation in leadership, the WSCF chose conference locations that contrasted with the European
sites where other ecumenical organizations gathered in the interwar period
(Oxford, Stockholm, Lausanne, and Edinburgh twice). Ten years after the

inaugural meeting in Northfield, and amid global anxieties about a "yellow peril" following Japan's military defeat of imperial Russia in 1905, Mott pushed for the federation to hold its 1907 conference in no other city than Tokyo.[39] And when it came to the choice of a venue for the 1922 meeting of the federation—despite disgruntlement from some Western delegates—he opted for another Asian location. In fact, the idea of Peking as a venue had been urged by Chinese student leader T. Z. Koo at the executive committee meeting in Holland the year before. Koo remained a major figure in the ecumenical movement and was later a plenary speaker at Oxford 1937 on the same evening as Reinhold Niebuhr. In 1922, he wanted the federation to take the opportunity "to give to the development of China the Christian impress."[40] But not all Chinese wanted the forces of Christianization to meet in Peking. The recently formed Anti-Christian Association harangued delegates from Shanghai on their way to the conference. A *New York Times* correspondent cited a manifesto released by the Hunan chapter of the association, which claimed, "The existing World Student Christian Federation Conference under the Chairmanship of Dr. Mott is promoted by the foreign capitalists who are aiming at enslaving Chinese millions through the shield of Christianity." The Peking government and Peking newspapers, however, were more favorably disposed toward the conference.[41]

The treatment of international relations at Peking foreshadowed much of what was to come in other ecumenical world conferences. First, there was no specific agreement on the issue of war, on whether Christ would permit Christians' participation in armed conflict. It was still a year before the release of Kirby Page's *War: Its Causes, Consequences and Cure*, and pacifism among student Christian groups had not yet reached the height of popularity it soon would. YMCA leader Sherwood Eddy had not yet declared his conversion to pacifism, and the WSCF chairman, Mott, never did. The federation's general committee thus concluded, "As a result of our discussion at the Peking conference, we declare frankly that we have not succeeded in reaching an agreement as to what our individual attitude ought to be in the event of war." This statement captured the pattern that characterized the ecumenical world conferences of the interwar period: Individual pacifism was never a defining or universally held principle of ecumenical internationalism.

More significant than the federation's disagreement over war was their broader take on the role of race relations in international life. The most noteworthy document to emerge from the Peking conference arose from the deliberations of a special section on "Christianity and International and Interracial Problems." Dominated by Japanese students, the group produced a text

known as the "Peking Resolutions." In it the students resolved: "We, representing Christian students from all parts of the world, believe in the fundamental equality of all the races and nations of mankind and consider it part of
our Christian vocation to express this reality in all our relationships."[42] The
adoption of a racial equality resolution authored by Japanese delegates stood
in stark contrast to the events of three years earlier, when the racial equality
clause suggested by the Japanese was taken out of the Treaty of Versailles during negotiations. Indeed, the Peking Resolutions can be seen as one small part
of the wider backlash to the "Wilsonian moment" described by Erez Manela.
Disillusioned by the broken promises of equality at Versailles, these students
were, in their own sphere, seeking to set right what President Wilson and Australian Prime Minister Hughes had deliberately left undone.[43] Ecumenical
internationalism, as revealed at Peking, did not primarily consist in advocating
pacifism or the League of Nations (which German members loathed), but, as
for World Tomorrow internationalists, it involved a more holistic analysis that con-
strued race relations as interconnected with international relations.

The Peking 1922 conference's emphasis on racial equality certainly appeared
to make an impression on American ecumenical leaders. It emboldened John
Mott to write scathingly about racism in the federation's internationally circulated periodical Student World following the conference. In a special themed
issue on interracial and international relations, also featuring Japanese internationalist Nitobē Inazō, Mott argued that racial hatred among Christians was a
form of "apostasy": It was equivalent to a denial of the faith. That such hostil-
ity "persists even under the shadow of cross-tipped church spires proves not
the impotence of Christ but the infidelity of his followers."[44] Francis P. Miller,
later Mott's successor at the WSCF, and a contributor to The World Tomorrow,
likewise reflected on the implications of what he heard at Peking. Also writing
in Student World, he anticipated with more specificity than Mott the ecclesiological critique of nationalism and racism later developed at Oxford 1937. A
"truly universal church of Christ," he argued, "takes no cognizance of political and racial discrimination, but is in eternal antagonism to that form of in-
growing patriotism now prevalent."[45]

Aside from the individual impacts on Americans such as Mott and Miller,
the WSCF and the networks arising from Peking went on to provide an important basis for the ecumenical internationalism of the 1930s. Many of those
who attended Peking 1922 and subsequent WSCF conferences in the 1920s
were in the position, and of the age, to assume leadership in the process of
generational change that swept through the ecumenical movement in the mid
to late 1930s. The Dutch ecumenist Willem Adolph Visser 't Hooft, later general

secretary of the World Council of Churches, and himself a leader in the WSCF, argued that the federation functioned as the real "nursery and brains of the ecumenical movement." The shapers of Oxford 1937—Oldham, Visser 't Hooft, the Frenchman H. L. Henriod, and Americans such as Reinhold Niebuhr and Henry Pit Van Dusen—all were engaged with WSCF study groups on theological and political problems throughout the late 1920s and early 1930s.[46]

Jerusalem 1928

The first "enlarged" international meeting of the International Missionary Council (IMC) in Jerusalem, in 1928, augmented the concerns raised at Peking with anti-imperialist critiques typical of 1920s missiology. The IMC was formed in 1921 to replace the temporary Continuation Committee of Edinburgh 1910. The central node in the John R. Mott–Joseph Oldham network (with Mott chairing the organization, and Oldham serving as its secretary), the council was a major pillar of interwar ecumenism and arguably the climax of both their careers.[47] One of the key tasks taken on by the organization, apart from publishing the *International Review of Missions* serially, was to plan for another world-scale missionary conference as a sequel to Edinburgh 1910. The result was Jerusalem 1928.

Although Jerusalem 1928 was the sequel to Edinburgh 1910, there were major differences between the two conferences—all of which reveal how much had changed in eighteen years in Protestant missionary ecumenism. Organizers assigned social and ethical topics such as "Industrial Problems," "Rural Problems," and "Religious Education" to specific sections—topics outside the ambit of Edinburgh's missiological focus. Moreover, the IMC's constitution, drafted by Oldham and adopted in 1921, committed the council to bring together forces to promote "justice in international and inter-racial relationships."[48] While organizers did not create a specific commission assigned to explore international relations as there had been at Peking and Stockholm, international issues such as imperialism, migration, and race relations received extensive treatment throughout other sections, especially the section on "The Christian Mission in the Light of Race Conflict."

In a related difference, Jerusalem 1928 saw a dramatic increase in participation from countries outside of North America and Europe. At Edinburgh, only 10 of the 1,356 delegates had been so-called "nationals"—the nomenclature used to identify those from non-missionary-sending countries. By contrast, the Jerusalem organizers imposed a cap on the number of delegates from send-ing organizations: They could only make up half the total of delegates; the other half had to be from agencies and churches elsewhere, with many in the latter category being women. Thus the IMC implemented a kind of early af-firmative action quota system.[49] As a result, one ecumenical historian saw Je-rusalem as "the first truly representative global assembly of Christians in the long history of the Church."[50]

The conference's logistical arrangements also fostered a greater mutuality among delegates than at Edinburgh. In choosing Jerusalem as the site—the conference took place over two weeks on the Mount of Olives—the council considered both its spiritual significance and its geographical location, a middle ground between East and West. The delegates shared meals together in the dining hall of the German sanatorium on the mount, a building also used for meetings, while most of the delegates slept and lived in a tent city also on the mount. Delegates from around the world addressed the three central worship services at St. George's Cathedral—including Helen Kim, dean of the Women's College in Seoul; Dr. Wei of China; Reverends Chatterji and Karunakar of India; and Professor Jabavu of South Africa. A *New York Times* contributor as-signed to the Jerusalem conference, Howard Bridgman, reported back to America: "It did not resemble the traditional missionary meeting known to our grandfathers. No map on the wall partitioned the world off into white and dark spots. . . . As to the composition of the assembly, moreover, there were more Chinese than English and Scottish put together. There were al-most as many delegates from India as from the United States. There were more Africans than French."[51] Such a composition made the conference uniquely placed among ecumenical conferences to give attention to race relations as part of international relations.

While during the conference the council passed a fairly standard statement opposing war—urging prayer and support, in the words of the contemporary Kellogg-Briand Pact, for the "renunciation of war as an instrument of national policy"—the most important contributions of the conference to ecumenical internationalist thought came in its treatment of race relations and imperial-ism.[52] The section studying "The Christian Mission in the Light of Race Con-flict" gave particular prominence to this issue.[53] As John Mott explained in his opening address to the conference, the leadership of this section was assigned to those who were deemed to be from areas in which race relations were con-sidered most fraught; nonwhite speakers were given the majority of roles.[54] The section featured two notable black Americans: John Hope, the president of Morehouse College, Atlanta, as plenary speaker, and Max Yergan, one of the leading figures in black American YMCA networks (and at that point, a missionary in South Africa and leader of the South African Student Christian Union), as chair of the section.[55] Its membership also included Jorge Bocobo, who, as well as being active in the Filipino YMCA and a staunch activist for Filipino independence, was a professor of law and later president of the University of the Philippines. Alongside Hope, Yergan, and Bocobo served Professor Davidson D. T. Jabavu of South Africa—the first black professor at the University of Fort Hare, and author of *The Segregation Fallacy and Other Papers: A Native View of Some South African Inter-Racial Problems* (1928).[56]

Speeches given before plenary sessions of the conference focused on the connection between race relations and international affairs. Taking the platform, Max Yergan laid out the problem of race relations in South Africa in the context of global empires and economics. "The whole of Africa south of the Mediterranean section, with the exception of Liberia and Abyssinia, has fallen under the political control of four or five of the larger powers of Europe."[57] Yergan went on to suggest that race relations had to be understood in light of economic factors: "We cannot escape from Africa's economic significance . . . her gold diamonds, oil, rubber, cotton." The economic relationship brought with it social changes. "The socialistic outlook of Africa has been challenged and in places replaced by the individualistic outlook of the West."[58] The larger picture was this: "Western life is thrusting itself upon the African, whether the African or the European desires it or not. This process could become ruthless."[59] Harold A. Grimshaw, a special delegate from the League of Nations' International Labour Office, and chief of that organization's Native Labour Section, agreed with Yergan. Speaking to the council on a separate occasion, he pleaded, "Our African brothers are under the rod of exploitation and Christianity is silent. You missionaries must speak and write, for public opinion is a great power."[60]

Other speakers in the Race Conflict Section emphasized the issue of economic imperialism. Jorge Bocobo directed attention to how the debate over Philippine independence depended on the vicissitudes of the American political system: "The Philippine question is the football of American politics . . . Our faults are magnified by the press and by American government officials." Yet Bocobo's underlying critique targeted economic imperialism. American capitalists wanted room to plant rubber on a large scale and were seeking to overturn laws limiting the holding of public land to two thousand acres. "The Washington Government is backing the plan of the capitalists. Since we have protested against these proposals, our autonomy, granted in 1916, has been largely withdrawn. Perhaps this step was taken to intimidate us into giving up this testimony."[61]

Delegates would also no doubt have read the special preparatory paper for the conference authored by Samuel Guy Inman. A longtime missionary to Mexico, Latin American scholar at Columbia University, and later a *World Tomorrow* contributing editor, Inman argued that the problem besetting the region was the influx of foreign capital. Loans, and the intervention they provoked, were the instrument of economic imperialism, and ought to be of chief interest to the missionaries.[62] Inman asked whether churches had considered how difficult it was to spread a missionary message when "in Santo Domingo and Haiti . . . the United States Marines ruthlessly establish martial law": when in Nicaragua "American bombing planes are destroying hundreds of Nicaraguan lives": and while in Colombia "citizens read our boasts of how we took Panama."[63] Inman's critique of American imperialism in Latin America was emblematic of the crossover between the *World Tomorrow* strand of internationalism with missionary ecumenists.

Howard Bridgman, the *New York Times* contributor attending and covering the Jerusalem conference, captured the character of the meeting as a space for anti-imperialist critique. With some bemusement, he outlined how the "West came in for some healthy berating from both Westerners and Orientals":

> The Indian Christians went out with a rather sharp stick for Britain. Not one of them apparently is reconciled to British rule . . . The American delegation had a similar shock a few minutes later when a delegate from the Philippines declared just as vigorously that his fellow-countrymen wanted to be their own rulers and looked eagerly forward to the time when the United States would fulfill its tacit promises to them. Hardly had he done speaking when the Japanese voiced resentment of the legislation of our Congress respecting the presence of Japanese on the Pacific Coast. Japan's delegates had hardly sat down when a woman from Korea, smarting under the statement just made that there was no racial prejudice in Japan, claimed the platform and in sweet but vigorous tones set forth Korea's objection to being under the domination of Japan.[64]

Despite the humor of Bridgman's tone, Jerusalem clearly did provide an opportunity in which the nexus between race, religion, and empire could be deliberated on with a relative degree of freedom and mutuality. The attendance of nonwhite delegates and the opportunities to share the platform and engage in dialogue and debate in sections and plenary sessions created a space for voices to be heard that would not have otherwise been heard so readily on the world stage.

Delegates to the Jerusalem conference also addressed their own relation to imperialism. Protection of missionaries could trigger military intervention just as easily as investments and loans. On this practical matter the conference came to an historic resolution: They urged missionaries to renounce the right for military protection from sending countries. With the naval bombardment of Peking still in living memory, the Jerusalem 1928 conference urged "upon all missionary societies that they should make no claim on their governments for the armed defense of their missionaries and their property."[65] British delegates opposed the resolution, but it passed with a majority.[66]

Just as remarkable in the climate of the 1920s was the council's statement about race relations in domestic politics. Here, in a decade characterized by a surge of white supremacist politics globally, the council opposed segregation, racially restrictive immigration policies, and unjust dispossession of indigenous lands.[67] This imperative derived from a belief that "any discrimination against human beings on the ground of race or color, any selfish exploitation and any oppression of man by man is, therefore a denial of the teaching of Jesus."[68] Yergan's influence, and that of his YMCA-flavored social theology, was plain in the leading proposition given in support of racial equality: "The Fatherhood of God and the sacredness of personality are vital truths revealed in Christ."[69] Earlier in the plenary discussion, Yergan had urged the council to commit itself to a "statement of belief in and practice of the sacredness of personality as taught by Jesus and the Christian faith." The language, shared with Kirby Page, Sherwood Eddy, and many other American latter Social Gospellers, reflected Yergan's immersion in the YMCA-social Christian milieu. It also reflected, as Glenda Gilmore shows, Yergan's "idealist" phase, before his turn toward Marxist realism in the 1930s.[70] But the statement did not merely rest on the personalism of the Social Gospel. Other notes of Christian racial thought made it into the document too. The ecclesiological reasoning pervading the Mott network and the World Student Christian Federation also found a place. "Our Lord's thought and action, the teaching of His apostles, and the fact that the Church, as the Body of Christ, is a community transcending race, show that the different peoples are created by God to bring each its particular gift to His city, so that all may enhance its glory by the rich diversities of their varying contributions."[71] Although the essentialism of ascribing particular gifts to particular races would be absent from Oxford 1937, this section of the statement came closer to the kind of language used in Oxford reports nine years later.

The statement urged churches to take action within their own lives, and within their home societies at large. It "confessed with humiliation" that, notwithstanding isolated examples of "prophetic action," churches were typically part of the problem.[72] But the statement also urged Christians churches to take steps in "creating, informing and influencing public opinion, by presenting their constructive plans before responsible administrative authorities, and, where necessary, by pressing for legislative action."[73] Rather then segregation, there needed to be the "utmost practicable equality in such matters as the right to enter and follow all occupations and professions, the right of freedom of movement and other rights before civil and criminal law, and the obtaining and exercise of the functions of citizenship."[74] Land policy and resource allocation had to be done in accord "with justice and with the rights of the indigenous peoples."[75] Then there was immigration. The council acknowledged some restriction might be expedient. However, "such restriction . . . should never make discrimination among intending immigrants upon grounds of color or race, neither of which can, in the opinion of this Council, be held to be in itself a legitimate ground for exclusion."[76] The council placed itself squarely at odds with the immigration policies of the United States and Australia, each at the height of their restrictive powers. Such an oppositional tenor had clear resonances with the tone of *The World Tomorrow*, and the magazine published an extensive and positive review of the conference in its June 1928 edition.

Stockholm 1925

The parallel ecumenical efforts of the Life and Work movement offered a different take on world affairs from that seen at Peking and Jerusalem. The "Universal Christian Conference on Life and Work," held in Stockholm in August 1925, did not emphasize so much the wrongs of Western imperialism and racism—matters on which, apart from minor exceptions, such as American missionary Sidney Gulick's contribution on white supremacist attitudes as an "ominous" cause of war, it was relatively quiet.[77] Instead, Stockholm featured hand-wringing deliberation on the status of national solidarity, cosmopolitanism, and international organization in Protestant theology. More than five hundred delegates attended from more than thirty-seven countries, with, according to organizers, all church communions and denominations around the world having been invited to appoint delegates. Organizers received a polite refusal from the Roman Catholic Church, but, in a turn of events rightly heralded as historic, representatives of the Greek Orthodox Church joined their counterparts from Western Christendom for the first time in centuries. Indeed, the Orthodox Church of Constantinople, known as the Ecumenical Patriarchate, had urged a rapprochement or fellowship between churches in the Patriarchal Encyclical of 1920, addressed "Unto All the Churches of Christ Everywhere."[78]

Organizers conceived the Stockholm conference as complementing the work of ecumenical organizations such as Faith and Order and the World Alliance for International Friendship through the Churches. The Swedish archbishop of Uppsala, Nathan Söderblom, who had more influence on the conference than any other individual, thought that it should be left to the Faith and Order conferences to attend to matters of doctrinal unity; meanwhile the Life and Work conference would help churches cooperate together at an international level in the realm of practical, social Christianity.[79] Churches, the Stockholm organizers argued, ought to cooperate on social and international matters "as if" they were already united.[80] The slogan famously associated with the conference was thus "Doctrine Divides but Service Unites"—a position with which Kirby Page and many American Social Gospellers sympathized.[81]

Söderblom and others in the organizing committee (composed of British, American, and European church leaders) also sought to relate the conference to the work already being done by the World Alliance for International Friendship through the Churches, with whom they cooperated extensively. The World Alliance had several national chapters established throughout Europe as well as the United States. It had been convened on the eve of the Great War to link the causes of supranational church unity and peace, and expressed the enthusiasm for international law and arbitration that swept throughout the peace movement—Christian and otherwise—in the 1910s, in the wake of the Hague peace conferences. Taking up the concerns of the World Alliance, the Stockholm conference made international relations a key part of its program, making it the subject of a themed section alongside others on economic and industrial problems and "social and moral" problems.[82]

However, despite the hopes of Söderblom and the other conveners, the discussions on international relations saw not unity but conflict. Theological differences refused to disappear. As Visser 't Hooft remarked, "service can only unite if you arrive at a common understanding of the service to be rendered."[83] Three major issues set British and American delegates at odds with their Continental counterparts: first, whether the League of Nations could be seen as something that was Christian in principle; second, what status nationhood and nationalism had in a Christian ethical scheme; and finally, the whole relation of ethical reform efforts to Christian faith itself. From the point of view of Continental Reformed delegates, the question was what, if anything, did American *aktivismus* have to do with the Kingdom of God?

During discussion in the international relations sections, delegates from France, Britain, and America gave overwhelming spiritual endorsement to the League of Nations. Many of the most influential British delegates at Stockholm had only the previous year been involved in the historic British "Conference on Christian Politics, Economics and Citizenship" (dubbed COPEC), a landmark in ecumenical thought regarded by the organizers of Stockholm as an important preparation for their conference. In hallowed Wilsonian tones, COPEC's reports described the preamble of the league's covenant as being like "the laws of Christ applied to nations."[84] Such British enthusiasm joined with the high hopes of Nathan Söderblom. Envisioning ecumenism as providing a "soul" for the League of Nations, Söderblom argued that if the church did not provide the animating spirit of the league, some other force would.[85] Americans such as Charles Brent concurred with the general plans for Christianizing the international system through disarmament and the league. So too did Frenchman M. le Pasteur Jézéquel, the general secretary of the National Union of Reformed Churches in France, who expressed the argument in the most provocative terms, asserting that "the Church ought to become the careful attendant of the League of Nations," and that there should be made a marking of the league in the liturgical calendar: "One Sunday in each year she [the Church] will invoke the benedictions of the Heavenly Father upon the holy enterprise."[86]

Such ringing endorsement of the recent Versailles settlement, coming predominantly from members of former Allied war powers, proved difficult for many German delegates to stomach. Animosity over the War Guilt clause in the Treaty of Versailles remained a burning issue. German delegates had promised in advance not to raise it in discussions, but as Söderblom's biographer, Bengt Sundkler, wrote, the issue refused to go away and instead "hung in the air like a thundercloud."[87] Eventually, Dr. Klingemann, superintendent of the Rhine Province, addressed it directly in what Visser 't Hooft remembered was a dramatic moment of attack.[88] "We only want our position to be understood," Klingemann urged. "Now remember," he said, "that disarmed we live in an armed world. We wait for the promised general disarmament to be able to believe in peace." While he was not opposed to the idea of a league in abstract terms, he concluded that, "in the present state of the League we cannot find religious power or any communion with the Kingdom of God."[89] Such a dour atmosphere surrounded debate over the league—with many Germans having to be urged not to leave the conference entirely—that delegates remembered the day of this conflict as "Black Tuesday."[90]

The debate over approaches to the league was closely tied to another conflict over the nature and validity of nationhood and nationalism. Unlike other world conferences, Stockholm did not publish separate reports from each topical section. Instead, the task was for the conference to distill the consensus, such as it was, into one final "message." One member of the committee charged with finalizing the draft message was George Bell, the bishop of Chichester, and later a delegate at Oxford 1937. "It cost many heart-searchings," Bell recalled, to bring it to completion. He did not deliver the text to the printers until 2 a.m., and even then it had four dissenting opinions attached.[91] The message offered assurance that the conference delegates had "set forth the guiding principles of a Christian internationalism." It would be "equally opposed to a national bigotry and a weak cosmopolitanism." Although capturing the middle way between two poles of opinion expressed by delegates, the statement covered over the anxious and lengthy debates that led up to it.

Scandinavian and Continental delegates on the whole displayed a reluctance to see an erosion of the virtues of patriotism, the "principle of nationality," and the church's identification with Christian nationalism. For others, mainly the Anglo-American delegates, universalism came a little more freely. Sir Willoughby Dickinson, who had been part of COPEC's International Relations Commission, and who represented the World Alliance for International Friendship, was unequivocal in his denunciation of nationalism. "The Son of God came into the world to save mankind. He recognized no frontiers, neither political, racial nor linguistic."[92] Similarly, the American bishop Charles Brent, a founder of the Faith and Order movement and the chair of the Commission on International Relations at Stockholm—a figure for whose whole theological approach the German theologians shared little enthusiasm—saw the promotion of universal brotherhood as simply something God was doing. "In aiming at the unification of the churches and at the brotherhood of the human race, we are not making a doubtful experiment but simply identifying ourselves with God's purpose." And, he added a dash of power-of-positive-thinking logic to counter skepticism: "If we approach it without misgivings we shall attain it much the sooner. God cannot do without man's cooperation."[93]

Many delegates from the German-speaking churches, deeply influenced by Reformed theology, were less concerned about God's ability to get by without human cooperation. And they were even less enamored with the vision of an internationalism that negated patriotism and love of nation. In response, they argued that true internationalism first required patriotism. Berlin University's Adolf Diessmann, one of the major influences on the conference and on world ecumenism and a figure who would have given much leadership at Oxford 1937 had he not died shortly beforehand, insisted on the importance of national particularity.[94] His arguments contained an implicit critique of Socialist internationalism when he urged that "the great ecumenical movement, in which we are all participating, does not aim at making a uniformly drab and inert mass of millions of standardized men out of the peoples and churches distinguished from one another by speech, by civilization and by historical experience." Rather, ecumenists had to "conserve and ennoble everything in the way of specific endowment which God has entrusted both to nations and churches, in order that we may co-operate together on the basis of the Gospel of Christ."[95]

Debates over the league and the nature of nationality manifested a deeper disagreement over the nature of Christian ethical thinking itself. Although the planners had hoped to leave theology and doctrine aside, doctrine came back to bite them. The issue that came to the fore in debates over the League of Nations was the relationship between the Kingdom of God and human action, and as a consequence, the relation between the Kingdom of God and history itself. Could human effort bring about the Kingdom of God through gradual progress and reform? Did heaven really have to wait until God's initiative, or could it be made—manufactured—by earnest effort and application of right principles here on earth now? Such was the message Continental delegates felt they were hearing from Anglophone delegates, especially Americans. Many went home to Germany after the conference reportedly finding American *Aktivismus* incomprehensible. They joked with each other that Americans believed the Kingdom was just around the corner if Prohibition and the Outlawry of War could be made to stick. Americans created similar caricatures of the Germans, including composing a song about their approach. Adapting the hymn entitled "Rise up, O Men of God," they sang:

> Sit down, O men of God
> His Kingdom He will bring
> Whenever it may please His will
> You cannot do a thing.[96]

The issue at stake was eschatology: different ways of relating the future Kingdom of God to action in the present historical situation. But as one of the best participant-historians of the ecumenical movement, Nils Ehrenström, wrote later, these differences over eschatology became mapped onto other labels such as Calvinism versus Lutheranism, or American activism versus German otherworldliness. At Stockholm, he argued, a "basic antithesis was revealed—partly theological, partly geographical and cultural—which in changing manifestations was to preoccupy the movement for many years to come."[97]

Conclusion

The three examples examined in this chapter together provide a portrait of the way ecumenical conferences functioned as a site and practice for the development of Christian internationalism in the 1920s. Clearly, across the different ecumenical organizations, various emphases emerged: the status of the League of Nations and the nature of nationalism at Stockholm 1925, and the importance of racial equality and imperialism at the conferences of the World's Student Christian Federation and International Missionary Council. Given the differences between the conferences, the ecumenical movement in the 1920s might better be seen as a plurality, as many "ecumenical movements," rather than one ecumenical movement. Indeed, ecumenism was only spoken of as a singular phenomenon from the late 1930s, around the time of Oxford 1937, when the idea of a World Council of Churches was proposed. This gradual shift from plural to singular only serves to underline further the way that Oxford 1937 joined and synthesized many disparate elements of 1920s ecumenical internationalism. Practically, the appointment of the IMC's Joseph Oldham as director of research at Oxford, and Oldham's subsequent coaxing of Mott into chairing the conference, meant that Oxford 1937 should be seen as not just a sequel of Stockholm 1925 but as a synthesis between the Stockholm approach and the Peking-Jerusalem approach that they had already shaped.[98]

There were several issues still to be resolved in creating such a synthesis. How would the European strands of the movement take on the concerns with race and imperialism predominating in the IMC and WSCF? How would Continental ecumenists work with American delegates whose Social Gospel internationalism they found incomprehensible? With the League of Nations' reputation severely damaged by its inability to act effectively against Japanese or Italian aggression in the 1930s, it was doubtful whether anyone could see the League of Nations as the vestibule of the Kingdom of God. And with the Nazi assumption of power in Germany, already stark differences between Continental and Anglo-American philosophies and theologies of nationality would demand to be addressed. Against such a backdrop, Oxford 1937 would have to articulate an internationalism fit for an age of despair.

Chapter 5

Race, Nation, and Globe
at Oxford 1937

Prayer at the Oxford 1937 conference was shot through with the language of supranational and supraracial solidarity. Many participants reported that they found the worship services—held in St. Mary's Cathedral every morning from 9:30—to be the most "unforgettable part" of the conference.[1] Although such services were voluntary—and while typically at such conferences delegates would treat them as free time—their large attendance at Oxford spoke of their importance to delegates.[2] The official prayer guide suggested that attendees engage in silent prayer on the theme of worldwide solidarity in the church. One such session offered the following prompts: "Una Sancta. A supra-racial, supra-national, supra-class community. The denial of this claim by nationalism and sectarianism. The growth of oecumenism."[3] Specially written liturgy positioned participants to consider their own role in the politics of race and nation, such as in the following order of service:

> L[eader]: Have I allowed my Volk heritage, through my own ignorance, pride and self-centeredness, to become "a middle wall of partition" between me and those of other races and cultures?
> Silence
> L: Have I been truly a brother to my fellow-men irrespective of caste, color, creed or nationality?
> Silence[4]

For Chicago University's Edwin Ewart Aubrey, "no part of the fellowship was more conducive to mutual sympathy."[5]

Such prayers and liturgies reflected the contemporary challenges ecumenists faced in 1937. The phrase "*Volk* heritage" used in the liturgy was a vital
indicator of the critical world situation in which the conferees met. The proposal for Oxford 1937 came about at exactly the time—and in direct response
to—the rise of the new professedly Christian nationalism in Nazi Germany.
When the new German government sought to establish a *Volkskirche* in 1934,
dissenting German Evangelicals, spurred on by the theological leadership of
Karl Barth, formed a breakaway, dissenting "Confessing" branch of the Evangelical Church.[6] Both the national church and the dissenters sought recognition
from the ecumenical movement. At the meeting of the Universal Christian
Council on Life and Work at Fanö, Denmark, in 1934, where the idea for
the Oxford conference was first proposed, the German crisis was dramati-
cally instantiated. Two rival delegations of Germans—one official, the other
unofficial—were present: the Confessing Church represented by Dietrich Bonhoeffer, and the German national churches by Bishop Theodor Heckel, who
was appointed by the new "Reich bishop," Ludwig Mueller. Daylong debates
at Fanö saw Heckel deflect heated criticisms over Nazi plans for a national
Reich church, especially from the American representative, Henry Smith
Leiper, foreign secretary of the American Federal Council of Churches.[7] Leiper
went on to play a major role in the preparation and postconference publiciz-
ing of Oxford's work in America.

Also present at Fanö was Joseph Oldham, who, at that meeting, was appointed head of the Advisory Commission on Research by the Life and Work
council. Oldham went on to become, in Visser 't Hooft's words, "the *auctor
intellectualis* of the whole enterprise." As Nils Ehrenström put it, he was "the
chief architect and outstanding exponent of the Oxford project."[8] Oldham's
appointment in the midst of the *Volk*-church controversy clearly shaped the
research parameters he set for the conference. In his *Church, Community and
State: A World Issue*, released the same year as the Fanö conference, Oldham
placed nationhood—the nature of *Volk*—at the heart of the contemporary
world crisis. As Oldham explained, the proposed conference title, "Church,
Community, and State," implied there was more at stake than the old question
of church and state. Now the larger issues concerned nationhood, or rather, the
very nature of the "community," his rendering of the word *Volk*.[9] It was more
than a German problem; it was, as the title of his work suggested, a world
problem: "What place in God's purpose does the nation hold? What is the
relation of the Church to the communal life with which its own life is in-
separably intertwined?"[10] It was more than merely abstract. Delegates from
Japan and China discussed supranational unity while their two nations were at

war. Attendees from Germany, the United States, and South Africa debated the normativity of racial equality while, at home, authorities and churches often practiced the opposite. In a world climate in which the structures of international community seemed near to collapse under the strain of economic isolation on the part of the United States; militarism and expansionism on the part of Japan, Italy, and Germany; and the general intensification of illiberal fascist politics in Europe, the task of Oxford was to draw Protestants together and articulate hope for supranational unity and community in theological terms.

But, what kind of theology? Under Oldham's guidance, Oxford 1937 marked the high tide of so-called neoorthodox theology in the ecumenical movement, or as I term it in this chapter, "postliberal" theology.[11] Although in many ways postliberal theologians remained embedded in liberalism, they nonetheless professed and sought to critique the theological liberalism in which they had been trained. Their critiques of liberalism's methods, outlook, and sensibility gave to the Oxford conference the language it used to voice its distinct version of Christian internationalism. Postliberal theologians not only emphasized Augustinian and neo-Reformed notions of original sin, they used that doctrine to insist that the relationship of God to the historical realm—to the state, to the nation, to all historical forms of community—had to be articulated in a constant and complex negotiation of "Yes-and-No," or rather, "No, *then* Yes." There could be no seamless identification of the Kingdom of God with the nation-state or with the League of Nations: neither with nationalism nor internationalism. But, if the dialectical "No" was aimed at the sin of national and racial idolatry, a revived idea of the catholicity of the church was to be the basis of the dialectical "Yes." That is, to engage in redemptive action and witness in international life meant beginning with what God was already doing: gathering into the church an ecumenical community transcending borders, nationalities, and race, which was, and would finally be, at the end of history, united in Christ. It was a vision at once universalist and also particularist—attending little to the relation of Christianity to the world's other faiths and featuring, still, in spite of its hopes, a decidedly North Atlantic focus.[12] But, because such a focus on a catholic ecclesiology differed in intellectual method from mainstream liberal internationalism, providing a way to speak of international community without either sacralizing or demonizing the League of Nations, it became a signature element of Oxford's postliberal political theology. In all the preaching and debating across sections and plenary sessions, Oxford 1937 was defined by the argument that ecumenical ecclesiology—with the conference process and shared worship as a kind of praxis—not only provided the setting for the articulation of Christian internationalism, it also provided the substance.

Sources of the Postliberal Consensus

In the world of transatlantic Protestantism surrounding Oxford 1937 there were arguably two main groups seeking to develop a theology that would reject liberalism: the stream of thought emanating from Continental Protestantism associated with the writings of Karl Barth; and the emerging "Christian realism" associated with Reinhold Niebuhr, his brother Richard, and a network of other "younger theologians" (a self-designation) from Yale Divinity School and Union Theological Seminary. Although, for understandable reasons, historians often group them together under the label "neoorthodox," these two groups developed distinct theological currents—not only different in flavor and method but also often mutually critical and mutually averse.[13] And yet, both met and combined, in a very important sense, to produce the Oxford consensus.

Of the two strands, *Krisis* theology, or "dialectical theology" associated with the Swiss professor Karl Barth, originated earliest, sweeping through ecumenical circles in the late 1920s.[14] Barth offered a radical critique of what he saw as the whole theological method of liberalism that had dominated the nineteenth century since the work of Friedrich Schleiermacher and a rejection of anything that reeked of Feuerbach's anthropocentric conception of religion.[15] At stake, for Barth, were the very foundational assumptions about God's capacity for self-revelation. God was radically *other* and would only be known through such self-revelation. As such, he would not speak through history or *Kultur*, nor through the Hegelian unfolding of ideas, still less through the Romantic historicist ideology of Nazism. Salvation, Barth argued, in a recapitulation of Reformation theology, had to come from beyond the horizon of human effort and knowledge: as an act of grace. Laying out the essential elements of his early thought, Barth's evocative commentary on the New Testament book of Romans became a touchstone for the movement—in Visser 't Hooft's terms, the "Barthian storm"—that surrounded his work. Sinful humanity stood, by default, he argued, under the judgment of God. "The wrath of God is the judgment under which we stand . . . *it* is the 'No' which meets us when we do *not* affirm it; it is the protest pronounced always and everywhere against the course of the world in so far as we do *not* accept the protest as our own."[16]

Importantly for Oxford 1937 and its deliberations on nationalism and world order, Barthianism not only meant opposition to Nazi nationalism, it also implied that notions of natural law, of universal moral order, or of natural theology could no longer provide a basis for Christian reflection on political order, as many nineteenth- and early twentieth-century Protestants had assumed. Christians, Barth argued, needed to reject methods of reasoning that claimed "to be theological, i.e. to interpret divine revelation," but "whose *subject* however differs fundamentally from the revelation in Jesus Christ and whose *method* therefore differs equally from the exposition of Holy Scripture."[17] Taking Barth's critique on board meant de-emphasizing, if not disbanding, appeals to ethical universalism in historical Christian international thought—whether Aquinas's treatment of a just war, the early modern theorizing of Grotius and Locke, or, especially, the generalized appeals to the brotherhood of man of late nineteenth-century liberalism. Such a concern with theological method was heard repeatedly in the deliberations at Oxford 1937, where delegates, especially from Germany, reiterated that the churches should not merely rubber-stamp existing liberal ideas about international life but should focus on discerning what ethical implications arose from divine revelation.

Meanwhile, a separate push toward a postliberal theology came from the emerging realist theologians in America, particularly from Reinhold Niebuhr and his colleagues in the Fellowship of Socialist Christians, *The World Tomorrow*, and another small but very important body called the Theological Discussion Group, whose life Mark Edwards has done tremendous work in capturing.[18] Although often deeply critical of Barthianism for being too biblicist, too pessimistic regarding human nature, and allegedly fostering political apathy, Niebuhr and his colleagues also launched an attack—with far less academic rigor, but more socially and politically directed energy—on what they called liberalism.[19] Scholars debate whether Niebuhr ever really detached himself from liberalism, but nonetheless this is what he professed to be his goal.[20] Liberalism, Niebuhr argued, rested on a fundamentally optimistic view of "the goodness of human nature, . . . [an] interpretation of human history in terms of the idea of progress, and a belief that collective behavior differs only in a certain tardiness in reaching the ideals of the latter."[21] The two aspects of liberalism against which he primarily reacted, then, were its view of human nature and, related to that, its progressive, optimistic outlook on human history. As he put it in the title of his famed magnum opus, he was concerned with a realistic appraisal of both the "nature and destiny of man."[22]

One of the central achievements of the Oxford 1937 conference was to bring together the very different Niebuhrian and Barthian postliberal theologies and apply them to Christian political thought. Without this, Oxford may well have been another Stockholm, just more badly exposed in its incapacity to address the world situation in meaningful terms. Moreover, the fusion of the two postliberal strands did not happen by accident. It took the careful planning and constant, diplomatic mediation of organizers, especially Joseph Oldham, to ensure both strands were well represented at Oxford, despite Barth's personal absence, and to see that the overlaps between both schools of thought were exploited.

Oldham was uniquely positioned to interpret one strand of postliberal theology to the adherents of the other and to bring them together. Not only did he have more than a decade of experience at the ecumenical International Missionary Council, he also had familiarity with theological life on both sides of the Atlantic, having trained in German language and theology after studying at Oxford.[23] Oldham did not fit squarely within either strand of theology. He had sympathies with aspects of Barthianism and yet also enjoyed a developing relationship with Reinhold Niebuhr, Henry Pit Van Dusen, and other American realists, not to mention a decades-long association and deep friendship with John R. Mott. Oxford 1937 provided Oldham with the opportunity to use his personal contacts, networks, and interests to bring together both strands. Since the early 1930s, he had been meeting regularly with a group of European and British theologians in a small study circle dubbed the "Christianity and Reality" group that included Swiss theologian Emil Brunner, who, although denounced famously by Barth, was, to others, Barthian nonetheless.[24] Meanwhile, in the early to mid-1930s, Oldham also courted American realists, crossing the Atlantic several times in his preparation for Oxford in order to co-opt Niebuhr, Van Dusen, and others into the Oxford project. Oldham attended retreats of their Theological Discussion Group (TDG) and, through it, mixed with other theologians—many already known to him—such as Paul Tillich, the famed theologian who had been exiled from Germany and was then at Union Seminary; Reinhold Niebuhr's brother, H. Richard Niebuhr, of Yale Divinity School; Georgia Harkness at Mount Holyoke College; and Francis P. Miller, the chairman of the World's Student Christian Federation. As late as November 1936, Van Dusen advised other discussion group members before their upcoming retreat that Oldham was "counting very heavily on the discussions of our group to assist him in thinking through the plans and preparation for the 'Oxford Conference.'"[25]

Oldham's connection with the TDG was one of the primary ways he gave American postliberal theology prominence at Oxford 1937. He appointed the discussion group's convener, Van Dusen, head of the American branch of the Oxford 1937 "Research Commission," giving him responsibility for coordinating the production and circulation of preparatory papers in America as part of the enormous international exchange in the lead-up to the conference. He also used a feature of Oxford 1937's delegation policies (not employed at Stockholm 1925) to ensure that a high proportion of TDG members attended the conference as specially "co-opted" delegates. The co-opting system allowed Oldham to influence the intellectual composition of the group to his liking, independent of the machinations of local denominations, which may not necessarily have been likely to appoint the likes of Niebuhr. Of the small membership of the TDG in America, a remarkable number went to Oxford 1937 as specially co-opted delegates: Reinhold Niebuhr, Henry Pit Van Dusen, John Bennett, Georgia Harkness, Edwin Ewart Aubrey, Samuel McCrea Cavert, Paul Tillich, and others. As such, the meetings of the TDG became a setting in which delegates rehearsed arguments that were taken up at Oxford 1937.[26] Oldham's program of engineered appointments changed the demographic face of ecumenism from what had been at Stockholm. No longer did the older generation of liberal internationalists like Charles Brent represent the American voice; ecumenism, from 1937, for at least two decades, became associated with the face of American realist theologians like Niebuhr and Van Dusen.

Around their differences, the two strands of postliberal theology shared common emphases, the forces of which were pooled and concentrated. Despite differences in the way they understood the Bible, both turned to it increasingly as a source—a fact more remarkable for the Niebuhrian American Social Gospellers than for the Continental evangelical theologians. The biblical turn came with a new emphasis on the classical, Reformation understanding of sin as original and universal. This was true, even for Niebuhr, who cited the book of Romans in his plenary address at Oxford to speak about political ideology as the sin of self-glorification.[27] And in contrast to what was seen as the unquestioned, perhaps unconscious, progressivism of the nineteenth century (and indeed of the 1920s), both the new postliberal theologies of the 1930s stressed the gulf between the historical process and the purposes of God. Rather than discerning God's immanence in the historical process, both strands of theology asserted God's historical transcendence.[28] The notion that history was somehow manageable through rational effort or that history revealed its own self-enclosed meaning—whether Hegelian, Marxist, Nazi, or simple small "l" liberal progressivist—was anathema to both groups.

And just like realism at *The World Tomorrow*, postliberal theology at Oxford 1937 was also characterized by new "feeling rules": in this case, a prizing of holy self-despair. Reinhold Niebuhr, by 1937 a renowned author, preacher, and lecturer on both sides of the Atlantic—approaching cult figure status among the British student Christian movement—highlighted this during his plenary address on the second evening of the conference, entitled "The Christian Church in a Secular Age."[29] As Charles Hurd, the special *New York Times* correspondent at the conference, reported, Niebuhr "threw aside his prepared manuscript" and spoke extemporaneously to great applause, focusing on the theme of despair. He called upon the conference to make a virtue out of spiritual necessity: "some of the most profound insights into religion have come when men no longer had a reason for believing in themselves."[30] Listening to Niebuhr speak, F. Ernest Johnson, a fellow American delegate attached to the Federal Council of Churches, scribbled in the margins of his conference handbook a quotation: "Only the man who is in despair has any use for the Christian gospel."[31] Niebuhr was not alone, far from it; the official introduction to the conference laid out in the Delegates' Handbook set the scene with this quotation: "Only out of a deep distrust and despair of self can the word be spoken which the world needs to hear and which it will be willing to hear."[32]

In what ways, then, did Oxford delegates apply this postliberal theology and sensibility to international thought? The work of two study sections, that on "Church and Community" and that of the "Universal Church and the World of Nations," shows how, through intensive deliberations, delegates promoted new formulations and proposals that squared with the emergent theology and filtered out older emphases—whether liberal internationalist or nationalist. Formally, their task was to distill the insights of the preparatory essays circulating before the conference—many authored by major figures in international affairs—into reports that the conference as a whole could endorse. As such, the section reports reflected, more than any other documents, the *process*, with all its attendant disagreement and agreement, of consensus building at the conference.

Political Theologies of Nation and Race

The special study sections that met morning and night most days were scattered across Oxford—some in lecture halls, some in the old library of St. Mary's Church, others in rooms of other churches such as St. Columba's Presbyterian. Each section had around a week to agree upon a long report and a short report that they were to submit to the whole conference in the second week. Translators in each section provided assistance in discussions where necessary.

Henry Smith Leiper recalled that most delegates understood English, while those who did not "huddled" during discussions around translators who gave almost instant translation into French and German. "It was," he said, "gratifying to watch the working of this system."[33] Within sections of eighty individuals each, drafting committees of between ten and fifteen people, chosen from a variety of countries and church traditions, were tasked with capturing the group's views. These multilingual committees produced drafts of the reports daily in English, German, and French, and worked late into the night on a regular basis. It was in these groups, Edwin Aubrey (a member of the Theological Discussion Group recruited by Oldham) felt, that "the real give-and-take of the conference took place." What had once seemed like irreconcilable differences became, in the context of actual conversation and shared laughter, smaller obstacles than first thought, he reflected.[34]

The most direct treatment of nationalism took place in the section called "Church and Community." Meeting in the chapter house of Christ Church, with Britain's Sir Walter Moberly, head of the University Grants Commission, as chairman, the organizers were charged with examining "the relation of the organized Church to the society of which it forms a part . . . and particularly of that unique form of social organism the English-speaking peoples call 'the nation' and the Germans 'Das Volk.' "[35] As resources for the discussions in section meetings, the delegates had with them the preparatory papers produced in the scholarly exchange before the conference. These papers, however, offered delegates no ready-made consensus. On the contrary, they illustrated the persistence of the opposition between Anglo-American rationalist and Continental historicist approaches to understanding nationalism that had preceded the conference. Unsurprisingly, most of the contributors, especially Anglophone writers, offered critiques of the Nazi views of community. Professor Ernest Barker, one of Britain's most renowned political theorists of the interwar period (and who also wrote a series of essays for the London *Times* on the Oxford 1937 conference in the lead-up), offered an ambitious and perhaps misguided attempt to "disprove" Nazism by pointing to its definitional inconsistencies, perhaps reflecting the concern with semantic precision characteristic of the English analytical tradition in which he was immersed. Nazi ideas were mistaken in supposing "blood and soil" explained the rise of communities, Barker argued, for there were plenty of exceptions to that rule. Community did not arise from nature, but was always voluntaristic, "in some sense, a human creation, superimposed on the natural or physical grounds of human existence."[36] Thus one could be a member of society and partner in community "whatever [one's] . . . blood or speech."[37] National Socialists erred in insisting that blood equated with *Volk*.

Barker's paper appeared to raise the ire of Hanns Lilje, general secretary of the World Lutheran Convention, and editor of *Die Furche*.[38] Without naming Barker, Lilje attacked Barker's views directly in his preparatory paper. "There is only one traditional theory of nationality," he argued, "which can be dismissed straight away as lacking in realism, namely the purely rationalistic explanation."[39] There was no mythical "rational exercise" such as a social contract to be found at the source of nationhood. Rather, "the characteristic feature of nationality lies precisely in its very quality of givenness or pre-existence; it is a state which exists prior to our considerations and decisions so that our nationality confronts us with a pre-existent claim."[40] Contrary to what Barker or anyone else might argue, blood and soil did matter, urged Lilje: they did, "as a matter of fact, form the natural foundations of a people."[41] But Lilje also argued that a sense of historical "vocation" or "mission" was an "integral part of the essence of a nation" in addition to blood and soil.[42] Although Lilje did not sympathize with the Nazi Party—and remained a part of both the Confessing Church and the ecumenical movement during and after the war—his apologia for national mission, given in the late 1930s, remains eerie even today. He returned again and again to the theme of the mystical, semidivine transcendence of the nation: "The mystery that shrouds the historical birth of a nation . . . transcends any merely rational explanation . . . It is possible that theologically this is the only fundamental doctrine that can be laid down about nationality, namely, that a nation receives its mission from the hands of God."[43] Yet in the context of the conference, both Barker's rationalistic position and Lilje's unapologetically Romanticist view of nationhood represented two extremes. Neither view reflected the consensus that emerged; instead, they highlighted the gap that had to be bridged.

Out of the collective process of section discussions, the report of the Church and Community section arrived at a dialectical reading of nationality and nationalism that better expressed the postliberal theological consensus than did either Lilje or Barker. The report concluded that nationality was one of the many "frameworks of life" that partook in both good and evil: "they are of God and yet also of human sin."[44] Some preparatory papers had debated this position biblically: Was nationality to be considered among the "orders of Creation," a natural gift alongside marriage, family, or society, or was it a result of sin in the world?[45] The final report—in its dialectical style—answered that it was both. National egotism, the conference report on Church and Community argued, provided a clear example of where nationality—"essentially a gift of God to mankind"—was transformed into something evil because of its "infection by human sinfulness." They thus concluded that a Christian ought to find himself in "perpetual tension and conflict. He accepts thankfully his community in order to live and to work in it and for it; yet if he would work in it and for it for Christ he must be in continuous protest against it."[46]

Indeed, the reports of the Oxford 1937 conference anticipated later scholarship on nationalism (such as that of Ernest Gellner and Anthony Giddens) in stressing the importance of modern social fragmentation as a contributing factor in the rise of nationalism.[47] Modern, secular, industrialized life, the Oxford delegates argued, had seen the disintegration of traditional modes of loyalties. With old loyalties gone, and no new ones to take their place, "the community life of mankind has been thrown into confusion." In the face of this disintegration, the world was now witnessing a range of new and desperate attempts to "re-integrate" communities, particularly in, but not restricted to, Germany, Japan, Russia, and Italy. People were seeking to meet their "primal need" for community and fellowship by creating new solidarities, new centers of life. Yet in the effort to reintegrate social life, the elevation of the nation to "supreme good" resulted in the "deification," or idolatry of the nation. This was dangerous, they argued, for "a false sacred, a false God, merely adds demonic power to the unredeemed passions of men. Though bringing about temporary and local unity it prepares for mankind an even worse and wider conflict."[48]

Similarly, the report argued, racial particularity constituted a gift, and racial pride and abuse a distortion of that gift. "The existence of black races, white races, yellow races, is to be accepted gladly and reverently as full of possibilities under God's purpose for the enrichment of human life." Guarding against any chance that this assertion could be interpreted as allowing for a relationship of hierarchical complementarity and inequality between races (as apologists for empire—even at Stockholm 1925—often propounded[49]), the statement insisted that "there is no room for any differentiation between the races as to their intrinsic value. All share alike in the concern of God."[50] Thus, in churches, "there can be no place for exclusion or segregation because of race or color. 'There is neither Jew nor Greek, bond nor free for ye are all one in Christ.'" As had the Race Relations report at Jerusalem 1928, the Church and Community report at Oxford 1937 urged that each local congregation be called upon to "realize at any cost in its own self that unity," a recommendation that generated opposition from the white South African contingent.[51] The "rebuke of deeds" needed to be brought against "the recrudescence of pitiless cruelty, hatred and race discriminations (including anti-Semitism)."[52] This statement contained one of the few specific mentions of anti-Semitism. Henry Smith Leiper later recalled an episode from the conference where such phrases "mysteriously" disappeared from the German translation upon the final presentation. "There was something of a mystery attached to the report," he wrote. "The English version included the words 'anti-Semitism' and the quotation from St. Paul, 'In Christ there is neither Jew nor Greek.' In the German translation both references were missing! Nobody could explain how that happened. The chairman, Sir Walter Moberly, assured all present, however, that it was purely an inadvertence, an unintentional oversight by the translator."[53]

Which Plan for International Order?

While the Church and Community section met each evening in the chapter house of Christ Church, the section on the Universal Church and the World of Nations gathered not far away at St. Columba's Presbyterian Church—off Oxford's High Street. The latter group had been directed to attend more to the positive parameters of ecumenical internationalism. Which proposals for international organization would fit with the postliberal theological framework? Of what would a Christian voice in international relations consist? Aside from having the involvement of several of the well-known ecumenical leaders at Oxford—John R. Mott, Joseph Oldham, Visser 't Hooft, and the Universal Christian Council's general secretary, Pastor Henry L. Henriod—the World of Nations section had also co-opted the help of several other notable "lay" figures in world affairs. These included, for example, Phillip Kerr, the marquess of Lothian, former secretary to the British prime minister and future ambassador to the United States; Alfred Zimmern, Oxford University's notable professor of international relations; Lord Robert Cecil, a founder of the League of Nations; J. V. Wilson of the secretariat of the League of Nations; and John Foster Dulles, known then for his experience at the Versailles negotiations and in international commercial law.[54] The section was chaired by the president of Princeton Theological Seminary, Dr. John Mackay—a former Presbyterian missionary to Latin America who in the future would become a key figure in the Church Commission led by John Foster Dulles advocating for American Christians to support the establishment of a United Nations Organization.

More important than the section's personnel were the conceptual tasks it faced. Delegates had to bring the theological consensus of the conference to bear on the problems of international law, organization, and politics. In approaching this task, the group faced a kind of impasse. Given the conference's overall critique of "national egotism" and nationalism, the section unsurprisingly and inevitably argued that national sovereignty represented an insufficient normative framework for political behavior. A key paragraph in the section's final report—later cited in several American church documents of the late 1930s and early 1940s (see chapter 7)—made this commitment plain: "So far as the present evil is political the heart of it is to be found in the claim of each national State to be judge of its own cause. The abandonment of that claim, and the abrogation of absolute national sovereignty, at least to that extent, is a duty that the Church should urge upon the nations."[55] The section's commitment to some form of universalism over mere nationalism was certain. But what kind of universalism? The pervasive critiques of liberal theology and politics coming from theologians made it uncertain what the answer to this question would be.

The preparatory papers of the World of Nations section gave an airing to many of the rival schemes for international order circulating in the 1930s. But tellingly, not all got an equal place—indeed, some received no place—in the final report of the section. The exclusion and inclusion of these schemes by and large reflected their compatibility with the postliberal methodological grid used at the conference: namely, the commitment to a dialectical reading of politics, and the priority of ecclesiological reasoning. The primary method available to historians for examining the filtering process is to compare the language and proposals of the two bodies of sources. Proposals and themes in the final reports were couched in language directly derived from respective preparatory papers. It is not difficult, for example, to identify the contributions of John Foster Dulles, Max Huber, or William Menn in the final report. On the other hand, proposals deemed less worthy of adoption by the section were often excluded entirely from the final report. They were conspicuous not only by their absence, but also by the presence of language in the report that implicitly conflicted with their suggestions. Other proposals appeared but had marginal, rather than programmatic, weight in the report—a diplomatic drafting technique that acknowledged a viewpoint without giving emphasis to it.

Among the schemes rejected by the World of Nations section was the idea of a federated world state—an idea made popular in the 1930s by H. G. Wells and which circulated in American internationalist discourse before and during World War II.[56] The man who attempted to put the Christian case for world federation to the delegates at Oxford was the marquess of Lothian, Phillip Kerr, future British ambassador to the United States. Kerr, like everyone else at the conference, shared a loathing for the idea of unmitigated national sovereignty. His paper, very uneven in quality, and yet somehow attaining the opening position in the published volume of papers in the Oxford series, laid out the merits of world federation. If the problem was the notion of national sovereignty, the solution, he argued, was a pooling of sovereignties. The problem with the League of Nations was that instead of changing the structure of national sovereignties, it merely presupposed and reinforced them. For Kerr, the logic of history demanded a new system, a new "common sovereignty." There was no other "ultimate remedy." Here Kerr echoed the absolutist tones of his compatriot, Wells. The world federation, said Kerr, would equate to "a state which, in its own sphere, will command the allegiance of mankind, will be able to legislate for, judge, and tax everybody while leaving the national state freedom to deal with affairs in the national sphere."[57] It is clear Kerr's proposals met opposition; he responded to what appear to have been very pertinent criticisms in the final section of his published paper (perhaps added in a rush, with no time to integrate his response to the criticisms throughout the essay).

Yes, Kerr acknowledged, of course there was a danger that this new world state itself could become tyrannical, and no, it may not have been the most "practical" solution. But here is where Kerr saw the role of Christianity. For as the church would focus on its mission and as the Spirit of the Lord would do His work, the conditions for world federation would naturally improve. Clearly unmoved by the other delegates' postliberal emphasis on the eschatological fulfillment of the Kingdom of God, Kerr suggested such progress would "inevitably produce the Kingdom of God among the nations of the earth."[58] Thus he offered a plan for a kind of church-sanctified World Federation: "When this Christian transformation of man through love and understanding of the One True God has gone far enough . . . the legislative, executive, and judicial functions of the world federation will be exercised under some kind of democratic control, and in accordance with moral and spiritual law, and without any of the despotic, repressive, illiberal features which would necessarily characterize a world state today."[59] With such a stubbornly optimistic tone in the context of 1937, one could be forgiven for reading Kerr as if nothing had changed in the ecumenical movement since Stockholm 1925. The Christian faith for Kerr, as for many Anglophone and French delegates twelve years earlier, appeared to be a means to a liberal-democratic end. It is clear, though, that his proposals were not taken seriously. The final section report made none but the slightest, passing mention, without endorsement, of his ideas on World Federation.[60] The theological filter of section discussions worked to block its influence.

Alfred Zimmern's call for the extension of the ethos of the British Commonwealth likewise failed to gain a mention in the report. For Zimmern, the British Commonwealth had an intangible, "spiritual" quality that made war between its members "unthinkable."[61] The same quality of relations could be found between other democratic nations such as the United States and Canada, Britain and the United States, or Britain and Switzerland, for example. The question was how, then, this sort of sense of social solidarity could be expanded in the interests of establishing a peaceful world order. Logically (not envisaging the asymmetrical warfare or terrorism of the twenty-first century), if such solidarity became universal, he argued, war would become unthinkable. For Zimmern, "the enlargement of the social conscience is the heart of the international problem." The task would begin with democratic nations, for in these nations the sense of social engagement was already active among citizens. The peace between democratic nations derived from a spiritual community of "common things." World order, Zimmern urged, "is not a matter of political architecture, of constructing courts and councils and assemblies and bodies and officials . . . but of finding means to mobilize the existing store of virtue and public spirit in such a way as to act as a permanent driving force in world affairs."[62] Zimmern, though not a theologian, had done his best to connect in his own way with neo-orthodox theology. The earlier part of his essay had attempted to engage with St. Augustine—a decade before Reinhold Niebuhr would discover the insights of his work as a basis for his realism.[63] Yet Zimmern's actual analysis and proposal was not really Augustinian in character. He appeared to lean more on Ernest Barker's reading of Augustine (the Cambridge professor also contributing to the Oxford conference), than on Augustine himself. Where Augustine had famously stressed original sin, Barker instead spoke of mobilizing the "existing store of virtue" in humankind, and came very close to identifying the Anglophone democracies with the essence of a Christian world order.

One figure whose proposals for world order did appear—but only in partial form—in the final section report was John Foster Dulles. Dulles, as will be discussed in chapter 7, became a pre-eminent figure in the resurgence of American internationalism during the 1940s. In his Oxford preparatory paper, Dulles expanded on one of his most dearly held and oft-repeated themes: the promotion of international structures that allowed for "dynamic change." His Oxford paper foreshadowed the book he published the following year, *War, Peace and Change*, and cast the problems of world order in distinctly mechanistic terms. The problem of lasting peace, Dulles argued, was that of finding a system able to distribute "dynamic forces" and provide suitable "outlets" to mitigate the "blockages" of national boundaries. National boundaries acted as artificial barriers that stood in the way of the natural flow of supranational forces.[64] Unlike Kerr, Dulles saw the notion of a world-state as out of reach, a "grandiose solution," and impossible so long as there remained cultural difference in the world. Yet his ahistorical, mechanistic outlook—with echoes of Adam Smith's trust in the invisible hand—perhaps displayed just as much optimism. Dulles's vision required nothing less than the management of the forces that made up global life: "Our requirement is not that there be no boundaries but that safety valves be cut through the barriers of boundaries so that human energy will diffuse itself peacefully and not be suppressed and compressed within a rigid envelope until a bursting pressure is maintained."[65] Dulles's safety valves mainly related to international commerce. Unequal distribution of resources caused conflict. More of the world's resources could be opened up through an extension of the mandate system, he suggested, without circumspection as to whose good such an open door would promote. Dulles pointed to the example of how the early United States balanced interstate commerce with a measure of state sovereignty. The model served as an example for how transborder flow could be balanced with stability. (American federalism remained a core paradigm for Dulles's internationalism.) Under such an arrangement, international currencies could be stabilized and made consistent and exchangeable. Migration restrictions could be loosened. Those changes would represent "apertures through which human energy and initiative may peacefully pass." Importantly, too, for Dulles, the dynamic nature of world politics, and the mistakes of the Treaty of Versailles, meant that new treaties needed to be made flexible rather than static, and able to be periodically updated.

Parts of Dulles's proposals found their way into the section report in a passage entitled "The Conditions of Peaceful Change." Stressing again that "the unequal distribution of bounties is one of the causes of war," the report called on Christian peoples to use the power of public opinion to ensure their governments made decisions that reflected a national sacrifice for the greater good. To make such judgments, it argued, churches needed better, less nationally biased information, another task to which the ecumenical movement could give themselves. The whole goal, though, was the creation of an "equality of opportunity" for countries and individuals in a worldwide marketplace. Free engagement in free trade, mediated by government, monitored by the power of enlightened public opinion, would bring peace and well-being for all.[66] Any efforts on the part of "less fortunate lands" to seek adjustments that reversed the current inequality to another inequality in their favor were unwelcome. What was needed was, in a negative and abstract formulation, the "removal of inequalities of opportunity."[67] While they were included in the final report, though, Dulles's proposals did not amount to a comprehensive scheme such as that of the League of Nations, the British Commonwealth, or a World Federation. They represented a footnote on the importance of free trade and legal flexibility to be built into any international organization. As such, they were simply placed, like many other inclusions in the final report, as one more point worthy of note, rather than an item of programmatic significance.

While the British and American preparatory papers offered variations on a liberal internationalist theme and did not achieve much prominence in the section's final report, a contribution from a German delegate more successfully captured the postliberal emphases delegates sought. Pastor Wilhelm Menn— later a member of the German war resistance—saw too much overlap, too much easy sanction, between the pacifist and internationalist work of the idealistic-humanitarian movements and the peace work of the churches. Over the last two centuries, he argued, there emerged "on the one hand, a half-conscious, half-unconscious secularization of Christianity by the reception of idealist and humanitarian elements, and, on the other, a widespread conscious or unconscious adoption and assimilation of Christian conceptions by humanitarian idealism."[68] Vague talk about the "unity of mankind" as the basis for world order represented a case-in-point. The general anthropological unity of mankind could not be the starting point for a Christian ethic of international order; instead, the church's response to the ethical problems of international life should begin with a theology of the church itself: "The one Church of Christ is a God-given, historical reality. That is the unshakable ground from which, and from which alone, we must begin our discussion of the Church and the international sphere, the questions it involves, the hopes it may engender, and the tasks which may have to be undertaken as a result."[69] Indeed, the difference in starting point could even be expressed in the language used. Menn's penchant for conceptual precision led him to distinguish "oecumenical" from "international." For "while the concept 'international' itself testifies to differences that for it are fundamental, and so contains an element of negation," he argued, "the word 'oecumene' characterizes the world as a unity."[70]

Menn did not seem to grapple with what such an ecclesiological orientation meant for those of other faiths. How would they relate to plans for international order that stressed the primacy of the Christian Church? Nonetheless, the World of Nations section report took up much of Menn's approach, and, like him, sought to emphasize the gap between mere liberal internationalism and ecumenical witness. Point II of the report reiterated Menn's distinction between "international" and ecumenical. "One starts from the fact of division and the other from the fact of unity in Christ."[71] More importantly, the next paragraph reflected Menn's concern with "starting points," arguing there was a qualitative distance between the political theology of ecumenism and ordinary political resources. The concern with the "sources" of political insight reflected postliberal theology's concern with the basis of revelation:

> The fact of the ecumenical character of the Church carries with it the important consequence that the Church brings to the task of achieving a better international order an insight that is not to be derived from ordinary political sources. To those who are struggling to realize human brotherhood in a world where disruptive nationalism and aggressive imperialism make such brotherhood seem unreal, the Church offers not an ideal but a fact. . . . True ecumenicity must be the goal of all our efforts.[72]

As the church formed part of the answer, it could not be left behind in the rush to change the world. This position represented a conscious distancing from the "churchless" activism of some Christian internationalists.[73]

The question of actual plans for international order still remained, however. In addition to those floated in the preparatory papers, the daily deliberations of the section also saw other proposals for peace and world order surface. Once again, delegates collectively rejected some, while they took up others and incorporated them into the final report. One notable rejection was the American proposal that war could be "abolished" as a system—much in the same way slavery had been. Apparently the difficulties in meaningfully implementing the Kellogg-Briand Pact had done little to assuage the triumphalism of Outlawry advocates. In any case, their position stood so far outside the theological consensus forming at Oxford 1937 that the "abolition" position did not even appear as one possible Christian view of war among others in the final report.[74]

The particular scheme that did receive most serious attention in the section discussions was the League of Nations. In their treatment of the league, though, Oxford delegates—unlike those at Stockholm 1925—applied their dialectical, "No-Yes" framework. Not only did a false deification of the nation need to be countered, they argued, so too did a false deification of the League of Nations. The report stated emphatically that "no international order which has been devised by human effort may be equated with the Kingdom of God."[75] Despite the dangers, though, particular plans still had to be evaluated and, if appropriate, supported. "It is erroneous to hold that our hope in the King-dom of God has no bearing upon the practical choices that men must make within the present order," the report urged.

Dispersed through the deliberations on the league was a distinct note of self-consciousness about earlier moments in Christian internationalism—a coyness about the culture of sacred reverence that had once surrounded the league.[76] As well as expressing dialectical theology, the warnings against idol-izing the league grew from particular observations made by figures involved at Geneva over the previous decade and a half. In his preparatory paper, Alfred Zimmern complained that he had witnessed Wilsonian idealism become a "reli-gion of internationalism."[77] Internationalists, he argued, had tended to elevate the league to "an object of aspiration, round which sentiments of a religious or quasi-religious character were allowed, and even encouraged, to gather."[78] In doing so, the league movement had only opened the way for reaction. "Wearied of stretching their aspirations beyond natural limits, men were open to the appeal of primitive and unthinking tribalism," which for Zimmern was "equally false and idolatrous."[79] Others who had lived and worked in Ge-neva agreed with Zimmern. Some delegates told the section meeting that they could recall "hundreds of people of a certain type—nicknamed 'the mystics'—who came to Geneva in the spirit of religious pilgrims, and who said: 'I believe in the League' with a kind of rapture as if they were saying: 'I believe in the Holy Catholic Church.' "[80] Reflecting these discussions, the fi-nal report of the section offered a clear rejection of the sacralization of the league. "The League is not a Church," it asserted. "The tendency," it argued, "to endow the League with qualities which it does not or cannot possess . . . has been responsible for much disillusionment and confusion of mind."[81]

Although the religion of the league received a major "no" from the con-ference, the continuation of the league as an international organization received an overall "yes." The World of Nations section report entirely rejected the no-tion that the league had failed, as some were arguing. It did accept that there were problems with the league's ability to foster compliance, as had become evident in the six years since the beginning of the Manchurian crisis. But im-portantly, the report insisted that the "idea on which the League of Nations was founded—that of international co-operation—has not been disproved." Indeed, "no alternative conception or method of comparable range has come to light in the intervening period."[82]

One figure who went further than any other in conceptualizing how support for the league could stand as an expression of the new ecumenical theology was Swiss international jurist Professor Max Huber. Before Oxford, Huber had already been a member of the Permanent Court of International Justice between 1922 and 1930, and its president from 1925 to 1927. At the time of the conference he held the presidency of the International Committee of the Red Cross, a position he occupied from 1928 to 1945.[83] He had published major works in the field of international law and was known for his views on the "sociological" basis of international law—a position he argued was an alternative to the major options of Natural Law and Legal Positivism.[84] Huber's contribution to the World of Nations actually came as a surprise to delegates in that section. It did not appear on the agenda of the section; instead Huber was chairman of the neighboring section, "Church and State." At some point during their deliberations, however, World of Nations delegates received a special memorandum from Huber, whose arrival one American attendee remembered as being "very helpful."[85] So helpful, in fact, that whole parts of Huber's memorandum were copied into the section's final report. The memorandum was later also included in the World of Nations section's published volume as a paper alongside the work of Dulles, Kerr, and Zimmern.[86] Among all individual papers, his best reflected the postliberal theological emphases of the conference and most directly influenced the emphases of the final section report.

Huber introduced the term "ethos"—which he used in a semitechnical sense to refer to the sociological basis of law—to the conference. This term remained associated with the conference and its reports for years and, as seen in chapter 7, was cited by American internationalists planning for postwar order. Within states, Huber argued, the rule of law was sustained by a combination of force and ethos. And "without an ethos no law can exist. . . . Continuity and dignity are given to law only by something which transcends law and external circumstances, namely, the sense of obligation which is found in the conscience of the human being who is subject to law."[87] In international life, Huber observed a lack of ethos; there was none that had sufficiently gained communal recognition so as to ground the rule of law. "The various political units into which the world is divided stand side by side without any organic connection."[88] Modern political thought had sought to compensate for the lack along two main lines. First, stretching from Grotius's work to Kant's *Perpetual Peace*, natural law thinking held the law of nature to be the "moral as well as . . . juridical basis for interstate relations." While using religious language on its surface, this was basically a secular movement, Huber asserted. Then, in the nineteenth century—alongside the development of legal positivism—there had arisen newer, more or less "utilitarian" approaches, which had "sought to base the order of state relations mainly . . . upon the economic and intellectual interdependence of the nations."[89] Both efforts at invoking a normative universalism to counter the claims of nation-states had problems, he argued. Whatever particular insights these philosophies might offer—"even when they contain elements which can be used by Christian thinkers"—they were inadequate as a Christian system as such, for their starting points were not distinctly Christian. Huber showed what Barthian theology sounded like when it met international jurisprudence.

Taking up the dialectical approach emerging at the conference, Huber argued that the New Testament held the state in dual regard: as both divinely sanctioned and potentially demonic.[90] Such a view meant Christians could neither elevate the state to ultimate status on one hand nor remove its significance entirely on the other. Given the dual character of the state, a "community of nations," rather than a world state or world federation was the best option. A world state, Huber warned—contra Kerr—while perhaps successful in stopping wars, would also result in an even greater demonic concentration of power and would not represent the dual nature of government. Huber concluded then that the League of Nations was a body whose essential idea was sound, even if it was marked by failures. It was a "torso" that might offer future growth.[91] But for a new League of Nations to work, argued Huber, it would need to be undergirded by a universalistic "ethos." Because an ethos was the product of a concrete community, Huber argued the supranational church, the ecumenical church, could function as a social base for the development of this international ethos. For unlike many political communities in the late 1930s, it was at least supranational in principle due to its permanent missionary character.

The final section report took up Huber's ideas in several passages. A portion entitled "Inherent Difficulties in the Establishment of International Order" reiterated, occasionally verbatim, Huber's analysis of the lack of "organic connection" between states.[92] "All law," agreed the report, "must be based on a common ethos—that is, a common foundation of moral convictions." Applying Huber's ideas on the role of the church in creating this ethos, the report concluded: "To the creation of such a common foundation in moral conviction the Church as a supranational society . . . has a great contribution to make."[93]

But characteristically for Christian internationalists of the interwar period, whether radical or ecumenical, the section's final report argued that institutional, legal, or political solutions, while necessary, did not alone go far enough. "The evil lies deeper down."[94] The problem of national and racial solidarities becoming idolatrous and dangerous would not be dealt with merely by the League of Nations. Rather, in order for the church to work against such forces, the report called for ecumenism itself to be promoted. "True ecumenicity must be the goal of all our efforts."[95] "Our starting point," it argued, "is the universal fellowship of Christians, the *Una Sancta*. All Christians acknowledge one Lord, whose claim upon them is to transcend all other loyalties. Here is the first obligation of the Church, to be in living fact the Church, a society with a unity so deep as to be indestructible by earthly divisions of race or nation or class."[96]

It was not that delegates naively assumed that such unity within churches was already in existence. They heard several addresses in plenary sessions describing the facts of disunity within the church. T. Z. Koo of China (who had been present for the passing of the racial equality resolutions at the Peking 1922 WSCF conference) argued in a plenary session that Western Christians discredited their faith by their persistent racial prejudice.[97] An American delegate, Samuel McCrea Cavert, earned some journalistic acclaim for making a similar point with "ironic humor" in his "perversion" (in the *New York Times* correspondent's words) of the Apostle's Creed. Cavert announced to the assembled delegates: "I believe in the Holy Catholic Church and regret that it does not exist." Delegates would have instantly recognized the first phrase as part of the creed and the second phrase as Cavert's replacement for what would normally read "the communion of saints." Cavert argued that any visitor to a church in the United States would find it difficult to see ecumenism lived out. The visitor would "not find Negro and white Christians worshipping together before God." Moreover, somewhat prophetically, given the wartime internment policies to come after Pearl Harbor, Cavert also predicted that the visitor would not "discover that American church members have such a sense of community with Japanese Christians as would stand the strain of much political tension between the United States and Japan."[98]

But all of these examples of actual disunity only served to add further fuel to the delegates' argument that ecumenical consciousness among the churches needed to be raised. Theirs was an endlessly elastic jeremiad. As the final section of the report stated, "The Church is by nature ecumenical, but few of its members have as yet come to realize the full implication of this fact."[99] Thus, when the proposal for a World Council of Churches organization was announced in a plenary session during the second week, delegates of the World of Nations section saw much room to "rejoice."[100] "The vastness of the proposal was staggering," reported one American delegate.[101] One of the key purposes of the proposed council, as stated in the proposal's aims, was to "promote the growth of ecumenical consciousness in the churches," the very thing members of the World of Nations section were calling for.[102]

True to the ecumenical world conference format, there was yet one more stage of distillation and consensus formation to come. Each section's findings had to be folded into one overall "Message," with the Church of England's Archbishop of York, William Temple, charged with writing the draft. Temple did little to alter the findings of the Church and Community section, and gave their antiracist strands full emphasis: "against racial pride or race antagonism the Church must set its face as implacably as rebellion against God."[103] Likewise nationality had been given to "enrich and diversify human life," but "national egotism is . . . no less than individual egotism, a sin against the Creator. . . . The deification of nation, race or class, or of political or cultural ideals is idolatry, and can only lead to increasing division and disaster."[104] In capturing the findings of the World of Nations section, Temple's summary stressed ecumenicity as the ground of Christian internationalism. As a community, the ecumenical church was "called to be in its own life a fellowship which binds men together and . . . overleaps all barriers of social status, nationality or race"; correspondingly it would "call the nations to order their lives as members of the one family of God."[105] In language directly borrowed from the World of Nations section report, the Message argued that the pursuit of international justice "must express itself in a demand for such mitigation of the sovereignty of national states as is involved in the abandonment by each of the claim to be judge in its own cause."[106]

Conclusion

Much of the significance of Oxford 1937 lay in the fusion of an old practice—ecumenical inquiry into international relations at world conferences—with a new controlling, theological framework. The theological consensus that emerged in preparations for the conference and that crystallized at the meeting gave shape to a distinct and enduring strand of Christian internationalism. Rather than focusing primarily on the elements of liberal internationalism, such as individual subjective rights, international law, and free trade, the Oxford delegates offered instead a theological critique of nationalism and racism as idolatry and collective "egotism." Whereas earlier Christian internationalists, particularly from Britain and America, had seen such liberal internationalist ventures as the League of Nations as near to an expression of the Kingdom of God, Oxford delegates renounced all such identification of world order schemes with the will of God. They promoted involvement with the league, but based on a dialectical no-and-yes outlook; falsely messianic hopes could repose in the league as much as they could in the nation-state.

The nature of the postliberal consensus formed at Oxford 1937—and the processes and practices that formed it—has implications for writing both American and international history. These largely arise out of the inability of conventional historiographical categories to contain and categorize such a phenomenon as the Oxford conference. Firstly, the consensus produced at Oxford was clearly no mere projection of American power or culture. Undoubtedly certain Americans influenced the formation of the consensus. The long and diffuse influence of John R. Mott through the WSCF and IMC has to be acknowledged. Out of the organizations connected with his brand of ecumenism emerged some of the general impetus and argumentation for a greater realization of supranational and transracial solidarity among Christians worldwide. More specific to Oxford, however, was the influence of the postliberal realist theologians such as Reinhold Niebuhr, Henry Pit Van Dusen, and John Bennett. Notwithstanding the input of this group of Americans, the consensus was a product equally, if not more so, of the emphases of Continental theologians and church leaders. Their suspicion of not only liberal Social Gospel activism but also Anglo-American rationalism in general greatly altered the conference's direction and language. The British also had a strong influence, and, in the final analysis, it appears to have been predominantly a mediating one. Organizers such as Oldham, Bell, and Temple deliberately sought to bring the American realist and Continental neoorthodox emphases together in a political-theological venture. Christian internationalism at Oxford bore the marks of Huber, Menn, and Oldham more than the know-how of Zimmern, Kerr, and Dulles.

More broadly, Oxford 1937 is a testament to why a strict disciplinary separation between church history and wider, secular narratives of twentieth-century international history is artificial, at best. Oxford 1937 does indeed belong in church history narratives, a fact of which church historians of the ecumenical movement have been well aware. Yet, historians of international social movements and international thought have not recognized that Oxford 1937 was not only an event in church history: It was an event in international history. It belongs just as firmly in the narratives of internationalist thought in the interwar period. It was a milestone in postliberal international thought, an important parallel and alternative to the institutionalist narrative of the same period offered by Dorothy Jones's *Toward a Just World*. As an ecumenical world conference, Oxford 1937 was a key practice and central node in an important network of cultural internationalists overlooked in works like Akira Iriye's *Cultural Internationalism and World Order*. As the gathering point for what became one of the most influential social movements of the 1940s, Oxford 1937 played a crucial role in the development of the moral norms with which a scholar such as Cecelia Lynch is rightly concerned.[107] Oxford 1937 could and should feature in such narratives. Oxford 1937 provided the normative framework for the engagement of many Protestant Christians in American and Britain in peace planning discourse and postwar reconstruction efforts, providing a platform on which neutralists and interventionists, pacifists and realists gathered in support of the establishment of the United Nations organization as the revived league they were looking for. The impact of Oxford 1937 on American wartime internationalism is the subject of the next two chapters.

Chapter 6

Oxford's Atlantic Crossing

In their planning for the Oxford 1937 conference, the American delegation commissioned Amerop Travel Services of Madison Avenue, New York City, to create transport packages for attendees. True to their charge, the agency offered their clients a range of possibilities for what to do after the conference. Initially, all delegates travelled together by rail back to London. Special sightseeing tours followed the next day, and a reception at Lambeth Palace the day after. Day three in London brought what many had considered would be the real climax of the Oxford conference: the final service at St. Paul's Cathedral. Henry Smith Leiper urged his fellow American delegates not to miss the promised "distinguished ecclesiastical procession." He declared, "The pageantry of this world gathering will be a treasured memory for many years to come."[1] Not only would it be an extension of the *communitas* experienced at the conference, it would offer a touch of the exotic for men of plainer Protestant American stock. Chicago's Edwin Ewart Aubrey was not disappointed: It was, he said, an "impressive public service," with a visit from the Lord Mayor of London. After being exhorted to "go forth" by the archbishop of Canterbury, Aubrey recalled the shared experience of delegates going out "into the London throngs, members of a deeper and wider fellowship than the Church had ever known before."[2]

Upon leaving London, delegates chose from a variety of tour packages. The main group took a series of small tours in the countryside—including a trip by launch on the Upper Thames—before returning on the ship that had taken them to England from New York weeks earlier. The French SS *Champlain* was chosen as the "flagship" for the party because of its "very desirable accommodations and facilities." A whole block of accommodation across the three cabin classes had been booked, so that, as during the earlier days of the Eddy Seminar, delegates could remain together as a party for the weeklong crossing of the Atlantic. Other delegates meanwhile enjoyed the summer weather motoring through the English Lakes district before attending the "World Conference on Faith and Order" meeting in Edinburgh beginning on August 3. Still others took options for further travel on the Continent. The most expensive and extensive tour ranged through Belgium, Germany, Switzerland, Italy, and France before allowing travelers to take the SS *Champlain* direct from Paris to New York.[3]

At various times between the end of July and early September 1937, as summer began to turn to fall, the American delegates to Oxford arrived by ship back in New York Harbor. They had taken much of their own thinking and their own distinctiveness to the Oxford conference. But now that delegates had crossed the Atlantic westward, what would they bring back? In what ways did they carry Oxford 1937 home to America? Since Daniel Rodgers's field-shaping work on the transfer of social policies and practices from Europe to America in the early twentieth century, the notion of "Atlantic crossings" has become in historical scholarship both a metonym and a metaphor for claims about larger historical forces and patterns.[4] Following Oxford 1937 delegates as they returned to the United States, literally crossing the Atlantic in a French luxury liner, allows us to ask about the larger ways in which they were or were not part of an Atlantic crossing, part of a diffusion of transnational currents. Conference attendees explicitly aimed to transport their findings home. The Life and Work movement in America aimed at nothing less than bringing the spirit and message of the Oxford and Edinburgh conferences "home to every community and parish in the nation."[5] But such a bold statement of purpose naturally begs the question of whether that would be possible: not simply whether such a move could be achieved logistically, but whether such a crossing was in fact achievable culturally and intellectually. Could the Oxford consensus take root and flourish in American soil?

This chapter and the one following together argue that Oxford had a profound influence on American mainline Protestantism in the late 1930s and early 1940s. At the very moment when American nationalist isolationism was reaching a crest in the late 1930s, American ecumenists used the message of Oxford 1937 to point Protestants in the direction of internationalism. It turned out to be vital that the Oxford conference had recognized a variety of views on war and had refrained from identifying any one view as legitimate. Between 1939 and 1941, when opinion in America polarized in the "great debate" over whether the United States ought to support the allies against Germany, Oxford 1937's critiques of nationalism and racism, its emphasis on practicing supranational and supraracial solidarity within churches, and its carefully framed support of international organization provided a discursive framework in which neutralists and interventionists, pacifists and realists could and did work together. Oxford 1937 predated the turn to the bipartisan internationalist consensus that emerged in American politics after Pearl Harbor. But precisely because of this timing, ecumenists were well positioned to take the lead in shaping American public opinion in the process of its reversal. The craze for peace planning discourse in early 1940s America, which saw ecumenical theologians and leaders like Dulles debate plans for postwar international order and American engagement in it, brought ecumenists into the center of American public debate with remarkable force. Many who had once been part of the rag-tag oppositional campaigns of *The World Tomorrow* now found themselves bastions of the establishment, courted by the state as it sought to mobilize opinion-shaping groups such as churches. Nor did they abandon all the political imperatives of earlier years; Oxford 1937's emphasis on opposing nationalism and racism in many ways extended and complemented earlier positions. But in its Atlantic crossing, Oxford 1937's Christian internationalism ultimately became fused with the new American internationalism, with the former often subsumed by the latter.

This chapter and the next provide complementary views of how the Oxford consensus both influenced American internationalism and was altered by it. Because of the scale of John Foster Dulles's work in this regard, chapter 7 is devoted entirely to his Commission on a Just and Durable Peace—the most influential internationalist Protestant publicity organization in 1940s America. The present chapter considers many of the other American ecumenists' efforts to disseminate Oxford 1937 to American churches and the wider public. Most particularly, it focuses on the way realist theologians around Reinhold Niebuhr—arguably the most intellectually influential of ecumenists at the time—both perpetuated the ecumenical project and changed it, with Niebuhr promoting what was essentially an Oxford 1937 political theology shorn of its ecclesiology.

Widening the Circle of Participation

Attempts to publicize the conference began before it ended. Walter Van Kirk, an American Lutheran theologian and prominent campaigner in the domestic peace and disarmament campaigns of the 1930s, took up a radio microphone on the fourth day of the conference. Not a fringe religious broadcaster, but the NBC network, broadcast Van Kirk's voice across the Atlantic.[6] "Hello America! Hello America!" Van Kirk called out. "I've been to all sorts of conventions and conferences but this one tops them all," he said. "There's drama here— the drama of a Church stacking itself against a world of war and preparations for war, economic injustice, racial persecution, and national bigotry." Reporting on some of the sights he had seen at Oxford and the sense of challenge he felt at the conference, Van Kirk mused that he "env[ied] the church historian of the future when he picks up his pen to tell the story of the Conference."[7] Van Kirk's broadcast on a mainstream national network dovetailed with the coverage of major newspapers such as the *New York Times*. Special correspondent Charles W. Hurd used wireless technology to file almost daily reports with the *Times* with headlines like "Fellowship Urged to Reclaim Church: Oxford Conference Hears Pleas for Vigorous Christian Band to Offset Nationalism."[8]

The publicity process continued once American delegates went home and wrote up their reflections in the smaller periodical press. Edwin Ewart Aubrey wrote a full and detailed—almost ethnographic—report of the conference for the major mainline scholarly journal, the *Journal of Religion*, conveying his surprise at the unity he experienced at Oxford and his sense of the achievements and limitations of the conference.[9] Reinhold Niebuhr wrote in his magazine, *Radical Religion*, that despite the fact that "one does not expect too much of an ecumenical conference, the Oxford reports achieved a remarkably high level of genuine Christian testimony."[10] Benjamin Mays, the African American clergyman and intellectual and president of Morehouse College, Atlanta, took space in the NAACP's *Crisis* magazine to offer his account of the experience, reporting that members felt themselves to be a part of a "universal church that transcends all national, racial or class barriers."[11]

The most intentional publicity efforts following Oxford came from the organization nucleus based in New York composed of the American branch of the Life and Work movement (which had convened Oxford), the American branch of the Faith and Order movement (which soon merged with Life and Work), and the U.S. Federal Council of Churches. This shared bureaucracy effectively became the headquarters of ecumenism in the United States. As will be seen in the next chapter, their publicity efforts crested with the work of the Dulles Commission. But across the board—Dulles included—their publicity efforts showed them positioning themselves as "mainline," as representatives of an authoritative international consensus that American localities needed to learn from. The assertion of mainline status involved both an argument—namely that they spoke for and to the center—and various attempts to socially embody that argument.[12] For ecumenists this implied a whole different conception of relating to the public than had characterized Page and *The World Tomorrow*'s counterpublicity efforts. Whereas the latter had marshaled forces outside of the mainstream in order to intervene in oppositional terms, ecumenists in the late 1930s and 1940s positioned themselves—with increasing success—in the role of mediation, dissemination, and education: the center radiating out.

Ecumenical headquarters immediately faced, of course, the difficulty of transferring something almost impossible to transfer: the conference sensibility and experience itself. Searching for other ways to pass on the Oxford experience, they published a swathe of pamphlets and publications such as *Highlights of Oxford* and the *Oxford Conference Study Series*. The latter contained texts and reports from the conference together with study questions and inside background material on the deliberations. At least group deliberations could go on in church halls and youth fellowships with the aid of a discussion guide. In the "World of Nations" study material, the authors offered discussants a detailed breakdown of that section's report and several questions. For instance, "Study One" asked:

> How far are we justified in speaking of the Church as supra-national? Have not the Protestant and Eastern Orthodox Churches in the past been conspicuously national rather than supra-national? If supra-nationalism is the true ideal for the Church, what modifications of our present practices and viewpoints are necessary?[13]

"Study Two" posed the questions:

> What can the Church do to induce States to modify their claims to absolute sovereignty? Is there any likelihood that the States will pay any attention to the Church's opinion in this matter?[14]

Bringing chapter and verse from the Oxford report to bear on that moral bugaboo of interwar Christian internationalism in America, the famed toast of Decatur and the slogan of the Chicago *Tribune*, the study guide also asked participants to consider whether the "point of view expressed in the words 'my country right or wrong'" differed from the positions elaborated at Oxford.[15]

Other kindred organizations made use of the publications of the Life and Work movement. The Race Relations department of the Federal Council of

Churches took up and repackaged the reports of the Oxford conference that had clear relevance to their own purposes. One of their pamphlets, entitled *The Church and Race: What Was Said at the World Conference on Church, Community and State*, rolled out extracts from the conference documents. From the "Message" it quoted: "Against racial pride or race antagonism the Church must set its face implacably as rebellion against God." The publication also included more extensive passages from the report on Community at the conference, such as the section's conclusion that "there can be no place for exclusion or segregation because of race or color."[16] The pamphlet, to position itself as mainline, stressed the large and representative nature of Oxford. "The report of the World Conference at Oxford," it claimed, "may be said to represent the mind of the Church across the world today. It was the most accurate—indeed the only—portrayal of the prevailing Christian conscience." Statistics were deployed on the front cover—well before readers were introduced to the challenge to segregation within: "110 separate Communions were represented; 325,000,000 Christians are enrolled in these Communions; 43 different Nations were represented; Every racial group was represented. Every continent was represented."[17] With such a weighty aggregation of numbers, it implied the question: How could Americans refuse to align with Christian world opinion?

In parallel with the pamphleteering and circulation of study guides, the Federal Council of Churches sponsored a speaking tour in February 1938, in which 165 Oxford and Edinburgh attendees together delivered 1,725 addresses before audiences that included 189 denominational bodies—a vast attempt at rendering the ecumenical consensus mainline.[18] But spreading the message was not all top-down. A new innovation that blended study group techniques with local participation also emerged: this was holding smaller, follow-up "replica" conferences. In these gatherings, ecumenists came closer to transmitting the conference sensibility that they had hoped to bring home. Doubtless, the process of digesting reports already produced at Oxford was a different experience from forging that same consensus via international translators in the halls of Oxford the previous year. Still, considerable local initiative and enthusiasm appears to have cropped up. Although there was some oversight from ecumenical headquarters in New York, it was the networks of local churches and state convocations of pastors that worked out their own approach to replica conferences. The town of Evanston, Illinois, which would, incidentally, later host the second assembly of the World Council of Churches in 1954, stood out for its efforts. The city of 65,000 people held its own mini-Oxford conference with 400 delegates in late November 1937. Organizers appointed delegates to the Evanston conference proportionally, one for every fifty church members, across a range of denominations. Just as at Oxford and Edinburgh, they split those in attendance into sections dealing with the topics covered at the world conferences. Edinburgh topics such as "The Grace of God and the Word of God" appeared in the program alongside Oxford topics such as "The Church and the World of Nations." Several speakers who had attended the actual Oxford and Edinburgh conferences addressed the Evanston group. The Evanston Ministerial Association felt the conference "surpassed our brightest hopes." They were particularly impressed by the "keen interest" in the reports of the Oxford and Edinburgh conferences. "We staged an experiment in unity and were rewarded by an experience of unity," they reported back to New York.[19] The practice of conferencing itself had become a way of participating in ecumenical unity.

Various kinds of follow-up meetings occurred all over the United States, each of which offered participants a small way of sharing the experience as well as the ideas of Oxford's deliberations. The churches of Oakland, California, held public meetings of several hundred people and weekly study seminars of 160, where participants examined the reports of the Oxford and Edinburgh conferences, week by week and topic by topic. The conference format was also molded into the weekly church fellowship group meeting. In New Britain, Connecticut, around 140 people met every week to share tea, social fellowship, worship, an analysis of an Oxford report, and an hour of discussion to conclude. When the city of Raleigh, North Carolina, hosted the State Pastors' Convocation of 1937, special seminars, public addresses, and radio broadcasts featured discussions of the Oxford and Edinburgh conferences. Groups from the Pacific Northwest as well as Wisconsin, Illinois, and the East Coast met in various ways to form discussion groups, permanent study circles, seminars, and replica conferences in the late months of 1937. Back in New York, the Joint Executive Committee expressed pleasure with such state-based action. Devolving to state organizations and local churches represented a "strategic element" in the follow-up to Oxford and Edinburgh. Groups were large enough to attract national speakers and were small enough to remain in touch with their state-based constituency. They brought clergy and laypeople into contact with the findings of the Oxford conference in a recapitulation of the conference experience itself.[20]

Realists as Ecumenists

One of the most obvious and lasting ways Oxford 1937 influenced American Christian internationalism was through the intellectual leadership of the cadre of realist theologians who were delegates. Evidenced through their presence at New York's Union Theological Seminary and in the pages of *Christianity and Crisis*, a journal of opinion convened in 1941, the salience of ecumenism to realists was clear.

In 1937, Charles Clayton Morrison, still editor of the respected American liberal Protestant magazine, *Christian Century*, opined that there was an over-representation of Union Seminary figures among the delegates to the conferences at Oxford and Edinburgh. Where, he asked, were the places for midwestern liberals? Henry Pit Van Dusen of Union Seminary replied to the magazine, arguing that the arrangements merely reflected the choice of the Europeans. Reinhold Niebuhr's invitation to be a plenary speaker, for instance, was due to the fact that he had generated more interest among the Europeans and the British than any other American.[21] But Morrison's complaint did have some merit. At Oxford 1937, Union, proportionally, was easily the most-represented American seminary. Given that around seven hundred delegates had to represent non-Roman Christianity around the world, the number of Union figures with influential roles in the plenary discussions and study sections was considerable. One of the six presidents of the whole conference, who were drawn internationally from Britain, the United States, India, France, Sweden, and the Eastern Orthodox communion (and all of whom received honorary DDs from Oxford for their work) was the aged Union scholar William Adams Brown. The president of Union, Henry Sloane Coffin, chaired Oxford's section on the Church and Education. Then there were the younger, realist theologians at Union. The international exchange of research papers had been filtered through the hands of Van Dusen, then professor of systematic theology and later president of the seminary. Reinhold Niebuhr and Paul Tillich (then a recent émigré from Germany who was professor at Union) were both delegates to Oxford, as was John C. Bennett, who took up a tenured position at Union in 1944. Not only did each of these Union faculty members attend the conference; most received places in the published volumes of reports and, in the case of Niebuhr and Van Dusen, speaking roles in plenary sessions.

Morrison was right in sensing that such an arrangement was no accident. As seen in the previous chapter, the principle organizer, J. H. Oldham, had deliberately targeted this Union-based network, attending the private and invitation-only gatherings of the Theological Discussion Group. Oldham was investing, to use another Manhattan metaphor, in rising stock. He enlisted the Union Seminary network just on the cusp of its rise to national prominence and, indeed, assisted it in that very rise. With its links to ecumenism, and particularly to the World Council of Churches, Union Theological Seminary in the 1940s–1950s achieved a place in public life that is difficult to imagine today. It became, alongside Yale Divinity School, the preeminent center for mainline Protestant theological education and research. Its faculty—particularly Niebuhr and Tillich—became public intellectuals, and Union itself grew in establishment status. The number of *Time* magazine profiles of Union faculty in the postwar years was remarkable for any institution of higher learning— let alone a theological seminary.[22] Niebuhr's rejection of an offer to work at Harvard University to remain at the seminary should be seen against this backdrop.[23] By inviting such a disproportionate number of individuals associated with Union, Oldham succeeded in enfolding an upcoming generation of theological thinkers into the ecumenical movement he sought to shape. President Henry Sloane Coffin, reflecting on his fifty years at the institution, observed the aftereffects of Union's representation at Oxford 1937. "Once enlisted in these ecumenical movements," Coffin said, "[Niebuhr, Coffin, Brown, and Bennett] could not demit responsibility."[24] Indeed, so complete was their absorption that, organizationally speaking, Mark Edwards is right to insist that these Christian realist theologians were really only "part-time liberal Cold Warriors but full-time pioneers of global Protestant ecumenism."[25]

A clear demonstration of Union's close relationship with the ecumenism of Oxford and the World Council was the way in which ecumenism crept into its curriculum. Henry Pit Van Dusen—even before he became president— began teaching a course in the field of systematic theology entitled Ecumenical Christianity. He offered it in the special springtime Accelerated Program of the 1944–1945 academic year, co-teaching with Henry Smith Leiper, the stalwart organizer and publicist of the Oxford conference and by then the American secretary for the World Council of Churches.[26] Leiper's long experience with the ecumenical movement—in the WSCF for over a decade and at the Life and Work meeting at Fanö 1934—would have helped bring students into contact with its inner workings. The next year, according to Union's course catalog, Van Dusen taught the course alone in a normal full-length semester. The catalog gave the following description of its subject:

An examination of the development and present status of the Ecumenical Movement both its life and thought. The origins of the movement in the nineteenth century. The sequence of Ecumenical Conferences—Edinburgh (1910), Stockholm, Lausanne, Jerusalem, Oxford, Edinburgh (1937), Madras, Amsterdam—their findings and influence. Ecumenicity at the community, national and world levels. The relation of the Christian World Missions and the Movement of Christian Unity. The possibilities of an ecumenical theology.[27]

The same year, John Bennett, an Oxford delegate and a recent, but long-awaited recruit to Union's Christian Ethics Department, taught a course entitled The Church and the World. It dealt with "aspects of the doctrine of the church which are most important for the relationship between the church and secular society," and "the social function of the church in transforming the social order." Bennett promised students "the results of recent ecumenical discussions will be examined."[28] Indeed, part of the expectation Reinhold Niebuhr had for Bennett's appointment was that he would teach Christian ethics by drawing on his experience and knowledge of ecumenical thought. To that end, Niebuhr co-taught a seminar on ethics with Bennett. Niebuhr would cover the church doctrines on ethics but Bennett, Niebuhr instructed him by mail, was to teach "what is actually done and what can be done on the issues of family, race, nation etc. . . . drawing particularly upon your experience in ecumenical Christianity."[29]

It was illustrative of the growing nexus of interests at Union that on Wednesday afternoons in the 1945–1946 academic year, Henry Pit Van Dusen taught his course on Christian ecumenism while one floor beneath him in Room 205 that same evening, Reinhold Niebuhr taught his special one-off course, Christian Ethics 242, Problems in Postwar Reconstruction. Union was in the mid-1940s becoming the center for an ecumenical-internationalist interpretation of international affairs. The first course purely on international relations at Union Seminary appears to have been the subject offered in the summer school semester of 1944 called Christian Ethics and International Politics (Christian Ethics, S254), taught by Hans Simons, professor of international relations at the New School for Social Research.[30] Outside of such specialized, sporadic units, however, students addressed international relations from an ecumenical point of view mainly in Bennett and Niebuhr's co-taught seminar, The Application of Christian Ethical Principles (Christian Ethics 231–232). This course considered—among other things—race relations, war, and international order and, importantly, placed them in the light of the "distinctive contribution of the church both ecumenically and locally."[31]

When not in the classroom, Union's realist theologians ran, from Union offices, another enterprise that made clear the nexus between ecumenism and their new Christian realist approach to international relations: the weekly *Christianity and Crisis*. Writing and editing journals of Christian opinion was, of course, nothing new for them. Niebuhr's original appointment at Union, financed by Sherwood Eddy, was tied to part-time work for *The World Tomorrow*. In the meantime, Niebuhr had edited *Radical Religion*, later renamed *Christianity and Society*, which earned him a following in Britain. One British reviewer in the *Expository Times* connected Niebuhr's *Radical Religion* to Oxford 1937, arguing that together they represented a new kind of "social gospel,"—one "that enters into the heart of the political conflict"—in contrast to the individualistic and apolitical stance of the popular "Moral Rearmament" movement.[32] All the while Niebuhr (and most of those around him) continued to write and editorialize for *Christian Century*, as well as for secular magazines such as the *Nation* and the *New Republic*. Yet, as Mark Hulsether documented in his work on *Christianity and Crisis*, the time came when Niebuhr grew too frustrated with *Christian Century*'s pacifist-isolationist position on the conflict in Europe to continue his relationship with the journal.[33] Niebuhr exclaimed to John Bennett in 1940, "I don't know whether it is my nervous condition but the *Christian Century* has gotten on my nerves to such a degree that I had to blow it off."[34]

Niebuhr and his collaborators positioned *Christianity and Crisis* in clear opposition to the *Christian Century* on what constituted a Christian analysis of America's role in the international conflict. For Niebuhr and his collaborators, pacifist isolationism—a position to which *The World Tomorrow* had contributed—had too exclusive a hold on the public mind as *the* Christian approach. The new eight-page, fortnightly "journal of Christian opinion," would help loosen the grip of this view, making clear that, contrary to *Christian Century*, a third way could be found between "holy war fanaticism" and absolutist pacifism, or "inaction," as they saw it. In the first edition, dated February 10, 1941, Niebuhr introduced the journal: "It is our purpose to devote this modest journal to an exposition of our Christian faith in its relation to world events."[35] The journal became the premiere site in which postliberal ecumenical theology was connected concretely to the causes of American internationalism and interventionism. The first issue of the magazine called for immediate backing for the passage of Lend-Lease legislation.[36] Nothing was more important than making sure the United States never again "refuses to assume some measure of responsibility for world order," another editorial urged.[37] One more editorial, bearing the marks of Niebuhr, employed dialectical reasoning in the style of Oxford 1937 to caution against "Holy War" ideology in which "unqualified sanctity is claimed for one cause against another."[38]

While historians have long recognized *Christianity and Crisis* as a significant exponent of the American interventionist viewpoint, they have not, on the whole, recognized its role in maintaining a connection with ecumenism post-Oxford 1937. As well as being a journal devoted to promoting internationalist politics, the journal maintained and developed its relationship with ecumenism across the Atlantic and in America. Its original six-person editorial board, chaired by Niebuhr, consisted of influential Oxford attendees John A. Mackay (the president of Princeton Theological Seminary who had chaired the World of Nations section) and Henry Pit Van Dusen as well as longtime World Student Christian Federation ecumenist Francis P. Miller. The next year the board added John Bennett and two key organizers of Oxford 1937—the Federal Council of Churches' F. Ernest Johnson and Henry Smith Leiper—to its number, linking *Christianity and Crisis* even more closely with the World Council of Churches on one hand and the ecumenical establishment in the United States on the other.

Indeed, as well as offering opinion on international politics, the journal also saw its function as providing news of Christian churches and missions around the world. This was a key informational practice called for in the World of Nations section at Oxford 1937 in the hope of raising "ecumenical consciousness."[39] The first issue, for example, contained reports that in Slovakia, sixty priests and ministers had been imprisoned by the pro-Hitler Tiso government, and that missionaries caught up in parts of Japanese-controlled China were being sent to "Free China" with the help of a new advisory committee. A special note examined the efforts of the provisional chairman of the World Council of Churches, William Temple, the archbishop of York, "universally recognized as a chief spokesman of ecumenical Christianity." Temple and a team of other ecumenists and former Oxford delegates, such as William Paton, George Bell, and Alfred Zimmern, had been working intensively throughout January in the lead-up to the Church of England's "Malvern Conference," where several major figures in British life, such as T. S. Eliot (also at Oxford 1937), Dorothy Sayers, and John Middleton Murry had participated in deliberations on what the war revealed about the "general condition of Western civilization." *Christianity and Crisis* saw the gathering as "momentous" in significance, and the editors promised to continue reportage of similar groups' work in the future.[40] Indeed, in future years these editorials were expanded and consolidated into a regular section called "The World Church: News and Notes," where speeches or correspondence from overseas were also printed alongside regular news. One of the tasks the journal took on, then, was to integrate American readers into the wider community—real and imagined—of ecumenical Christianity. Positioning itself as a conduit of "world" Christianity only furthered *Christianity and Crisis*'s move to the mainline establishment.

At both Union Seminary and *Christianity and Crisis*, the new Christian realism associated with Reinhold Niebuhr and colleagues grew out of, and maintained, ongoing connections with ecumenical Christianity post-Oxford 1937. The growing influence of this group of intellectuals and their articulation of Christian internationalism formed a vital part of Oxford 1937's Atlantic crossing. Yet what did their "realism" amount to in relation to the wider project of ecumenical internationalism? Did the controlling, methodological commitments at Oxford 1937 maintain an influence on the realists' thinking into the 1940s? A look at Niebuhr in particular—undoubtedly the most influential of the realist theologians, the one who became the most preeminent public intellectual—offers a way of answering this question.

Niebuhr and the Oxford Legacy

One key aspect of Oxford 1937's significance is that it spurred the emergence of a trend in which British and American ecumenists began to interpret international relations in a new disciplinary register. Decidedly nonscientific, the register offered instead a humanistic (in a disciplinary, not ideological, sense) reading of the "tragedies" and "ironies" of the large-scale histories of civilizational crisis. It was a distinctly historico-theological reading of international life, one that emphasized paradox and dialectical argument—one that sought to relate the theological themes of God's transcendence and humankind's finitude and sinfulness to the precariousness of the contemporary historical situation. It was a far cry from the later, scientific grants-based university study of international relations in the 1960s.[41] As such, Oxford 1937 needs to be seen as a factor in the rise of what international relations scholar Roger Epp termed the "Augustinian" moment in international thought in the 1940s. Just as St. Augustine had done in his *City of God* in explaining an earlier civilizational collapse, 1940s Christian intellectuals such as Niebuhr, in the face of their own imminent civilizational catastrophes, attended afresh to the doctrines of sin and to the dialectical relationship between the "City of God" and the "City of Man."[42] Not only Niebuhr but also other seminal and founding figures in the "English School" of international relations, such as Martin Wight and Herbert Butterfield, owed their historico-theological outlook in part to the ecumenical movement. One of Martin Wight's most penetrating and most theological treatments of the Cold War, for example, appeared not in an international relations journal such as *International Affairs*, but in *Ecumenical Review*, the periodical of the new World Council of Churches, established in the aftermath of Oxford.[43]

Niebuhr's work in particular demonstrated the ongoing influence of the dialectical framework developed at Oxford. Although there were signs of a theological turn already in his earlier book, *An Interpretation of Christian Ethics*

(1936), written with the influence of his brother H. Richard and colleague Paul Tillich in the background, Niebuhr's works became more firmly set within formal theological discourse from 1939 and into the 1940s.[44] In the process, his critique of nationalism, long a theme in his writing, also became more theological in structure and tone, echoing more closely the language used at Oxford 1937. In his most widely celebrated theological work, the two-volume *Nature and Destiny of Man* (1941–1942), nationalism appeared firstly as collective egoism, a position that essentially extended his early 1930s argument in *Moral Man and Immoral Society*. However, Niebuhr added to this older layer of argument a new layer of more explicitly theological language with clear parallels to the Oxford reports. For example, the Oxford "Message" had argued "national egotism" was "a sin against the Creator of all peoples and races," and that the "deification of nation, race or class, or of political or cultural ideals" was "idolatry, and can only lead to increasing division and disaster."[45] Niebuhr's *Nature and Destiny* identified a "temptation to idolatry implicit in the state's majesty."[46] Dangerous forms of "self-deification" occurred when a social group made "pretensions of itself as the source and end of existence."[47] These could have been lines and phrases straight out of the Oxford 1937 reports. While it may be tempting to see the ecumenical movement as merely echoing Niebuhr's arguments, close reading of the sources lends that interpretation very little plausibility. It is far better to understand the influence as mutual and two-way. Niebuhr absorbed the ecumenical critique of nationalism even as he helped, along with others, to shape its character.

While Oxford's critique of nationalism had primarily been shaped with Nazi Germany in view, one of Niebuhr's significant contributions was to apply the dialectical structure of its thinking to American messianism in foreign policy. Even in early Cold War writings, as he was calling for "responsible" use of American power abroad against Communism, he frequently qualified his seemingly war-ready outlook with a call for churches to work against the Christian nationalism that routinely flourished in the shadow of war. In *Christianity and Crisis* in 1948, he challenged Americans' tendencies to treat democracy as a "religion." Americans extolled democracy's virtues and were "apprehensive about the perils to which it is exposed, pour maledictions upon its foes, rededicate themselves to its purposes and claim unconditioned validity for its ideals."[48] Niebuhr, to be sure, urged in his wartime work *Children of Light, Children of Darkness*, that democracy probably constituted the best available option for organizing a government. His famous aphorism in that work had suggested: "Man's capacity for justice makes democracy possible. Man's tendency to injustice makes democracy necessary."[49] But, in "worshipping" democracy, he warned, Americans became tempted to "identify the final meaning of life with a virtue which we possess, and thus to give a false and idolatrous religious note to the conflict between democracy and communism."[50] Later, when Republican supporters of General Douglas MacArthur wanted American military force taken into China, Niebuhr saw a strategic miscalculation premised on a moral and theological mistake: namely, on an "idolatrous conception of the perfection of American democracy, and its appeal to other peoples."[51]

Niebuhr's approach to questions of international order and world organization in the 1940s, although he did not acknowledge it, also elaborated elements of the World of Nations section report at Oxford 1937. Niebuhr spent much of the 1940s lamenting the legalist character of peace planning discourse and the failure of many—both Christian and non-Christian internationalists—to pay attention to "organic" factors when they designed blueprints and constitutions for world order. In the prestigious *Foreign Affairs* magazine, he wrote about the "illusion of world government." Niebuhr rejected entirely the rationalist account of government as being created by fiat—by some act of social contract. And he went on to challenge the efficacy of any potential world government to create a world community. "Governments cannot create communities for the simple reason that the authority of government is not primarily the authority of law nor the authority of force, but the authority of community itself. Laws are obeyed because the community accepts them as corresponding, on the whole, to its conception of justice."[52] Such arguments recapitulated the Church and Community section's rejection of rationalism in its account of government, and sounded uncannily close to Max Huber's influential contribution to the World of Nations section. Applying his long-held views on the sociology of law, Huber had argued, "continuity and dignity are given to law only by . . . the sense of obligation which is found in the conscience of the human being who is subject to law."[53] International law and organization had little chance of being effective while nations "stand side by side without any organic connection."[54] Niebuhr's critiques of rationalism and legalism were of the same cloth as the European contributions at Oxford 1937—closer perhaps than he knew. But in either case, many of the distinctive emphases of his 1940s realism should be seen as continuous with the political-theological consensus formed before the war at Oxford 1937, and not merely as unique to him.

An important element of discontinuity, however, existed between Niebuhr's thought and the Oxford 1937 consensus. As seen in the previous chapter, the dialectical reading of nationalism was only one of the two controlling methodological commitments at Oxford. The other was the priority of ecclesiology. The Oxford reports and proceedings were permeated with the argument that the doctrine of the Universal Church was to form the starting point for political reflection. In Niebuhr's case, this element went missing in the Atlantic crossing. Although it is difficult to prove the absence of an idea, the marginal place of ecclesiology in Niebuhr's writings can be appreciated when seen in contrast with those around him. Henry Pit Van Dusen, or "Pit," as Niebuhr referred to him, wrote a special piece relating ecumenism to international order as part of a compilation put together by the Commission on a Just and Durable Peace (examined in the next chapter). His abstract stated his position tightly: "the Church is itself, a body which overriding all man-made barriers, unites in fellowship and understanding those of every nation and class. The supra-national (ecumenical) quality of The Church is more than a theory: it is a fact. It provides a unique foundation and experience upon which to build a better world order."[55] Van Dusen was cautious not to overstate the case in the actual article. The church was not a political instrumentality, and ecumenical Christianity was still frail. But the presence of this type of argument in 1942 demonstrated its currency for others in Oxford's Atlantic crossing.

Niebuhr seldom appeared to reason in such terms. He shared the basic commitment of the Oxford consensus as to the necessity of some political expression of world community, but his arguments rarely, if ever, started with the nature of the Universal Church. World community was, instead, for Niebuhr, a demand of the present historical situation. In his *Nature and Destiny of Man,* what he saw as the slow evolution toward the realization of world community appeared as one more illustration of the way the historical process contained within itself both the promise of justice and the frustration of that promise. It provided an object lesson in the way that the ethical "ideal" was always both transcendent and immanent to history.[56] Writing in *Christianity and Crisis,* Niebuhr argued that a Christian "hears the divine command in every new historical situation." The imperative arising from the historical situation in 1942 was clear: "The Christian ought to know that the creation of some form of world community, compatible with the necessities of a technical age, is the most compelling demand of our day."[57]

The absence of ecclesiology in Niebuhr's thought became apparent in the divergent interpretations he and theologian Karl Barth gave of the Cold War. When Niebuhr and Barth both appeared at the Amsterdam world conference of 1948, a successor of Oxford 1937 and the inaugural meeting of the World Council of Churches, the issue uppermost in discussions was what could ecumenical Christianity say about the growing divide between the so-called Christian West and the Communist East. Delegates asked what churches in East Germany and Hungary should do in relation to Communism. Did Communism represent the same totalitarian threat as had been represented by Nazism? Niebuhr, writing in the Henry Luce magazines *Time* and *Life* had answered "yes" to that question since late 1946. But Barth and others on the Continent, such as Joseph Hromadka and Martin Niemöller, answered no: This was a different situation and called for a different response. According to Barth, Americans such as Niebuhr came to the Amsterdam meeting not with the Gospel but with a kind of "Christian Marshall Plan."[58] Barth, according to Niebuhr, insisted so much on the transcendence of God that he made theology irrelevant to actual political engagement. But aside from their differing assessments of Communism, the key difference between Niebuhr and Barth's approach lay in the place each gave to the Universal Church. In Barth's political writings of the period, the church remained as the controlling framework: He wrote about the church to the church. In the wake of Amsterdam 1948, Barth pointed out to critics that "the church is *not* identical with the West" and that the "Western conscience and judgment is not necessarily the Christian judgment."[59] If churches today did as the Western pundits and politicians asked of them, and offered a clear word against Communism, he argued, all they would be doing would be engaging in superficial and useless sanctification of the Western cause, which would continue on its own way with or without the church in any case. "It could only be a matter of merely dabbling in politics and expressing badly certain completely unclarified and imperfectly grounded *Western feelings*. The Christian-political confession today must consist precisely in the *renunciation* of such partisanship" (emphasis in original).[60] Interpreting texts such as these to his Union Seminary students in New York, Niebuhr warned that Barth's insistence on the transcendence of the church over all political systems resulted in a "blurring of distinctions between good and evil in the political order."[61]

Niebuhr's Cold War writings, in contrast to Barth's, hardly featured the church as a framework at all. Instead, other historical and political frameworks filled the absence. In pieces such as his 1943 article in *Christianity and Crisis*, Niebuhr addressed the "Anglo-Saxon" international community of Britain and America, who needed to recognize their historical destiny and take responsibility for laying the basis for postwar world order.[62] In other writings, rather than the worldwide "Christian Community" that Barth had focused upon, Niebuhr essayed upon the "moral and spiritual content of the North Atlantic Community." Such was the title of a specially commissioned essay he wrote for the American Council on NATO in 1954—one which sounded remarkably close to the line being pushed through U.S. Information Agency Channels in Western Europe at the time.[63] But more important and more typical than these extreme examples was the implicit subjectivity of readers in his mainstream works. The identity of the communal "we" in Niebuhr's work wavered ambiguously between church and nation—with the latter arguably receiving the final emphasis. His landmark study of the Cold War, *The Irony of American History* (dusted off and reprinted with endorsements from then Senator Barack Obama in 2007), was a prime example. Here Niebuhr employed Oxford 1937's dialectical and postliberal critique of all progressive modern views of history. He called for "a religious sense of an ultimate judgment upon our individual and collective actions" in order to "create an awareness of our own pretensions of wisdom, virtue or power."[64] But, essentially, while Niebuhr retained Oxford 1937's dialectical critique of idolatry, he applied it not to an ecclesiological but to a national framework. Unlike Barth, the "we" was not the community of the Church Universal but the community of foreign-policy-making Americans.

Undoubtedly Niebuhr was one of the most politically and intellectually influential figures in the transfer of Oxford 1937 ecumenism into American wartime internationalism. The contours of his thought reveal just how vulnerable the ecclesiological emphasis of Oxford 1937 was to what Richard John Neuhaus argued was America's baseline "ecclesiological deficit."[65] The problem may have been more acute in Reinhold Niebuhr's work. As Mark Edwards notes, Francis Pickens Miller had identified Niebuhr as someone who had "no theory of the Church," as early as his *Moral Man and Immoral Society*.[66] But, as will be seen in the next chapter, Niebuhr's Oxford-without-church approach was typical of a wider pattern and was shared by others, including John Foster Dulles.

Conclusion

Stepping back from focusing on Niebuhr and his churchless realism, though, the wider impact of Oxford 1937 on American ecumenists in the 1940s lay in its provision of a framework in which realists and pacifists cooperated and articulated a shared Christian internationalism. Following the proliferation of little replica conferences around the United States in 1937–1938, the Federal Council of Churches convened several important larger-scale national conferences of churches that signaled the importance of Oxford 1937's legacy. In 1940, they called for the first of what became an important series of "National Study Conferences" on war, peace, and international relations. On one hand, with ongoing links to the provisional World Council of Churches in Geneva, the move was an attempt to keep internationally connected ecumenical discussion going even in the face of war in Europe. On the other, the National Conference provided an important forum in which to bring together those who were in danger of splitting even further from one another as a result of divergent views of the war now ensuing in Europe. By 1940, former Oxford 1937 delegates were active on both sides of the debate over whether America should affirm neutralism or support the Allies against Germany at possible risk of war. With mutual antipathy growing between groups like Charles Lindberg's America First Committee and William Allen White's Committee to Defend America by Aiding the Allies—in whose service Niebuhr, for example, had enlisted—the tension within church ranks between interventionists and pacifists was growing ever more palpable. As a strategy to reach across the divide, to unite and reorient Protestants around a shared project, the Federal Council gave the conference and those that followed—Delaware 1942 and Cleveland 1945—a decidedly futurist orientation. Just like President Roosevelt's "Four Freedoms" speech and the U.S. and UK's jointly issued Atlantic Charter both did in the months following, the conference avoided the question of American involvement in the war in favor of discussing American involvement in a future postwar international order. This, as Ronald Pruessen notes, allowed pacifists and interventionists to come together and to affirm the elements of the internationalism they shared.[67]

As the Philadelphia conference's final "Message to the Churches" indicates, Oxford 1937 provided a banner under which Christian internationalists of pacifist and nonpacifist conviction rallied, and a basis upon which they asserted their shared support for American international engagement. Oxford 1937 gave them the political-theological framework to articulate support for an American internationalist program in the future, not in the Providentialist terms of Henry Luce's "American Century," but in ecumenical language that worked precisely against such national self-deification. The first item on the conference's final "Message," and the basis for all that followed, rejected, in principle, what delegates saw as the isolationist mentality and policies of recent years. "The United States for its own sake and for the sake of humanity will have to renounce its political and economic isolation and identify itself with other nations in the creation of a world government."[68] Although the phrase "world government" would not have sat well with Oxford delegates, the Philadelphia attendees made explicit their debt in the very next sentence. "In taking this position," they continued, "we subscribe to the declaration of the Oxford conference

(1937) that 'A true conception of international order requires a recognition of the fact that the State, whether it admits it or not, is not autonomous, but is under the ultimate governance of God.'" The Message went on to critique modern statism and nationalism in terms similarly indebted to Oxford 1937. It opposed any way in which the state was "deified and made an object of worship." On the other side, it called upon the churches to be mobilized to support the quest for "an international system of government." With clear echoes of Oxford 1937, it argued that, "The Churches, which in themselves transcend national frontiers, have a peculiar responsibility to help expand men's loyalties."[69] Even before the attack on Pearl Harbor, Oxford provided a framework for pro- and anti-interventionists to gather and articulate Christian internationalism as a call for a renewed American internationalism.

In March 1942, with U.S. entry into the war having defused tensions over the question of intervention, realists and pacifists again gathered in a National Study Conference—larger and more elaborate in scale, but still indebted to Oxford in style and theme—to hammer out the elements of their Christian internationalism. At the "National Study Conference of the Churches," held on the Delaware, Ohio, campus of Ohio Wesleyan University under the Federal Council's organizational leadership, representatives of twenty-six denominations came together—including American Lutherans, Northern Baptists, members of both branches of the Presbyterian Church, the Reformed churches, the Evangelical synods, Disciples of Christ churches, and the African Methodist Episcopal Zion and the Colored Methodist Episcopal Churches. Importantly, too, the Federal Council invited several of the old, familiar para-church organizations in the Christian internationalist networks to send delegates, such as the American Friends Service Committee (which had been closely associated with *The World Tomorrow* in earlier years), the Church Peace Union, and the World Alliance for International Friendship. The national YMCA and YWCA sent representatives, as did the Student Volunteer Movement and Foreign Missions Conference.[70]

With such a mix of personnel, Delaware offered a synthesis of *World Tomorrow*-style anti-imperialist and antiracist critiques with Oxford 1937 ecumenical internationalism—indeed it showed how intertwined the strands had become. Delaware's final "Message," shaped, as David Hollinger notes, by stalwart pacifist and former *World Tomorrow* contributing editor A. J. Muste, appealed to "fellow citizens to recognize now the crucial importance of justice in race relations in our own country as . . . essential to world peace."[71] Rather than narrating the story of a benign, well-intentioned isolationist United States drawn by others into a war, the report cast the United States as complicit in the breakdown of the peace through the character of its race relations. It was notable that the conference ratified and approved the following statement only months after the attack on Pearl Harbor: "We remind our fellow Christians of the appeal of the Japanese for recognition of racial equality at the time of the Versailles Peace Conference. The refusal of that plea and the imposing of such restrictions on immigration as embodied in the Immigration Act of 1924 are recognized as factors contributing to the breakdown of peace."[72] The Message went on to condemn lynching, segregation, and "unequal treatment" of black Americans, acknowledging "with profound contrition the sin of racial discrimination."[73] The United States could not "safely be trusted" with planning peace "so long as our attitudes and policies deny peoples of other races in our own or other lands the essential position of brothers."[74] Such a conceptualization of race relations as integral to international relations had characterized Christian internationalism throughout the 1910s–1930s, whether traced from Sidney Gulick to Sherwood Eddy, Kirby Page, and *The World Tomorrow*, or from John R. Mott, Joseph Oldham, and Max Yergan at Jerusalem 1928 to T. Z. Koo and Benjamin Mays at Oxford 1937. It was still present three years later at the 1945 "National Study Conference on the Churches and a Just and Durable Peace" (held in Cleveland, Ohio), whose Message called for repeal of the Oriental Exclusion Act and the forwarding of antidiscrimination policies in the United States, and which stated that not only did the Japanese empire need dismantling but that Christians needed to demand that the "imperialism of the white man shall be brought to the speediest end."[75]

At the same time, the Delaware conference's concern with "the relation of national sovereignty to some kind of yet-to-be-created transnational political authority," which Hollinger rightly observes was of "chief" importance at the gathering, was a clear legacy of Oxford 1937.[76] The Message urged the mitigation of the norm of anarchic national sovereignty by means of international organization, but importantly it highlighted the provenance of its ideas as differing from other non–church-based "One World" internationalists gaining popularity. Rather than drawing on popular notions of world federation or the like, delegates deployed phrases made ubiquitous at Oxford five years earlier to ground its case: "It is the purpose of God to create a world-wide community in Jesus Christ, transcending race, nation and class."[77] It is telling that it was not only members of the influential realist group like Henry Pit Van Dusen who insisted on such ecclesiological language in linking ecumenism to internationalism. Writing in the *Christian Century* in 1939, A. J. Muste sounded more like Oxford 1937 than his erstwhile opponent in the debate over war, Reinhold Niebuhr. Entitling his essay "The True International," he reflected on the positive development that in 1939 the visible church was "becoming a more faithful replica of the invisible"; it was no longer the secular radicals who stood out for their opposition to totalitarianism, but ecumenical pastors like Germany's Martin Niemöller. Still, he urged, the church needed to stop offering to members merely an experience of being part of a "sanctified Rotary Club," and instead, through "mighty and joyous discipline," lay claim to being the "True Scarlet International of those 'who have washed their robes and made them white in the blood of the Lamb' and among whom is neither Aryan, Negro, Slave, Japanese or Malay."[78] The Philadelphia and Delaware conferences of 1940–1942 reveal some of the greatest impacts of Oxford 1937's Atlantic crossing. Realists represented but one strand in a wider tapestry of Christian internationalist thought that took up the Oxford consensus as a framework to envisage and call for a future domestic and international—indeed, in recent parlance, "intermestic"—order built on an eschewal of racism, imperialism, and nationalism, American varieties included.

Chapter 7

The Dulles Commission, the UN, and the Americanization of Christian Internationalism

"Only a few Americans will sit at the peace table but you and every other American may have a part in determining what is done at the peace table. . . . Help mobilize public opinion in your community for a pattern of world order in which the spirit of Christ may dominate the relations between both men and nations."[1] Thus read the instructional pamphlet introducing the "Christian Mission on World Order," convened by the Federal Council of Churches' Commission on a Just and Durable Peace in October–November, 1943. As a "mission," the campaign drew on the styling of American revivalistic evangelism, featuring crusading techniques such as sermons, Christian music, and youth events. But new content filled the traditional format. On church bookstore displays at mission meetings, according to the instructional pamphlet, there were not to be standard Bible-study materials or evangelical tracts but instead bestselling internationalist books such as E. H Carr's *Conditions of Peace* and Wendell Willkie's *One World*, as well as the pamphlets of the Commission on a Just and Durable Peace. Similarly, when five thousand people filled the Cathedral of St. John the Divine in New York City for the mission's opening service on October 29, they heard not only from the commission leader, the Presbyterian layman John Foster Dulles, but also from Republican Senator Joseph H. Ball of Minnesota, a key architect of the congressional "B2-H2" resolution (named after its four sponsors, of whom Ball was one), which called for the allied countries to form a permanent international organization after the war.[2] Ball dubbed the Mission on World Order "the greatest crusade since Jesus sent His twelve disciples out to preach the brotherhood of man."[3]

With rhetoric that was less ambitious, but which still underscored the bipartisan ethos of the mission, Undersecretary of State Sumner Welles sent along a message to be read at the church meeting in which he reminded attendees of his government's strong commitment to collective security. This mission, though crusading in style, did not aim to convert individuals to Christianity but was, rather, part of the Dulles Commission's aim to mobilize churches as an electoral bloc in support of the emerging internationalist consensus. The mutual courting of church and state and the ideological linking of God and nation were exactly what commission leader Dulles was working for.

Peace-planning discourse not only provided cohesion within Christian internationalism, it became the vehicle that propelled American Christian internationalists further into the center of public debate over American foreign policy in the Second World War. Mainline Protestants increasingly sought to position themselves in a "proprietary relationship" with the nation and state in the 1940s.[4] But, reflecting several wider political shifts and developments, the state increasingly sought a proprietary relationship with the church too. State Department figures were naturally interested in the Dulles commission's seemingly prodigious capacity to steer Protestant public opinion. Publicity and communications techniques were at the fore of their new "cultural diplomacy" initiatives.[5] And they no doubt recognized the importance of generating favorable public opinion for postwar international organization. An internal report from 1944 showed they were watching; it noted, "The Churches constitute the largest aggregation of groups in the United States expressing opinions on international relations issues."[6] Add to that the broader wartime impulse on the part of the federal government to enlist civil society in the service of building morale, and the interest of the state in courting churches appears even stronger.[7] More specific partisan imperatives also played a role, such as the Republican Party's hasty turnaround from isolationism to internationalism between 1941 and 1944. Dulles' blend of Republican *and* internationalist credentials made him an appealing figure to many wishing to see the GOP change tack. And no less important was the Roosevelt administration's desire to avoid another 1920-style electoral disaster. Roosevelt needed all the help he could get in generating bipartisan support for a new international organization and in avoiding the fate of Wilson.[8] Across the political spectrum, from Foggy Bottom to Capitol Hill, politicians and bureaucrats found they had good reason to take notice of mainline Protestants.

The attraction was mutual, however. Churches relished their proximity to power and their increasingly establishment status. They interpreted the cataclysm of war as offering an historic opportunity to shape the founding of a whole new postwar world order on Christian principles. By the end of the war, church leaders who had been at Oxford 1937 were operating on the inside of policymaking discourse, sharing platforms with the State Department and exchanging photo opportunities with the Truman White House. The radical internationalism of *The World Tomorrow* had stood in an oppositional relationship to the Republican foreign policy consensus of the 1920s, exposing through its muckraking journalism what it saw as the tendrils of American imperialism, nationalism, and militarism. And, the ecumenical internationalism of Oxford 1937 had not been primarily aimed at shaping governmental policy but at discerning and expressing the church's witness in an age of catastrophe. In contrast to both, the Christian internationalism of the 1940s self-consciously sought to operate in a position of mutual influence with governmental discourse—and, to a remarkable extent, it succeeded.

The Commission on a Just and Durable Peace was established by the Federal Council of Churches (FCC), with Dulles appointed immediately as chair, at a meeting in Atlantic City in December of 1940, one year before the Pearl Harbor attack. The work of the commission, to be sure, involved many major figures in 1930s and 1940s Christian internationalism, including most American Oxford 1937 delegates, such as fellow Presbyterian John Mackay, John Bennett, Reinhold Niebuhr, Henry Pit Van Dusen, Samuel McCrea Cavert, Walter Van Kirk, and many more. Yet both the success of the commission and the changes it wrought in the intellectual approach of Christian internationalism were due to Dulles more than any other individual or group of individuals. As Henry Pit Van Dusen recalled it in an oral history interview: "It was recognized that this was really a one-man show. It really was his [Dulles's] Commission. It produced a series of documents. . . . Every one of them originated on one of his yellow lawyer's pads, on which he wrote his memoranda. . . . The Commission was really a rubber stamp for his ideas."[9] Dulles biographer Ronald Pruessen is right, then, in suggesting that historians follow the media styling of the time in calling the organization the "Dulles Commission."

Although the new commission was connected to and inspired in part by members of the Federal Council's "Department of International Justice and Goodwill"—a body dating back, in various incarnations, to the period before the First World War—the FCC established the new commission as an ad hoc independent body, reporting directly to its executive committee.[10] The body's independence contributed further to it becoming a vehicle for Dulles's particular vision for world order.[11] With two former secretaries of state in the family, with extensive experience in international affairs, and with his enthusiastic involvement in ecumenism—representing the United States at Oxford

1937 and a later meeting of the provisional World Council of Churches meeting on the "International Situation" in 1939—Dulles was a clear choice for Federal Council leaders. His main qualification, as Andrew Preston notes, was his ability to straddle the divides that threatened to wrack ecumenical Protestantism during the war: He was neither a pacifist nor an interventionist; he blended realism, at times incoherently, with liberal idealism.[12] Although a Republican, Dulles was a fervent Wilsonian, eager for a "second chance" at forming an international organization. As such, he had already been assigned the delicate role of keynote speaker in 1940 at the Philadelphia National Study Conference (which was discussed in chapter 6). As one of his biographers, Mark Toulouse, rightly suggests, Dulles had become, by 1940, the most influential layman associated with the Federal Council of Churches.[13] At Atlantic City that year, he became head of a new institution almost custom-made to fit him.

The Oxford 1937 experience clearly had an impact on Dulles, who called it his "great enlightenment." As Toulouse narrates it, the effect of Oxford was heightened by the contrast between Dulles's experience there and his attendance just prior at the International Studies Conference of the League's Institute of Intellectual Cooperation in Paris.[14] The juxtaposition of the discordant nationalism he saw at Paris and the sense of transracial and transnational unity he felt at Oxford compelled him to conclude he had been wasting his time with other internationalist ventures: They were an "experience with futility."[15] The way forward lay in the churches countering the "petty instincts" of nationalism.[16] Indeed, in his major work of the 1930s, *War, Peace and Change*, penned in 1938 and published in 1939, Dulles drew on Oxford 1937 language to critique national "deification"—a distinctly Oxford term—whereby the "nation has to a marked degree pre-empted the role of that higher spiritual entity with which every man desires to feel some identification."[17]

Just as Dulles's own work provided a conduit for Oxford 1937 emphases, so did the commission he came to lead. The Federal Council clearly positioned the new organization as an outgrowth of Oxford 1937's ecumenical internationalism, and its early pronouncements reiterated the key dialectical emphases of the Oxford conference. In its founding statement, for instance, produced at Atlantic City in December 1940, the Federal Council argued that Christians needed to maintain a permanent tension between national identity on one hand and solidarity with the worldwide church on the other, a tension between the cause of Christ and the pretensions of the state. In words drawn almost directly from the Oxford 1937 report of the Universal Church and the World of Nations section, the statement reminded its church constituencies that "the spiritual and social gains to be expected from any national victory are never so decisive or so permanent as to justify, as an act of expediency, identifying the cause of Christ with the cause of the nation. . . . Let us not give unto Caesar a spiritual allegiance which belongs only to God."[18]

The first official "act" of the commission also revealed the influence of Oxford 1937 in particular and ecumenical internationalism in general. The commission published a compilation of peace-planning pronouncements from around the world in a booklet entitled *A Just and Durable Peace.* The very act of this gathering and reissuing positioned the commission as an American component in a wider ecumenical movement. The publication included several British statements, such as that of the Church of England's Malvern Conference in January 1941 and a joint statement of Catholic and Protestant church leaders in December of 1940. By far the most common and important element among the documents, however, was the critique of nationalism and the normative legitimacy of national sovereignty that had emerged at Oxford 1937. The commission's booklet included the report of the World of Nations section on the need for churches to call for "the abrogation of absolute national sovereignty."[19] It added a pronouncement from the Study Department of the Provisional Committee of the World Council of Churches that drew on Oxford in calling for national sovereignty to "find its counterbalance and limitation in international solidarity."[20] And the booklet included the report of the recent Philadelphia conference, whose message had stated unequivocally: "we subscribe to the declaration of the Oxford Conference." In gathering these various reports, the commission placed itself downstream from Oxford 1937 and located itself as one instantiation of the wider ecumenical movement. Indeed, one of the commission's stated aims at its foundation captured this practice: namely, to maintain "contacts with the Study Department of the World Council of Churches."[21]

While several biographies of Dulles and other works on the churches in wartime have addressed the details of the commission's work, they have not, on the whole, tended to place it in the context of the Oxford 1937 consensus from which it emerged, and from which it came to differ. While scholars such as Heather Warren have noted the observable connections between Oxford 1937 and the Dulles Commission, they have not been as attentive to the deeper, less obvious ways the commission substantively departed from its origins. Andrew Preston's probing treatment of Dulles argues for an essential continuity between the ecumenism of Oxford 1937 and the Dulles Commission's work in the mid-1940s. In contrast, I argue in this chapter that Dulles in fact "Americanized" ecumenical internationalism in significant ways. Under Dulles, a body originally devoted to study on the part of churches became a publicity and lobby bureau directly aimed at brokering a relationship between a Christian electoral constituency and Washington foreign-policy makers. Dulles's view of the churches became an increasingly instrumentalist one as he sought to mobilize them as a political base that would legitimize American state-run internationalism. Rather than stress postliberal theology and its attendant ec-clesiology of the Universal Church, Dulles altered the commission's language so that it framed its politics in terms of a universal "moral order"—a set of principles deemed to be derived from Christian sources and yet assumed to be so general as to be readily observable by any reasonable person. Jesus took the form, not of the uncompromising historical pacifist of *The World Tomorrow*— nor of the reconciler of races through his blood—but of a resolute moral vision-ary who embodied the best principles for building an international political organization.[22] Importantly, under Dulles's influence, the commission over time altered the negation implied in the structure of Christian internationalist thought: no longer was the critique directed at nationalism; "responsible" inter-nationalism was now cast in opposition to "selfish" isolationism. For a while, the two forms of internationalist critique coexisted and overlapped. But as American internationalism once again assumed its hegemonic form in the postwar period, the "yes" to American world leadership eventually undid the "no" toward Christian nationalism that had characterized the whole sweep of ecumenical and radical Christian internationalism in the interwar period.

Moral Order

Tensions between these ecumenical origins and John Foster Dulles's newer approach were apparent in the commission's convening of the second National Study Conference of the churches, in Delaware, Ohio, March 1942. While the study conference form was continuous with post-Oxford practices, and while ecumenical and radical elements of Christian internationalist thinking appeared in the reports, the Delaware conference also saw newer emphases emerge—emphases that came from the yellow legal pad of the commission's chairman. Dulles used the Delaware conference to unveil the commission's "Statement of Guiding Principles" on a just and durable peace. Included in the final conference "Message," and sitting in odd juxtaposition with the cri-tiques of imperialism and race (discussed in chapter 6), the document turned out to be programmatic of the commission's agenda over the next three, crit-ical years. "We believe that moral law, no less than physical law, undergirds our world," the introduction to the principles argued. "If mankind is to escape chaos and recurrent war, social and political institutions must be brought into conformity with this moral order." The document gave no real account for the provenance of this view of moral law. It clearly evoked a natural law style of thought, yet without acknowledgment of that tradition (still less without the modesty of its just war subset). It was the very kind of talk that Barthians like Menn and Huber had opposed at Oxford 1937. This was not postliberal ecumenism, but rather a distinct blend of theological liberalism, Presbyterian moral law universalism, and American exceptionalism that, as Malcolm Magee has shown, Woodrow Wilson best exemplified.[23]

The "Guiding Principles" linked the notion of moral order to many emphases circulating in liberal internationalism more broadly. Principle 4 linked the moral order to international organization. "Implicit in the moral order" was a "true community of nations."[24] Consistent with the arguments Dulles had made at Oxford, the principles called for the organization and supervision of economic interdependence, freedom of trade, and shared access of resources. While the Bretton Woods arrangements were still years away, the commission was already in dialogue with Leo Pasvolsky, a special assistant to Secretary of State Cordell Hull, then assigned to the National Resources Planning Board. Remarkably, as Hollinger points out, Pasvolsky, in attendance at the commission's Delaware conference, circulated a draft that outlined his board's and Roosevelt's later thinking on people's "rights" to economic and food security.[25] Other principles promoted disarmament and Wilsonian notions of anticolonialism, key pillars of internationalist campaigning in the interwar years. And, with their emphasis on moral order, the principles also linked to another kind of universalist discourse emerging afresh in the 1940s—that of universal human rights. Other commission members, such as O. Frederick Nolde, would go on to play a significant role in the drafting of the Universal Declaration. For the time being, the statement simply offered a general framework that affirmed that the rights of "racial and religious minorities of all lands" needed to be safeguarded and that "freedom of religious worship, of speech and assembly, of the press, and of scientific enquiry and teaching" were "fundamental to human development and in keeping with the moral order."[26]

In couching their principles in the language of Wilsonian moralistic universalism and nationalist exceptionalism, Dulles and the commission seemed to hint that war itself would be overcome by America playing a leading, redemptive role on the world stage. The principles made clear that if there was to be a moral order in international life, then "a very heavy responsibility devolves upon the United States" to make that happen.[27] They offered a tone of contrition for what they saw as the destructive, irresponsible use of American power in the isolationist interwar period. It was "a matter of shame and humiliation" that there had been too much concentration on the national "self." A true Christian internationalism was the opposite of "selfish," isolationist nationalism. Left unexplored was the question of how the United States might act in the future toward other nations who interpreted the universal moral order in terms different than its own. World leadership allowed for the possibility that the United States might have to assume the role of moral policeman. The tension was hidden, though, behind the argument that American power was not to be used in service of itself. The American flag, as Wilson had said two decades earlier, was not that of an imperial nation-state; it was "the flag of humanity."[28]

Just as the principles began implicitly to cast Christian internationalism as a subset of American internationalism, they also reframed the churches as a component of a national citizenry. The task of the hour, according to the "Statement of Guiding Principles," was to awaken the electoral power of Christians as a foreign policy constituency. As guiding principle 12 stated, "Christian citizens" had to "seek to translate our beliefs into practical realities and to create a public opinion which will insure that the United States shall play its full and essential part in the creation of a moral way of international living." Further recommendations in the report envisaged the commission brokering an internationalist consensus in America by using the "Statement of Guiding Principles" in two directions: both to provide "governments with a formulation of the spiritual bases for eventual armistice and peace proposals" and to "provide Christians with criteria for appraising specific armistice and peace terms."[29]

That these emphases sounded more American than ecumenical—mobilizing a national, democratic citizenry instead of focusing on a theology of the Universal Church, propounding a general and universally valid set of moral order "principles" instead of any particular theology, and calling for America to exercise its unique national responsibility—was not a fact lost on those listening at the time. The apologetic tone prefacing the conference's report provided evidence of this. Sure, "delegates endeavored to think ecumenically," an opening rider explained, but "it is recognized that the Conference delegates were Americans." There was no way the delegates could "claim immunity from the influence of American tradition and thought," it explained.[30]

Further evidence that the emphases were seen as more American than ecumenical came at an extraordinary meeting between the commission and a group of "Foreign Churchmen" in New York in 1941. Discussing the guiding principles, which were at that time being drafted, many of the international ecumenical church leaders present found American pretensions to universality hard to swallow. It was "very difficult for American Christians to make any contribution," argued Dr. Otto Piper of Germany, formerly a member of the Oxford 1937 World of Nations section. "Most Christians, even your committee, start on the assumption that America is in possession of the Christian truth and all other nations are mistaken about it." Yet, he reminded them, "the American way of life is not necessarily the right way of life for some other country." When the war ended, he predicted, it would be "difficult for America to translate their feelings and their ideas to other nations."[31] Adolf Keller, a major European figure in the ecumenical movement, founder of the International Institute of Christian Social Action in 1928, and a longtime leader in the Life and Work movement, which had convened the Oxford conference, echoed that view. He raised, in more subtle terms, the general problem of universality and otherness: "[W]e must make an effort to understand the deeper nature and subconscious psychology of other nations. It is not enough to project our 'imago' of what they are, upon their inner deeper life and values. A constant attempt of a deeper translation of another life must therefore accompany our moral judgment and political activity."[32] Claims to universality could inadvertently override the otherness of the other. With warnings such as these ringing in their ears, the commission leaders' defensive tone in framing the Delaware report months later was hardly surprising.

Despite other ecumenists' mixed feelings about Americanization, Dulles continued the process with vigor. He appeared to feel little ambivalence or hesitation about his new approach, and it came to dominate even further as he exerted his own control over the commission's direction. Behind-the-scenes minutes from the commission's Committee of Direction show the way in which Dulles consistently agitated for the commission to change its mission from "study" to the kind of public opinion brokerage between church and government he envisaged. At a meeting of the commission in the Gramatan Hotel in Bronxville, with a number of high-profile internationalists present, such as Clyde Eagleton of Columbia University and C. C. Morrison of the *Christian Century*, Dulles downplayed the need for any further "study." The time was such, he argued, that "we would not accomplish the purpose for which we were set up if we merely study blue prints of some future world order."[33] The commission needed to devote itself to reaching more people, to creating greater influence with the public, and to leveraging that very public influence in its relationship with government officials. The mission was no less than "the education of the American people to acceptance of these principles and their implications, and the bringing of these principles to the attention of those in government who have responsibility for action."[34] Dulles argued that, in his thirty-five years of contact with foreign-policy makers, he "had never known a time when such officials were as responsive to the view of the Christian community" as today. He offered, to finish, a biblical image—of Moses's aides supporting his limbs during battle—that eminently captured the kind of partnership between church and government he envisioned. "[T]here is an important governmental element that wants the same thing that we want, and we must hold up their hands."[35]

For Kirby Page and *The World Tomorrow*, of course, the state was certainly not equivalent to Moses, and the churches were certainly not to be its assistants. Although they too had sought to mediate relations between foreign-policy makers and churches in earlier years—for example, through the mass surveys of clergy—those relations had been intentionally discordant and oppositional. While *The World Tomorrow* and Dulles similarly sought to "educate" and mobilize American Protestants to be interested and informed on foreign policy, and while they shared some informational practices, such as the use of study guides, lectures, and pamphlets, it was crucial for Dulles that his mainline project be diffused and mediated by publicity so centrist and mainstream (so non-"counter") that not even the White House or State Department would dare ignore it.

Holding up the Hands of the State

Dulles began to get everything he wished for in 1943. That year the commission began to move into precisely the mediating role he called for. While the commission engaged in several high-profile enterprises—such as the Princeton "Round Table" of international church leaders, for which General Douglas MacArthur, in contrast to his response to *The World Tomorrow*, allowed Australian delegates to use a U.S. bomber as transport to attend—the most significant work came with the production of their famous "Six Pillars of Peace" statement. The release of the Six Pillars sealed the transition of the organization from an ecumenical study institute to a national publicity bureau. The Six Pillars became the foundational document, the touchstone, for all the commission's later, more specific commentary on proposals for postwar international organization, and it was this program that became their most famous product. Indeed, the pillars developed a brand recognition wider than the commission itself.

Having worked on his own with pencil and legal pad for months (if not years, as he alleged), Dulles began to circulate a draft of a set of "political propositions" in early 1943. The Six Pillars were basically a shortlisted selection of the thirteen guiding principles issued at Delaware the year before. But Dulles hoped this shorter version, shorn of the language of morality, would generate even greater levels of assent, framed as they were, not merely on the basis of religious reason but on the grounds of secular political reason as well. The pillars would address Christians, but Dulles hoped they would find an even wider appeal with the "great mass of people who are Christian-minded, but who are not regular church-goers."[36] The Six Pillars had to do, respectively, with the need for an international political organization, the need for an international economic organization, the need to ensure the changeability of any peace treaty, the need to frame national autonomy instead of colonial rule as an ultimate "goal," the need to provide for international control of military establishments, and the need to create an institutional guarantee of individual rights to religious and intellectual liberty.[37] The fusion of universalism and national particularism that had surfaced earlier in the commission's work was even more pronounced in the Six Pillars. Although the political principles were derived from seemingly universal moral principles, the commission's first pamphlet introducing the Six Pillars narrated the situation in national terms. The opening quotation came not from the commission, nor from scripture, nor even from a church declaration, but from *The Federalist* of 1787. The passage underlined the special responsibility "reserved to the people of this country, by their conduct and example, to decide whether societies of men are really capable or not of establishing good government from reflection and choice . . . or accident and force."[38]

The commission disseminated the Six Pillars through a combination of older church-based educational methods and newer techniques aimed at reaching a wider public. As with the Oxford 1937 reports, and with *The World Tomorrow* itself, the Six Pillars became the subject of special, local church discussion groups. Commission staff prepared an eighty-five-page "Study Guide" based on the Six Pillars, together with an "Instruction Manual for Use with the Six Pillars of Peace Study Guide" offering insights on educational technique.[39] Study groups composed of church youth, for example, could examine one pillar per week in the same way that many American follow-up conferences had examined one report of the Oxford conference per week in late 1937. Accompanying graphs and images (often supplied from cooperating internationalist organizations such as James Shotwell's Committee to Study the Organization of Peace) and statements from political leaders such as Sumner Welles and

Winston Churchill peppered the guide. On the commission's count there were around twenty thousand people involved in local committees whose purpose was to coordinate such discussion groups.[40] If each of those people had overseen the involvement of ten to twenty participants, numbers would have neared a quarter of a million people.

Church discussion groups aside, the media campaign associated with the Six Pillars began to attain for the commission the public reach and centrist influence Dulles hoped for. An initial mass mailing of sixty thousand copies of the statement to church ministers was accompanied by a further two thousand copies being sent to newspaper editors. Newspapers from across the country and internationally took up the opportunity and reported favorably on the release of the Pillars. Many, such as the *New York Herald Tribune* and *New York Times*, afforded front-page coverage to the story.[41] Even across the Atlantic, the London *Times*, much to the delight of the commission staff, editorialized in favor of the commission's work.[42] The centerpiece of the commission's publicity campaign was its engagement of the services of major public figures to write a series of articles on the pillars—an effort to snowball the growing economy of eminence by association on which the commission thrived. Writers included personalities such as Harold Dodds, president of Princeton University; Arthur Hays Sulzberger, publisher of the *New York Times*; and politicians from both major parties, such as the Republican governor of New York, Thomas Dewey, and Sumner Welles.[43] Coming one per week, with one writer per pillar, the articles were published in an estimated ninety-six newspapers with a combined circulation of around 5,400,000. They found their place in a further sixteen religious periodicals before being repackaged together in a booklet and redistributed once again—not unlike *The World Tomorrow*'s earlier compilation of "reverberations and re-reverberations" after its surveys.[44]

The wide political acceptance of the Six Pillars served Dulles and the commission in their lobbying of the White House from 1943. Although President Roosevelt had authorized secretive State Department planning for postwar order to go on in the background, he remained publicly evasive and vague on details about international organization. The Dulles Commission made it their aim to bring him out on the issue. On successive visits to the White House, Roosevelt expressed broad approval of the general ideas, but insisted on the need to be realistic about the kinds of detailed form that such a postwar organization might take. No doubt he was wary of letting what he later called "perfectionist" criticisms derail the project and damage his chances for reelection in 1944. But still the commission urged that the basic—and to their eyes, bland—commitments to continued Allied cooperation after the war, as seen in the Moscow and Tehran declarations of 1943, give way to plans for a peace that would be, in their terms, more "curative and creative."[45] A peace needed to have in mind the reconstruction of the larger social and international order—the moral principles espoused in the Six Pillars—if it were truly to be just and durable, they argued.

Interweaving Church and State, 1944–1945

One reason President Roosevelt could ill afford *not* to listen to the commission—and needed to appear to pay attention to them—lay in Dulles's associations with the Republican Party. Dulles's meteoric rise in public life was not due only to his remarkable instinct for generating success and influence through the publicity campaigns at the commission. To a significant extent, his political influence in 1944–1945 resulted also from the particular apertures and opportunities that opened in the rapidly evolving Republican Party between 1940 and 1944. Wendell Willkie's tilt at the presidency in 1940, followed by the celebrity status he attained through his travelogue-style, bestselling internationalist text *One World* (1943), signaled to other Republican hopefuls that an internationalist platform was the way forward.[46] When Governor of New York Thomas Dewey sized up his bid to become the next Republican nominee to run in the 1944 election, he realized he needed to boost his foreign policy credentials. His friend "Foster," who was, like Willkie, an internationalist Republican, was an obvious choice to enlist for help.

Dulles's work with Dewey led to a far greater role than mere campaign management. As foreign policy adviser to the Republican nominee in 1944, Dulles found himself in the delicate position of being able to shape much of the character of public debate over foreign relations. At stake in particular was the political fate of the Dumbarton Oaks conference, where, between August 21 and October 7, representatives of China, Great Britain, the USSR, and the United States met to plan ways of turning the United Nations alliance into a postwar international organization. Given his ecumenical internationalist constituency's anti-imperialism, Dulles potentially might have seized the political opportunity afforded by the election to paint Dumbarton Oaks as a mere meeting of imperialist, amoral Great Powers—which, to some extent, it was. Could Dewey and Dulles outflank Roosevelt on internationalist peace plans? With the polarized League of Nations debate and electoral disaster of 1920 in mind, the incumbent Democratic administration had reason to worry. Roosevelt's efforts in selling the Dumbarton Oaks proposals—in which

1,900,000 copies of the proposals, specially commissioned speakers, radio programs, and explanatory films were nationally disseminated—reflected this political anxiety.[47] Ahead of Dumbarton Oaks, then, Roosevelt had Secretary Hull reach out to the Dewey-Dulles team to arrange a kind of electoral cease-fire that would preserve the proposal from becoming political fodder. Dulles and Hull met three times in Washington D.C., in August to iron out the details of an arrangement that saw both parties agree that Dumbarton Oaks should be treated as a "nonpartisan" issue.[48] According to the *Washington Post*, Hull had wanted the statement simply to say that the subject of future peace should be "kept entirely out of politics." But Dulles had insisted that the agreement not preclude public discussion on a "nonpartisan basis."[49] The campaign offered a prime opportunity for public education.[50]

Preston argues that Roosevelt and Hull politically cornered Dulles—effectively silencing him from expressing dissent until the election was over. They reminded Dulles that if he scuttled Dumbarton Oaks then the one chance at a viable international organization would be jeopardized.[51] There was an element of such success for FDR; Dulles did sound closer to being an apologist for the proposals in late 1944. But on another level, though, the deal brought Dulles even closer to policymaking processes. In exchange for committing to nonpartisanship, Dulles was to be fed confidential reports from the State Department on the progress of the Dumbarton Oaks conference itself. His papers show he received secret copies of results of the Dumbarton Oaks discussion at least as early as September 11, as well as an early release of the final proposals on September 27—ahead of the conference finishing on October 7. Not happy just to watch on, Dulles also submitted to the conference, through State Department channels, his own proposal for a "peaceful change" mechanism to be included in the postwar settlement.[52]

Observers at the time rightly noted the significance of the bipartisan internationalist consensus that crystallized in the 1944 election as a result of these deals. The *Washington Post* praised the Hull-Dulles agreement as "one of the most significant developments in American political history." The editors saw the possibility of making American involvement in a postwar organization just as nonpartisan as the Monroe Doctrine.[53] Yet just as significant for the trajectory of Christian internationalism was the fact that Dulles was ushered into the inner circle of the campaign and given access to the State Department while remaining in his job with the church commission. Dulles did in fact offer his resignation to the Federal Council of Churches upon sensing the likelihood of further involvement with Dewey. But the council declined. The president, Henry St. George Tucker, passed on the Executive Committee's "earnest hope" that Dulles would continue in his position as chairman. Taking up Dulles's language of citizenship, President Tucker said "we sincerely believe that it is not only proper but desirable for Christians, in their capacity as citizens, to seek to implement through political action the ideals to which they are committed." Later, fellow commission member and president of Princeton Theological Seminary John Mackay wrote to commend Dulles on his role with Dewey, expressing hope that "some day, in the not too distant future, [Dulles might] take up the responsibilities of Secretary of State."[54]

In the meantime, as commission chairman, Dulles helped lead mainline Protestantism toward a qualified endorsement of the Dumbarton proposals, bringing Christian internationalism even closer to the government. Using the Six Pillars as a kind of "checklist," he and the commission brokered public opinion in the way Dulles had long envisaged. That is, the Six Pillars—conveniently enumerated—provided a list of criteria against which government proposals could be tested. Such a mechanism allowed Dulles to balance "perfectionism" in church ranks (to use President Roosevelt's term) against the lack of perfection in what government plans actually delivered. While Dumbarton Oaks, with its bare-bones emphasis on collective security between former allies, fell short of many internationalists' hopes, the commission could, and did, argue to the effect that the achievement of some pillars was better than none, and that it was best to retain what was already achieved and apply pressure to have the rest of the checklist completed. "The important thing," Dulles wrote to Charles Clayton Morrison, whose *Christian Century* was associated with the so-called perfectionist viewpoint, "is that Christian forces be united to seek the one thing which seems to me to be both essential and practical, namely, a world organization which at least faces in the direction of dealing affirmatively with some of the basic causes of war. If it faces in that direction then we can keep pushing to get more."[55]

While Dulles secured the Federal Council of Churches' endorsement of the Dumbarton Oaks proposals relatively quickly and easily, the real test came at the larger "National Study Conference on the Churches and a Just and Durable Peace" in Cleveland Ohio in early 1945. As reflected in its name, the Cleveland meeting was the sequel to the earlier Delaware, Ohio, study conference of 1942, where Dulles had unveiled his statement of Guiding Principles. As at the earlier conference, the inclusion of a wider body of churches and religious groups lent the conference a more inclusive, and at times more radical, character than the commission.[56] The topics that concerned delegates proved as diverse as those in attendance. The conference came out more radically than the commission had on economics, imperialism, and race relations.

In economic life, its reports argued, the United States had a way to go in addressing poverty and needed to adjust some of its most sacredly held beliefs: "Private property was not an absolute right but a right qualified by public interest."[57] In the arena of race relations too, Christians needed to work on problems at home: "It is strongly urged upon churches and church members that they wage a continuing campaign against race prejudice in all its forms." Churches should seek to have the civil rights of Japanese-Americans upheld and should campaign for legislation providing for a permanent Fair Employment Practices Commission, the repeal of poll tax laws, and the provision of housing support on a nondiscriminatory basis—all major planks of wartime civil rights agitation.[58] The content and the flavor of these proposals went well beyond the Dulles Commission's political range. The question at stake, then, was what such a gathering would say about the Dumbarton Oaks proposals. If any group seemed likely to find the proposals failing in their morality, it would be this one.

To press his defense of Dumbarton Oaks, Dulles used media channels, now available to him as Republican politician, to try to draw fellow Protestants into line. In the *New York Herald Tribune*, he warned the churches that their "perfectionism" tended to have a "paralyzing effect upon our actual practice of international cooperation."[59] In a radio address on Cleveland's WJW station on the opening evening of the Cleveland conference, he presented the Dumbarton Oaks proposals not as malevolent, but as vulnerable. "There is much risk that, as things now stand, the Dumbarton Oaks Proposals will never be more than words."[60] Whatever its strengths or weaknesses, the Dumbarton Oaks plan needed protection from the pincer of abstract American idealism on the one hand and the realities of Great Power cynicism on the other.

In the end, Dulles had his way, and the Cleveland conference provisionally endorsed the Dumbarton Oaks proposals in its final "Message." But this message utilized Dulles's checklist technique to state that its endorsement was only partial and conditional. The statement recommended "that the churches support the Dumbarton Oaks Proposals as an important step in the direction of world cooperation," but because "we do not approve of them in their entirety as they now stand," they added another enumerated document: a nine-point list of "measures for their improvement." Thus the checklist of the Six Pillars became supplemented with another list of nine points. The "Cleveland Nine," as they became known, encompassed calls for a preamble to be added to the proposed United Nations charter that would frame the task of the organization in view of "present and long range purposes of justice and human welfare," for "a special Commission on Human Rights and Fundamental Freedoms to be established" and for "eventual universal membership" of "all nations willing to accept the obligations of membership."[61] Strikingly, all three proposals—universal membership, a human rights commission, and a preamble—were effected at the San Francisco conference in coming months.

Having found himself interpreting the churches' opinion to the state, and the state's to the churches, Dulles's interweaving of the two increased even further in 1945. In contrast to Cordell Hull's grudging dialogue earlier, the new Secretary of State Edward Stettinius Jr. (who had chaired the Dumbarton Oaks proceedings) pursued John Foster Dulles, seeking his appointment at the upcoming San Francisco "United Nations Conference on International Organization" scheduled to start in late April.[62] When Stettinius initially proposed that Dulles act as a general adviser to the U.S. delegation, Dulles declined, stating that he would prefer to "advance the great purpose of that Conference" in a private, nonofficial capacity through the FCC's commission. Stettinius insisted—saying his request was "concurred in by the President"—that Dulles would best serve the conference by acting in an official capacity.[63] Dulles in the end assented. Stettinius responded in glowing terms: "I know of no one in American life who is better qualified than you are to aid your Government in this undertaking, perhaps the greatest of all time."[64]

Dulles had gone from the achievement of fostering bipartisan dialogue and cooperation in mid-1944 to working for the very State Department with whom he had made that agreement. His employment—although "without compensation," apart from $25.00 per diem—meant that this time he would suspend his role as chairman of the commission. He made it clear in a press release that at San Francisco he would not be representing the churches qua churches. The Federal Council tried to persuade him to retain his position as chair, citing the same benefits as earlier, but this time Dulles refused.[65]

Dulles's temporary resignation from commission work and church work, though, was nominal. He fitted his work at San Francisco in between church crusades and other events. Indeed, rather than conflicting, his state role and his church role became mutually reinforcing. Dulles surrounded his involvement with the State Department at San Francisco—where he worked closely with fellow Republican, and recent convert from isolationism, Senator Arthur Vandenberg—with church events devoted to the themes of world order and international organization.[66] Just three days before the San Francisco conference convened, the Oakland Council of Churches took advantage of Dulles's proximity and launched their own version of the earlier Mission on World Order: a crusade-style meeting held in the Oakland Auditorium Arena with Dulles as keynote speaker. The "Dulles Meeting," as it was known, was broadcast on three separate radio networks. Leaflets bearing Dulles's portrait advertised his promised address on "The Beginning of World Order." The programs for the day's events even devoted a page to the nine-point recommendations emerging from the Cleveland conference, underlining just how ubiquitous the "Cleveland Nine" had become. The hymn list combined the particularism of *America the Beautiful* ("*America! America! God shed His grace on thee*") with the universalism of *In Christ There Is No East or West*—a mix that well characterized Dulles's internationalism and that of his commission.[67]

After the San Francisco conference, with the new charter drafted and needing ratification by the U.S. Senate, Dulles used the checklist—the Six Pillars and the Cleveland Nine—to argue that the list had indeed been ticked. Protestant Americans needed to throw their support behind the new United Nations organization. Clause for clause, Dulles argued, the proposed international organization matched the wishes of the commission and its constituents. Dulles's personal papers show him forming the basis of his argument. In pencil markings scrawled over a draft of the new UN Charter, he systematically matched provisions in the charter against the Six Pillars and Cleveland Nine. For example, he matched Article 55 of the charter with pillar 2 as seeking to promote international economic stability. Article 14 of the charter, on peaceful adjustments, he related to pillar 3. Article 73 echoed the demands of pillar 4 on the ultimate goal of autonomy—and the list could go on.[68] Moving from his personal pencil markings to the public square, Dulles distilled his conclusions. To the *Dallas Morning News*, in a specially commissioned piece, Dulles argued that the Six Pillars—drafted all those years ago—had now found their fulfillment. The "new world organization follows in large measure the program which for two and one-half years millions of Protestant Christians of America have been thinking about and working for."[69]

Such congruency in views only helped to cement further the commission's establishment influence. Having gone ahead of the Roosevelt administration's public stance on international organization in the early 1940s—in fact, having begun to call for international organization way back at the Oxford conference when neutralism was at its peak—ecumenical internationalists were now as mainline as they came. As Dulles's personal trajectory as a hybrid church-government figure continued, he drew the commission further into the orbit of establishment politics with him. For instance, when President Truman appointed Dulles to attend the Foreign Ministers' conference in London in September-October 1945 as an official member of the U.S. delegation, Dulles immediately returned to brief the church commission on his observations on the state of the postwar world.[70] Soon afterward, President Truman personally chose Dulles to represent the United States as an alternate delegate at the first meeting of the UN General Assembly in 1946. Once the meeting ended, Dulles returned to try to find some time to confer with the busy president on the happenings at the first assembly.[71] The president, though, was keeping himself occupied with meetings like that of the Federal Council of Churches in Columbus, Ohio, where he traveled to speak in person. Times had changed drastically: only three years earlier, President Roosevelt had begrudgingly accepted visits from the Federal Council of Churches at the White House; now the new president would travel to attend a meeting of the same group held in the Midwest. A personal letter from Truman to Dulles gave some further indication of the stature the commission had now attained as an organization: "No man would willingly decline the opportunity to meet with a group which stands, as you do, for the highest values in American life. . . . If today, we Americans have a clearer understanding of our place in the world community, a stronger sense of fellowship with other peoples—as I believe we have—it is due, in no small part to the advanced position in international thinking taken by the Federal Council of Churches of Christ in America."[72]

Conclusion

While the San Francisco conference managed to pass the Dulles Commission's 1940s checklists, it should also be seen as fulfilling the more long-range proposals arising from Oxford 1937. At that conference, the World of Nations section report and the final Message had argued churches should work to promote the mitigation of unrestricted national sovereignty. The best way of doing that, it argued, lay in reviving the League of Nations. With the inauguration of the United Nations Organization, what had seemed a distant goal in 1937 achieved institutional reality—though how effective it would be in restricting national sovereignty remained to be seen. The Dulles Commission's campaign for international organization, which had begun before Pearl Harbor and before the new political consensus of 1943–1944, should be seen as a major part of Oxford 1937's Atlantic crossing. It represented one of the most practical political expressions of the ecumenical internationalism emanating from the Oxford conference. In mobilizing churches to support the building of an international organization, Oxford 1937 succeeded in crossing the Atlantic. In other ways, however, it was not so successful.

During the war—and particularly through the final two years, as public debate over international organization crystallized—the structure of Christian internationalist thought in the Dulles Commission was reconfigured. The movement's critical target shifted. No longer was the "no" against nationalism, the identification of the cause of Christ with the cause of the nation, as the 1940 Atlantic City statement had said; now it was against selfish isolationism. Such a negative shift was accompanied by the rising prominence of a positive theme in Dulles's work. His vision for a functional "national faith," first articulated at Oxford and later referred to in his commission work, laid the foundations for his later, influential rendering of the Cold War as a battle between rival faiths.

The mystery of how Dulles turned from internationalist to cold warrior has intrigued historians for decades. How did one who appeared so thoroughly imbued in his Christian-ecumenical experience at Oxford in 1937 become implicated in one of the most stridently ideological foreign policy chapters in American history? How, asks Mark Toulouse, did Dulles undergo a transformation from "prophet of realism to high priest of nationalism?"[73] In fact, Dulles's basic intellectual framework for relating Christianity to American nationalism remained unchanged. At the level of this deep structure of thought, Dulles's Christian nationalism in the Cold War period represented a logical extension of his internationalism in the interwar and wartime period.

Dulles appeared, on one level, to be entirely in accord with the Oxford consensus. Attesting to the deep impact the conference had upon him, Dulles also reiterated its critique of nationalism in his 1939 work, *War, Peace and Change*. On another level, though, Dulles's work, even at Oxford, contained elements all along irreconcilable with this wider consensus. Specifically, Dulles's idea of the nature of the relationship between Christianity and nationhood stood at odds with the dialectical and ecclesiological emphases that postliberal theologians had insisted upon at the conference. In his Oxford 1937 paper, Dulles revealed to all who cared to look that his reasoning did not start with the church, it started with the nation seeking resources in the church. Religion would provide the resources needed for internationalist reform. Mobilizing people for such a program required great spiritual energy, he argued. Looking at the so-called Christian West, the home of the liberal internationalism for which he called, Dulles observed a severe lack of zeal. Where was the "power of the spirit" seen in the sacrifice of Italians and Russians for their government, he asked. "What of the democratic nations? What of the so-called 'Christian' nations? They boast of high ideals but have they the spiritual fire . . . ?" While it was the task of reason to *design* a system for world betterment, it was the "task of spiritual leadership" to mobilize people for success in the project.[74] Without using so many words, then, Dulles called for a non-substantive civil religion that would provide the spiritual resources required for national progress.

Dulles's idea that a nation-state had the capacity and need for something called a "faith" also came to the fore in his commission work in the early 1940s. Dulles made clear the role he envisioned for Christian faith in the whole internationalist enterprise to fellow commission members: "Our primary task, as I see it, is a task to imbue the American people with some great dynamic faith which will carry them forward. Out of that we can get the strength which is needed to create and perpetuate the kind of post war order that we need." American leadership in creating world order would "only result from a sense of mission in the world."[75] Dulles was not talking about churches but about "the American people." Nor was he talking about a particularistic Christian faith but rather "some great dynamic faith." The content of the faith was not so important—and here he sounded close to Eisenhower ten years later—as long as it created a sense of American "mission in the world."

Dulles's instrumentalist view of civil religion was clear in the way he compared America's apparent spiritual exhaustion to the vitality of other great powers. Looking at the three greatest powers of the last century, Great Britain, France, and the United States, one could see, Dulles suggested, that they each "had a power and influence far out of relation to their numbers." This was where "faith" came in: "The source of that influence was that each of these three peoples had a sense of mission and of destiny in the world." The problem was that the previous world war had "burnt out" the faiths of Great Britain and France, and Americans had "no abiding faith in anything" since the last great source of idealism, President Wilson. Americans had lost their belief in national mission. Dulles went on to draw even more extraordinary inferences from the course of world events in recent decades. With the pall that fell over the world following the last war, there had emerged what he saw as a spiritual vacuum. Rising to fill that vacuum were several new "faiths" around the globe, the most vital being in Germany, Japan, and Russia. The idea that Communism and fascism were forms of "religion" was not new. It had been the central argument of Reinhold Niebuhr's speech at the Oxford conference in 1937, and had characterized his analysis as far back as *The World Tomorrow* days. But Dulles's conclusions from this analysis reached an unsurpassed level of pragmatism. The other "faiths" in Germany and Japan were evil in that they were based on race supremacy and other errant doctrines. "But at least they were faiths which gave their people, for the time being, a strong fervor and for which they were willing to sacrifice and die."[76]

Dulles did not reserve this argument for the behind-the-scenes planning of the commission; he published the substance of his speech in a booklet on the postwar world. "The American people face grave alternatives," he wrote. They had no discernible faith as such and thus faced the prospect of exhaustion in their fight against other, evil, "alien faiths." Americans needed a faith if they were to fight on and win. Thus the critical question was: "Will that faith be a righteous faith or an evil faith?"[77] Showing little hesitancy about casting faith as a component of national might, he diagnosed the source of American weakness: "It is lack of such a faith which has made us weak. To recapture such a faith will make us strong."[78]

Clearly, then, Dulles distinguished—perhaps unconsciously—between an American "sense of mission" and the false "deification" of nations he and others critiqued at Oxford 1937. Somehow the two were separate for him. In *War, Peace and Change* he had taken up Oxford's critique of nationalism, applying it to other countries, but not to America. Here he stood well apart from Niebuhr, Page, Miller, or any number of the *World Tomorrow* community. National deification for Dulles was something other countries did. America, on the other hand, represented part of the solution. Where Dulles did write of nationalism in America, he wrote of the "nationalist" ambitions of individual states, which had been successfully overridden by the experiment in federation. The history of federation in the United States "constitutes a significant illustration of the extent to which exaggerated national conceptions can be shrunk through the opening up of boundaries."[79] Americans did not engage in nationalism; their history held the key to ending it. Here Dulles fit a wider pattern in 1940s internationalism. As historian of public opinion Ralph Levering shows, although many Americans by 1943 accepted internationalist politics, they did so by retaining a belief in "the special virtue of the American experiment and those participating in it."[80]

Little wonder then that Dulles was so appealing to Henry Luce, the influential editor of *Time* and *Life* who coined the term the "American century." Luce argued, in his now famous 1942 essay, that "because America alone among the nations was founded on ideas and ideals which transcend class and caste and racial and occupational differences . . . America alone can provide the pattern for the future."[81] And it was Luce who spotted in Dulles's thinking a way to give language and meaning to the nature of the early Cold War. In a *Life* editorial in 1946—in an edition that covered the Federal Council of Churches' recent meeting on world order with a portrait photo of President Truman pasted in the middle—Luce surveyed the policy positions that were emerging in both parties. For Luce, the recent trend of "get tough" speeches regarding

Russia lacked a certain something. Senator Vandenberg asked, "What is Russia up to now?" Secretary Byrnes promised America would not "stand aloof." And Joseph Kennedy called for a tougher foreign policy in geo-strategic terms. But for Luce none of these figures got to the real issue. "In Mr. Kennedy's political geography the U.S. and Russia appear to be just a couple of nation-states trying to come to terms." But, Luce opined, "Russia is not just a nation-state." And, in order to have any chance in opposing Russia, America also needed to see itself as more than a nation-state. Russia's ideology could not be beaten "by force or by bargains; it can only be opposed by another ideology. If we aspire to real equality with Russia in the years ahead, we must, like Russia, have higher claims than peace and broader claims than nationhood."[82] The one voice on the political scene he liked best was that of John Foster Dulles. According to Luce, Dulles recognized that American foreign policy needed a "balance to the Communist idea, what Hamilton called an 'active principle' on our side."[83] What Luce liked most about Dulles's internationalism was his desire to restore the "missionary sense" to foreign policy.

Dulles's gradual shift from ecumenical internationalist to cold warrior should be seen as one more way in which Oxford 1937 was transformed in its Atlantic crossing. In Dulles's work, to be sure, the support that Oxford delegates had given to the idea of international organization remained, with notable success. But Dulles's notion of a national faith completely undid the two methodological commitments of postliberal theology at Oxford. Whereas Niebuhr had retained a dialectical reading of nationalism but had let the ecclesiology slide, Dulles gave way on both emphases. Identifying Christianity as a national faith contradicted the dialectical theologians' stress on God's transcendence over all political entities. Even more so than Niebuhr, Dulles's work strikingly illustrated Richard Neuhaus's allegation that the ecclesiological deficit in American Christianity tends toward an "ecclesiological substitution of America for the Church through time."[84] The nation *was* the church for Dulles.

Conclusion

Neglected Genealogies

Much has changed since historian Jon Butler complained, rightly, in 2004 that scholars had given too little attention to religion's place in American life after 1870. As if to answer Butler's lament, a torrent of scholarship on religion has since left its mark, not just on fields such as U.S. foreign relations but on the entire disciplinary trajectories of history and international relations. And yet, there is a way in which Butler's memorable image of twentieth-century religion as a "jack-in-the-box" phenomenon still warrants attention. Because of a lack of consistent analysis of deeper continuities and coherences—of the way the sacred constantly interacts with the secular—religion can still tend to appear episodically, in parcels of surprise.[1] Despite welcome exceptions, in the works of Andrew Preston, David Hollinger, and Mark Edwards, for example, historians give most attention to jack-in-the-box moments: to missionary reformers and imperialists in the early twentieth century, to Wilsonian apologists in 1919, or Cold War Christian nationalists.[2]

The way to redress the jack-in-the-box tendency, as Butler suggests, is to better attend to the deeper fabric of religious continuity in twentieth-century America. Excavating sites of collective deliberation such as *The World Tomorrow* and Oxford 1937—which both fall temporally and logically between jack-in-the-box moments—offers a way of doing just that. Taking a thematic look at the period between the Great War and the Cold War, I conclude here by asking where Christian internationalists fit. Theirs was not merely a "religion" story; they interacted over the long term with several critical aspects of national and international life. Here I focus on four: race, empire, nation, and realism.

Empire

It has become a stale historiographical commonplace to locate Christian missionaries within the history of imperialism and to simply stop there, as if the imperatives of historical periodization licensed the termination of the narrative. As Andrew Preston demonstrated in his *Diplomatic History* survey, "If any topic in the history of American foreign relations has had its religious aspects thoroughly examined it is the role played by Christian missionaries in the turn to formal imperialism in the late nineteenth and early twentieth century."[3] The association goes back at least as far as Arthur Schlesinger Jr.'s classic essay on "The Missionary Enterprise and Theories of Imperialism" in the 1970s.[4] One problem with this simple relationship—aside from the unilateral modeling it implies—is that it artificially disjoins missionary imperialists in the 1900s from missionary anti-imperialists in the 1920s, even when they are the same people, happening to appear in two apparently distinct historical periods. Frank Ninkovich's lucid and otherwise very helpful textbook exemplifies such a division. Missionaries appear in the book's narrative of U.S. imperialism in China in the early twentieth century, yet they disappear when the subject of interwar "Progressive Anti-Imperialism" is taken up in a later chapter. In fact, missionaries such as Mott and Eddy, at work in China only ten years earlier, should be seen as figuring among the key constituencies of Progressive anti-imperialism.[5] The pattern, of course, extended beyond China: Sidney Gulick's opposition to the "white peril" of imperialism in the Pacific from the vantage point of missionary work in Japan and Samuel Guy Inman's critique of "imperialistic America" in the *Atlantic* following his work in Mexico are examples of a wider pattern.

Both the ecumenical and radical strands of interwar Christian internationalism fostered and promoted an anti-imperialist program; and both had direct links to the missionary enterprise. *The World Tomorrow*, with its didactic muckraking and its persistent attention to the use and abuse of the Monroe Doctrine, clearly formed a major component in the crystallization of anti-imperialist sentiment among sections of the American foreign policy public in the 1920s. As a home to Kirby Page, Sherwood Eddy, and Samuel Guy Inman, it functioned as a hub for the articulation of missionary anti-imperialism. The importance of *The World Tomorrow*—and the need for it to be recognized more widely in mainstream historical writing—can be seen obliquely, for example, in the near collision Robert David Johnson has with the periodical in his work on the interwar "Peace Progressives." When surveying what he identifies as an anti-imperialist intellectual alliance around Senator Borah and colleagues,

Johnson does not account in any coherent way for missionary or Christian internationalist elements. This is so despite the fact that Kirby Page worked as one of Borah's de facto publicists, and even though Johnson explores the work of the Committee on Militarism in Education and the Fellowship of Reconciliation, two of the principle organizations, filled with radical Protestant clergy and YMCA preachers, housed at *The World Tomorrow*.[6] The same is true for Mary Renda's and Virginia Williams's accounts of anti-imperialist thought in the 1920s. Both touch on missionary anti-imperialist Samuel Guy Inman, for example, yet both fail to place him in the wider missionary anti-imperialist milieu to be found in radical Christian internationalist networks such as that of *The World Tomorrow*. By atomizing the individual, the movement is rendered invisible.[7] Nor do any of the above accounts come near to identifying ecumenical world conferences such as Jerusalem 1928 as sites for the promulgation of an anti-imperialist critique. Yet the latter afforded a historically significant voice not only to white missionaries but also to Filipino, African American, and Asian Christians as well.

Not only would accounting for interwar Christian internationalism complicate simplistic renderings of missionaries as imperialists, it would also help explain, in part, the nature of anti-imperialist campaigning itself in the 1920s. Several of the major differences between the anti-imperialism of the 1890s and that of the 1920s reflected the character of Christian internationalism. Opposition to the colonization of the Philippines and Puerto Rico had largely revolved around arguments concerned with either preserving the racial purity of the United States or the exceptional nature of the American experiment.[8] Neither concern drove the arguments of Kirby Page or *The World Tomorrow*. Indeed, for them, the nature of anti-imperialist critique was inextricably tied to the question of racial justice. Nor can their anti-imperialism be seen as a simple extension of the anticolonialism of Woodrow Wilson's Fourteen Points, although the latter no doubt added to the ambient climate in which Christian internationalists made their arguments. There is no evidence either of direct citation or indirect influence of Wilson upon these radical Christian internationalists' 1920s anti-imperialism. Indeed, their view that race relations constituted international relations fundamentally distinguished them from Wilson. It also should be remembered that many of the instances of U.S. military intervention that Christian internationalists opposed, such as those in Haiti and Mexico, had commenced at the instigation of President Wilson. Rather, the anti-imperialism evident among *World Tomorrow* writers and among ecumenists at Jerusalem 1928 should be seen primarily as an intensification and radicalization of what had already begun to emerge in missionary analysis of world politics in the 1910s. All this is not to say that Christian internationalists were the only figures involved in making anti-imperialist arguments linked to racial justice in the 1920s. Exposés run by the *Nation* magazine of the U.S. occupation in Haiti in the early 1920s provide examples of a wider pattern.[9] And the tide of anti-imperialist opinion clearly rose high enough for U.S. imperialism to become a factor in both the 1928 and 1932 presidential elections. But historical scholarship has not done a thorough job of taking stock of the substance of interwar anti-imperialism in general, and still less of missionary anti-imperialism. The currents evident in *The World Tomorrow* and the early ecumenical conferences point to a movement that should be recognized as part of the history of anti-imperialism in both U.S. and international history.

Race

Interwar Christian internationalism should also be seen as an important factor in activism concerning racial politics. A raft of historians have recently called upon scholars to recognize the longer history of the civil rights movement, to get beyond a narrow focus on the "classical" period of 1950s nonviolent direct action. Glenda Gilmore's work locates the roots of the civil rights movement in Communist and popular front radicalism in the interwar period.[10] Jacquelyn Dowd Hall suggests that the social politics of the New Deal era need to be taken into account as a backdrop to the 1950s.[11] Alongside Communism and the New Deal, however, scholars also need to look to interwar Christian internationalism—both the radical and ecumenical strands.

The World Tomorrow had several strong connections with liberal, intellectual-led civil rights groups such as the NAACP and the National Urban League throughout the 1920s and 1930s. *The World Tomorrow* followed and published NAACP research reports, including the latest statistics on lynching and other releases on black poverty.[12] It profiled W. E. B. Du Bois and praised the success of *Crisis* magazine in its series of biographies of "Adventurous Americans," and NAACP secretary William Pickens served as contributing editor.[13] *The World Tomorrow* also enjoyed links and mutual endorsements from the National Urban League's *Opportunity* magazine. Charles S. Johnson, the editor of *Opportunity*, served on the Editorial Council of *The World Tomorrow*. Advertisements for *Opportunity* regularly appeared in *World Tomorrow* pages, and Johnson contributed a hopeful article on "Recent Gains in Race Relations" in the series "Recent Gains in American Civilization"—a series to which historian Charles Beard and philosopher John Dewey also contributed.[14] Johnson and

Opportunity wrote in to commend the journal: "We welcome *The World To-morrow* under the editorship of Kirby Page and Devere Allen. We can think of no magazine of its kind that is doing work with quite the same magnetism for results."[15]

The World Tomorrow's position on race was relatively simple: It castigated the Jim Crow South and applauded the rise of the "New Negro." In a June 1927 editorial, for example, Page railed against America's "complacency" in race relations. One well-meaning liberal minister from a southern state had informed him that he thought the South was "doing all it can for Negroes." "Doing all it can!" Page retorted: "With lynching still a frequent practice! With millions of colored people in economic peonage! With racial segregation and discrimination prevalent!"[16] *The World Tomorrow* supported the cultural and political mobilization of blacks in efforts such as unionist A. Philip Randolph's organization of the Pullman Porters' Brotherhood in 1925.[17] It published fiction from Zora Neale Hurston and opinion from Alain Locke.[18] But it was Wallace Thurman, a colleague of Langston Hughes in the literary scene of the Harlem Renaissance, who had the strongest connection to the journal. Not only did Thurman work in the offices of *The World Tomorrow* for several years, he published an evocative assessment of Harlem life in its pages and took out advertising space for his short-lived journal, *Fire: A Quarterly Devoted to Younger Negro Artists*.[19]

Connections between the community of *The World Tomorrow* and civil rights activists continued well after that journal's demise. The Fellowship of Reconciliation, which was the original founder of *The World Tomorrow* and the organization closest to the periodical throughout its life, provided much of the basis for the founding of the Congress on Racial Equality (CORE) and its Freedom Rides. Moreover, when *The World Tomorrow* ceased to publish, several of those formerly involved with it, such as John Nevin Sayre, A. J. Muste, and Harold Fey, launched *Fellowship* as a replacement. When, in the 1950s, *Fellowship* functioned as a site for the articulation of a nonviolent Christian approach to civil rights advocacy—featuring Martin Luther King Jr.—it was extending what had been a concern and practice of *The World Tomorrow* more than two decades earlier.

Not only the radical Christian internationalism of *The World Tomorrow* but also ecumenical internationalism should be seen as antecedents to the later civil rights movement. Successive ecumenical conferences operated as sites for a collective articulation of belief in racial equality precisely at a time when politically and culturally the opposite belief had acceptance in the highest places. In their cowritten book, *Drawing the Global Colour Line* (2008), Australian historians Marilyn Lake and Henry Reynolds identify a sense of "imminent loss" of white power and prestige pervading politics in "white men's countries" in the early twentieth century. Rightly, they demonstrate that white politicians and their supporters in Australia, America, and Africa predominantly responded by insisting that the "global color line" be drawn more distinctly—in stronger tones—by means of immigration and various other population laws. But alongside—and in counterpoint to—the probing narrative offered by Lake and Reynolds, we can see elements of ecumenical Protestantism working against the global color line.

A comparison of two trans-Pacific journeys illustrates this point. Lake and Reynolds give great prominence to narrating former Australian prime minister Billy Hughes's 1924 tour of the United States in which he sought to foment solidarity over the virtues of maintaining white racial purity. Only five years earlier, Hughes had colluded with Woodrow Wilson to block the Japanese proposal for a racial equality clause in the Treaty of Versailles.[20] Now, according to Hughes, both Australians and Americans, perched as they each were on the Pacific Rim, still faced the peril of "watering down the bloodstream of race."[21] As Lake and Reynolds show, the example of the White Australia policy was lauded by American academics calling for restrictions on Japanese landholding and immigration to the United States.[22]

Just two years after Hughes's jaunt, another journey based upon promoting entirely different ideas of race occurred. John R. Mott sailed south to speak to Australians about "The Race Problem." According to his biographer, Mott's address to the Australian Missionary Conference in Melbourne in 1926 represented his "definitive address" on race.[23] The national gathering of missionaries had only just resolved that "the only effective way of saving and developing the aboriginal natives of Australia is by a policy of strict segregation under religious influence."[24] Yet, Mott opposed segregation and race-based immigration restriction directly, arguing, "the Christian spirit is necessarily missionary and inclusive, and cannot be content to let any barriers permanently remain between man and man."[25] He ranged across many pragmatic reasons to promote racial inclusiveness, but, true to his evangelical heritage, he weighted his arguments most heavily on the Bible. In a conclusion rife with New Testament allusions, Mott insisted that the very person and work of Christ pointed toward racial unity: "By His Incarnation, by the all-inclusiveness, or comprehension of His gospel and Kingdom, by His breaking down the middle wall of partition on the Cross, opening the Kingdom of Heaven to all believers, by the world-wide sweep of His Pentecostal program, and by the witness and sacrificial working of His living body, the Church, He reveals Himself as the

One through whom the unity of the human race is discovered and realized."[26] Mott left his audience in Melbourne with a call to a crusade, an "uncompromising warfare against everything which experience shows tends to produce racial misunderstanding and strife . . . against all unjust or unequal racial arrangements, laws and practices."[27]

Mott constituted only one part of a greater collective argument for racial equality being promulgated internationally. Mott's colleague J. H. Oldham, the architect of the Oxford 1937 conference, insisted on the idea of racial equality in his *Christianity and the Race Problem* (1924).[28] He had earlier attacked the links between race and national mythology in his *World and the Gospel*, published in 1916.[29] His 1924 work, however, went further. Oldham reminded readers, quoting German historian-theologian Ernst Troeltsch, that Christianity, "in virtue of its belief in a personal God, possesses an idea of personality and individuality which has a metaphysical basis and is proof against every attack of naturalism or pessimism." Christians needed to insist on the "the truth of equality"; racial and national barriers had to be broken down, for "God has no favourites."[30]

A close look at the ecumenical world conferences makes clear that Oldham and Mott did not just make these arguments as individuals. In opposition to the official position of Billy Hughes and Woodrow Wilson, the Japanese-led group of student ecumenists at the World Student Christian Federation conference in Peking in 1922 resolved: "We, representing Christian students from all parts of the world, believe in the fundamental equality of all the races and nations of mankind and consider it part of our Christian vocation to express this reality in all our relationships."[31] Six years later, at the Jerusalem 1928 conference, the study group devoted to The Christian Mission in the Light of Race Conflict, led by Max Yergan and other black ecumenists, insisted that "any discrimination against human beings on the ground of race or color, any selfish exploitation and any oppression of man by man is . . . a denial of the teaching of Jesus."[32] All "Christian forces," they argued, were bound to work to "preserve the rights of peoples," and to foster "equality of social, political, and economic opportunity."[33] Again, at Oxford 1937—with the question seen in a new light against the Nazi ideologies of race and nation—delegates concurred in declaring that "against racial pride or race antagonism the Church must set its face as implacably as rebellion against God. . . . The deification of nation, race or class, or of political or cultural ideals is idolatry."[34]

Following the thread of ecumenical world conferences through to the post-1945 period further highlights the continuities between interwar Christian internationalism and 1950s civil rights agitation. Having been impressed by his experience of racial equality at Oxford 1937, African American intellectual Benjamin Mays remained in the World Council of Churches network, becoming elected to its Central Committee at Amsterdam 1948 for a five-year term. At the next ecumenical world conference, held at Evanston, Illinois, in 1954, only months after the *Brown v. Board of Education* Supreme Court decision, Mays was assigned the task of responding to the South African defense of segregation with a speech of his own at the conference. Echoing earlier arguments from W. E. B. Du Bois, Mays attributed the modern idea of race to the long history of imperialism: The practice of exploitation had produced the illusion of superiority.[35] No biblical or theological basis existed for white supremacy or segregation, Mays argued, "for it was Paul who declared . . . nineteen centuries ago that God made of one blood all nations of men."[36]

Nation

Inquiry into the nature and status of the nation—and correspondingly, the critique of and protest against nationalism—lay at the conceptual center of interwar Christian internationalists' collective project. Engaging with this question enmeshed Christian internationalists in a wider global intellectual phenomenon. They asked their questions within a dynamic process whereby crises in global politics correlated with crises in international thought, provoking new and competing visions of world order. Wilsonian, Socialist, feminist, Pan-Islamist, and Pan-Asian internationalisms each emerged, proffering their visions of international or regional order. Of course, no necessary contradiction existed between the rise of nationalisms and internationalisms; often they developed in symbiotic partnership, especially in the case of the Wilsonian variety in the United States.

Both nationalism and internationalism responded to what we might consider (using terms adapted from Cemil Aydin) the "long crisis of normative legitimacy" in world order.[37] The delegitimizing of Western imperialism in the late nineteenth and early twentieth century grew into a crisis in the very fabric of international life in the early to mid century. Such an atmosphere of crisis and flux provided the conditions in which Christian internationalists attended to the deeper questions of nationhood and nationalism. For some, such as Kirby Page and others in the *World Tomorrow* community, the crisis shocked them into adopting an oppositional relationship to the dominant national myth of Christian America as a benevolent presence in world affairs. Combining revisionist history, anti-imperialism, and fresh attention to Jesus's response to first-century global politics, they saw the nationalism of large imperial powers such as the United States as a dangerous and alternative religion to Christianity. For others in the emerging ecumenical movement, the crisis caused them to freshly historicize nationalism. "It is only because we had grown up in a world where the doctrine of unfettered national sovereignty was accepted as an axiom," wrote the authors of the International Relations report at the ecumenical "COPEC" meeting in Britain in 1924—an intellectual precursor to Stockholm 1925—"that we failed to realize its moral perverseness and intellectual absurdity till it brought Europe clattering down about our ears."[38] For the study section on Church and Community at Oxford 1937, modernity had aggravated the problem even further. Disintegration of traditional modes of loyalty and community in modern life led, they argued, to false attempts at reintegration, such as modern nationalism. When, as a result, people elevated the nation to a position of "supreme good," they dangerously created "a false sacred, a false God," which only served to add "demonic power to the unredeemed passions of men."[39]

Clearly then, with the exception of John Foster Dulles, the subjects examined in this book are not to be seen primarily as purveyors of American nationalism and exceptionalism. Historians' long-standing focus on religion's role in structuring and nurturing American nationalist ideology—a project that has spanned generations of scholars from Sacvan Bercovitch and E. L. Tuveson to the present—has resulted in a tendency to merely amass further examples of the trend. Under the composite weight of such examples, the relationship between Protestantism and nationalism consequently takes on the appearance of being linear, permanent, and irrevocable. By contrast, the antinationalism of the Christian internationalists discussed in this book reveals an alternative structure of thinking not accounted for in that master narrative. In their critique of all nationalisms, including the American variety, interwar Christian internationalists illustrate what Daniel Rodgers argues was an "intellectual shift, a sense of complicity within the historical forces larger than the United States: a suspension of confidence in the particular dispensation of the United States from the fate of other nations."[40] Alongside their engagement with the politics of anti-imperialism and racial equality seen above, their critique of nationalism and exceptionalism created a third link connecting Christian internationalists to a wider intellectual and political landscape.

Realism

Recovering interwar Christian internationalism also undoes the jack-in-the-box aura surrounding two of the most prominent individuals to emerge from the movement midcentury, John Foster Dulles and Reinhold Niebuhr. In the very moment that international historian Glenda Sluga rightly identifies as the "apogee of internationalism," World War II and its aftermath, both Dulles and Niebuhr brought Christian internationalism to its greatest influence.[41] Dulles crystallized and marshalled ecumenical Protestant opinion into a vital electoral force in American public debate over international organization and, in doing so, helped forge the new centrist, internationalist political consensus that framed American foreign relations for decades. American public response to Dumbarton Oaks and San Francisco would likely have taken on a very different complexion had not the Dulles Commission managed to cobble together the strands of anti-imperialism, legalism, and realism circulating in the powerful mainline Protestant establishment in 1944–1945. Indeed, Dulles's essential success in doing so further cemented mainline Protestantism's social power and establishment status—as their mutual admiration with Truman shows.

Meanwhile, Reinhold Niebuhr emerged as the country's preeminent public theologian, a Cold War intellectual whose realism was so pervasive that it "provided a historical basis and rationale for the tone, the outlook, the unsaid, and often unconscious assumptions of this period."[42] Still employed at Union Theological Seminary, and having once written for *The World Tomorrow* and the Fellowship of Socialist Christians, Niebuhr found himself at different times appointed to George Kennan's long-range strategic research center, the Council on Foreign Relations, as well as U.S. delegations to the United Nations Educational Scientific and Cultural Organization.[43] Hans Morgenthau, perhaps the country's most significant theorist of realism in international relations, labeled Niebuhr the "greatest living political philosopher of America."[44]

Reframing these individuals within the context of interwar Christian internationalism allows us better to see the origins and character of their seemingly prodigious contributions. In particular, Niebuhr's prescient critique of American exceptionalism and national self-idolatry during the early Cold War should be seen as having its roots in the discursive arenas and networks of interwar Christian internationalism—not least in the radicalism of *The World Tomorrow* and the dialectical political theology of the ecumenical movement of Oxford 1937. In both enterprises, Niebuhr played a major and influential role. But, importantly, as has been demonstrated, the influence was mutual; his was not the only voice and it cannot be properly heard in isolation. In the extraordinary revival of contemporary interest in Niebuhr in the 2000s, many have rightly pointed to Niebuhr as a figurehead in an emerging call for a humble, or "ethical" realism.[45] But on this very point, Niebuhr needs to be seen not as a lone individual calling for national humility but as one exponent of a wider movement that, for decades, made it a central task to critique and puncture the pretensions of all nationalisms, including America's.

Similarly, Niebuhr's realism—not merely his tolerance for war, but his theoretical prioritizing of political over legal factors in international life—is rightly acknowledged as seminal in mid-twentieth-century international thought in the United States. As Mark Mazower notes in his landmark *Governing the World*, Niebuhr's realism "spilled over" from theology into academia and the world of policy as part of a wider pattern in which "the 1940s saw theologians exert unparalleled authority in public debate about the direction of American foreign policy."[46] Tellingly, in this same passage, Mazower goes on to identify the currents of German realism crossing the Atlantic in the 1930s as a *separate* source of realism's rise—one, in fact, which beat Niebuhr and the 1940s American theologians to it. Leaving aside the fact that Morgenthau expressed great indebtedness to Niebuhr for the character of his realism (which is in itself significant) the Oxford 1937 conference shows that 1940s theologians like Niebuhr were not separate but were actually conduits for the transfer of the very kind of Continental realism Mazower identifies. At Oxford 1937 they encountered and engaged with German and Swiss critiques of Anglophone rationalism and legalism, and in the work of Huber and others they saw the necessity of prioritizing the political and social over the legal. Realism's rise in postwar America should be seen as shaped in significant part by the Christian internationalism of the prior two decades.

And yet, the story is not simply linear or teleological. While Dulles's and Niebuhr's output represented the high-water mark of Christian internationalism's public prominence, their contributions ultimately aided the containment of the movement's critical power. Precisely by absorbing and claiming the rhetorical and intellectual contours of interwar Christian internationalism in service of their advocacy for 1940s *American* internationalism, they subverted the former's basal commitments. Both, ultimately, in different ways, made imperialism safer for American Protestants. Dulles, as Richard Immerman has shown, never *named* the emergent Cold War American empire as an empire, but nonetheless positioned the United States as "the 'group authority' for the symbolically named 'Free World,' making the rules, insisting that they be followed, and guarding against all trespassers by exercising its power, its spiritual, ideological, economic, and most important, military power."[47] Such a role for America—as guardian of international order—sprang, for Dulles, "from an almost parental desire to protect his offspring."[48] On the other hand, Niebuhr— as his writings make plain—acknowledged the rhetorical significance of anti-imperialism. He retained the term well into the Cold War, aptly naming that conflict as a battle between rival anti-imperialist imperialisms.[49] But his use of the category, even as early as the 1930s, tended toward abstraction and toward a consideration of conceptual moral and cultural dilemmas rather than toward protest over concrete spatial and political formations.[50] When in World War II and afterward he identified U.S. imperialism as merely the most preferable imperialism on offer, he effectively made imperialism something that was everywhere and nowhere at all, containing the critical power of the term by its very adoption.[51]

Finally, in connecting the state to Christian internationalist values, both Niebuhr and Dulles—particularly the latter—helped foster the very deification of the nation they had once formally opposed. In their respective ways, both anointed the state as a divine servant, and made, not merely empire, but civil religion too, safer for Protestants. Each figure's ecumenical internationalism was, as has been shown, distinctly churchless. With ecumenism shorn of ecclesiology, the nation took the place of the church and became guardian of the *ecumene*. Precisely when the American state sought legitimising narratives with which to frame its new projection of power in the world, Dulles and Niebuhr, wittingly or not, supplied the goods. Their disengagement of Protestant internationalist ideas from the narratives, practices, and enterprises in which they were originally embedded enabled the state to appropriate them, claiming the mantle of bearer of Christian values "in the service of a set of relations acclimatized to aggression."[52]

A Lost Civilization?

Having begun with the jack-in-the-box metaphor, I close this discussion with another image. It comes from a reviewer of Graeme Smith's work on Oxford 1937, who used the phrase "lost civilization" to describe the world of the Oxford conference. Oxford 1937 held intrinsic fascination, the reviewer suggested, because it was foreign and forgotten to the religious landscape of the late twentieth and early twenty-first centuries.[53] His image poses the question of whether the significance of interwar Christian internationalism lay in its alien character relative to the present day or in its contributions to the wider world. The answer, of course, is a combination of both. *The World Tomorrow* and Oxford 1937 did not merely flourish and die within their own self-enclosed, isolated realities. Interwar Christian internationalists engaged with and left their mark on four vital aspects of twentieth-century international life—on the politics of race, empire, nation, and realism, as this book has attempted to show.

Yet, in another way, their legacies do come to us as fragments of a lost civilization. The sense of lostness is more than nostalgia for a buzzing New York-based Christian Left periodical making headlines for its anti-imperialist surveys, or for the *communitas* experienced by steamship-traveling delegates sharing sacraments in other tongues at world conferences. The gulf that separates us from their civilization is intellectual and theological, as well as cultural. From this side of the 1950s, when God and Nation were forcefully rejoined in American political culture, the relative distance forged and maintained between the two in the interwar moment makes it an alien place indeed.[54]

Notes

Introduction: Missionaries, Mainliners, and the Making of a Movement

1. Sherwood Eddy, "Why Missions?," *The World Tomorrow*, January 1928, 18.

2. Eddy, "Why Missions?," 18.

3. John R. Mott, "Expectations," Address Delivered at the Meeting of the International Missionary Council, in *Addresses and Other Records*, vol. 8 of *Report of the Meeting of the International Missionary Council at Jerusalem, March 24–April 8, 1928* (London: Oxford University Press, 1928), 25.

4. Cited in Robert E. Speer, *The Finality of Jesus Christ* (Fleming H. Revell Company, 1933), 315.

5. W. A. Visser 't Hooft, "The 'Christian' West," in *God Speaks to This Generation: Being Some of the Addresses Delivered at a Conference on International and Missionary Questions, Birmingham, 1st to 7th January, 1937* (London: SCM Press, 1937), 41.

6. See, for example, Eddy, "The New Korea: A Development," *Churchman*, December 23, 1922, 17, copy in George Sherwood Eddy Papers, Record Group No. 32, Special Collections, Yale Divinity School Library (hereafter cited as Eddy Papers), Box 6, Folder 106; Eddy, "The Worst Government in the World," *Christian Century*, October 22, 1925, 1302–4; Eddy, "The New Map of Europe," in *The Christian Advocate*, December 24, 1925, 1578–80. For *New York Times* coverage of Eddy's views, see "Amazing Renaissance Is Now Sweeping All Asia," *New York Times*, November 23, 1913, SM14.

7. For Eddy's account of the seminar, see Sherwood Eddy, *A Pilgrimage of Ideas: Or the Re-education of Sherwood Eddy* (New York: Farrar & Rinehart, 1934), 183–99; and Sherwood Eddy, *Eighty Adventurous Years: An Autobiography* (New York: Harper and Brothers), 128–51. See also Rick L. Nutt, *The Whole Gospel for the Whole World: Sherwood Eddy and the American Protestant Mission* (Macon, Ga.: Mercer University Press, 1997), 201–17.

8. Eddy, *Eighty Adventurous Years*, 128.

9. F. Ernest Johnson, untitled manuscript, in Eddy Papers, Box 21, 6.

10. "A Traveling Seminar," *Christian Century*, September 23, 1926, 1159.

11. "An Announcement: Study Pilgrimage to Europe," *The World Tomorrow*, January 1927, 39.

12. "A Traveling Seminar," *Christian Century*, September 23, 1926, 1159.

13. See Eddy, *Pilgrimage of Ideas*, 184. "Seminars Below the Rio Grande," *The World Tomorrow*, April 19, 1933, 384.

14. Ben Cherrington's name is in the guestbook for 1921, held in Box 23, Eddy Papers. On Cherrington, see "Culture Division," *Time*, August 8, 1938, accessed June 27, 2013,www.time.com /time/magazine/article/0,9171,931422,00.html; and Justin Hart, *Empire of Ideas: The Origins of Public Diplomacy and the Transformation of U.S. Foreign Policy* (Oxford: Oxford University Press, 2013), 24.

15. Reinhold Niebuhr, *Leaves from the Notebook of a Tamed Cynic* (1929; repr., Cleveland, Ohio: Meridian, 1964), 67–68.

16. James T. Shotwell, "Introduction," in *The Study of International Relations in the United States; Survey for 1934*, ed. Edith E. Ware and James T. Shotwell (New York: Columbia University Press, 1934). See also Brian C. Schmidt, *The Political Discourse of Anarchy: A Disciplinary History of International Relations* (Albany, N.Y.: State University of New York Press, 1998). Akira Iriye, *The Globalizing of America, 1913–1945*, vol. 3 of *The Cambridge History of American Foreign Relations* (Cambridge: Cambridge University Press, 1993), 105. William C. Olson, "The Growth of a Discipline," in *International Politics, 1919–1969*, ed. Brian Porter (London: Oxford University Press, 1972), 3–29.

17. Harry Emerson Fosdick in *Christian Century*, January 19, 1928. Cited in Kirby Page, *National Defense: A Study of the Origins, Results and Prevention of War* (New York: Farrar & Rinehart, 1931), 204.

18. David R. Swartz, *Moral Minority: The Evangelical Left in an Age of Conservatism* (Philadelphia: University of Pennsylvania Press, 2012), is one such welcome exception. For the wider pattern, see Richard M. Gamble, *The War for Righteousness: Progressive Christianity, the Great War, and the Rise of the Messianic Nation* (Wilmington, Del.: ISI Books, 2003); John Fousek, *To Lead the Free World: American Nationalism and the Cultural Roots of the Cold War* (Chapel Hill: University of North Carolina Press, 2000); and Dianne Kirby, *Religion and the Cold War* (Houndmills, Basingstoke, Hampshire: Palgrave, 2003). William Inboden explores and applauds the role that Christian values played in the framing of U.S. foreign policy goals in the same period in *Religion and American Foreign Policy, 1945–1960: The Soul of Containment* (Cambridge: Cambridge University Press, 2008).

19. I am drawing here on Merold Westphal's interpretation of Marx in *Suspicion and Faith: The Religious Uses of Modern Atheism* (Grand Rapids, Mich.: W.B. Eerdmans, 1993), 143.

20. About the "white peril," see G. Sherwood Eddy, "Present Day Social and Intellectual Unrest," Address to the Student Volunteer Movement, in *Christian Students and World Problems*, ed. Milton T. Stauffer (New York: Student Volunteer Movement for Foreign Missions, 1924), iii. Cited in Rick L. Nutt, *The Whole Gospel for the Whole World: Sherwood Eddy and the American Protestant Mission* (Macon, Ga.: Mercer University Press, 1997), 189. See also Sidney L. Gulick, *The White Peril in the Far East: An Interpretation of the Significance of the Russo-Japanese War* (New York: F. H. Revell Company, 1905).

21. Immanuel Kant, "Toward Perpetual Peace," in *Toward Perpetual Peace and Other Writings on Politics, Peace, and History*, ed. Pauline Kleingeld (New Haven, Conn.: Yale University Press, 2006).

22. Compare W. E. B. Du Bois, on the global dimensions of the "problem of the color line" in *The Souls of Black Folk* (New York: New American Library, 1903), and Thomas Knock's discussion of "conservative internationalists" in *To End All Wars: Woodrow Wilson and the Quest for a New World Order* (New York: Oxford University Press, 1992). Glenda Sluga's *Internationalism in the Age of Nationalism* (Philadelphia: University of Pennsylvania Press, 2013) also surveys an important racially focused alternative to legalism in "The International Turn," 11–44.

23. For examples of the use of the term in the interwar period, see William Pierson Merrill, *Christian Internationalism* (New York: Macmillan, 1919); Sidney L. Gulick, "The Foreign Policies of the United States and the Success of Foreign Missions," in *The Missionary Outlook in the Light of the War*, ed. The Committee on the War and the Religious Outlook [Federal Council of Churches of

Christ in America] (New York: Association Press, 1920), 280–91, 288. See also the "Message" of the Universal Christian Conference on Life and Work, Stockholm, 1925, which claimed church delegates from around the world had "set forth the guiding principles of a Christian Internationalism." This Message, discussed further in chapter 4 of this volume, is reprinted in *The Ecumenical Movement: An Anthology of Key Texts and Voices*, ed. Michael Kinnamon and Brian E. Cope (Geneva: WCC Publications, 1997), 265–67. See also Jun Xing, "Christian Internationalism in the Crucible: 1931–1935," in *Baptized in the Fire of Revolution: The American Social Gospel and the YMCA in China, 1919–1937* (Bethlehem, Penn.: Lehigh University Press, 1996), 125–51; and Heather A. Warren, *Theologians of a New World Order: Reinhold Niebuhr and the Christian Realists* (New York: Oxford University Press, 1997), 71.

24. E. B. Sweeney, "Nationalism and Internationalism through the Churches: The Catholic Church and the Promotion of Peace Attitudes," *Journal of Educational Sociology* 10, no. 6 (February 1937): 341–42.

25. See David A. Hollinger, *After Cloven Tongues of Fire: Protestant Liberalism in Modern American History* (Princeton, N.J.: Princeton University Press, 2013); David Sehat, *The Myth of American Religious Freedom* (Oxford: Oxford University Press, 2011); Elesha J. Coffman, *The Christian Century and the Rise of the Protestant Mainline* (New York: Oxford University Press, 2013). William Hutchison's earlier discussion of the Protestant establishment is indispensable: William R. Hutchison, ed., *Between the Times: The Travail of the Protestant Establishment in America, 1900–1960* (Cambridge: Cambridge University Press, 1989).

26. Markku Ruotsila, *The Origins of Christian Anti-Internationalism: Conservative Evangelicals and the League of Nations* (Washington, D.C.: Georgetown University Press, 2008).

27. As well as Ruotsila, see the early chapters of Timothy P. Weber, *On the Road to Armageddon: How Evangelicals Became Israel's Best Friend* (Grand Rapids, Mich.: Baker Academic, 2004), for an introduction to early twentieth-century dispensationalist interpretations of world affairs.

28. Swartz, *Moral Minority*.

29. Fred Halliday, "Three Concepts of Internationalism," *International Affairs* 64 (1988): 187.

30. Sluga, *Internationalism in the age of Nationalism*, 4.

31. Micheline Ishay, *Internationalism and Its Betrayal* (Minneapolis: University of Minnesota Press, 1995), xxi.

32. Manfred Jonas in "Internationalism as a Current in the Peace Movement: A Symposium," in *Peace Movements in America*, ed. Charles Chatfield (New York: Schocken Books, 1973), 176.

33. Sondra R. Herman, *Eleven against War: Studies in American Internationalist Thought, 1898–1921* (Stanford, Calif.: Hoover Institution Press, Stanford University, 1969).

34. Sondra Herman in "Internationalism as a Current in the Peace Movement: A Symposium," 172.

35. See, for example, Warren F. Kuehl, *Seeking World Order: The United States and International Organization to 1920* (Nashville, Tenn.: Vanderbilt University Press, 1969), and *Keeping the Covenant: American Internationalists and the League of Nations, 1920–1939* (Kent, Ohio: Kent State University Press, 1997).

36. Richard H. Pells, *Radical Visions and American Dreams: Culture and Social Thought in the Depression Years* (New York: Harper & Row, 1973).

37. Pells, *Radical Visions and American Dreams*, 148–50.

38. This argument has been made about the treatment of interwar peace movements more generally by Cecelia Lynch in *Beyond Appeasement: Interpreting Interwar Peace Movements in World Politics* (Ithaca: Cornell University Press, 1999), and by David Hollinger in "The Realist–Pacifist Summit Meeting of March 1942 and the Political Reorientation of Ecumenical Protestantism in the United States," *Church History* 79 (2010): 654–77.

39. Donald B. Meyer, *The Protestant Search for Political Realism, 1919–1941*, 2nd ed. (Middletown, Conn.: Wesleyan University Press, 1988). Meyer's unwillingness to be seen as "recommending" Niebuhr's theology, as critics had earlier charged, was signaled in his introduction to this second edition, xviii.

40. Meyer, *The Protestant Search for Political Realism*, 260–61, and chap. 14.

41. Heather A. Warren, *Theologians of a New World Order: Reinhold Niebuhr and the Christian Realists* (New York: Oxford University Press, 1997). Mark Thomas Edwards, *The Right of the Protestant Left: God's Totalitarianism* (New York: Palgrave Macmillan, 2012); and Edwards, " 'God Has Chosen Us': Re-Membering Christian Realism, Rescuing Christendom, and the Contest of Responsibilities during the Cold War," *Diplomatic History* 33 (2009): 67–94.

42. Edwards, *The Right of the Protestant Left*, 4.

43. These earlier histories include Charles Chatfield, *For Peace and Justice: Pacifism in America 1914–1941* (Knoxville: University of Tennessee Press, 1971); *Kirby Page and the Social Gospel: An Anthology*, ed. Charles Chatfield and Charles DeBenedetti (New York: Garland, 1976); and *Devere Allen: Life and Writings*, ed. Charles Chatfield (New York: Garland, 1976).

44. Kirby Page, *Kirby Page, Social Evangelist: The Autobiography of a 20th Century Prophet for Peace*, ed. Harold E. Fey (Nyack, N.Y.: Fellowship Press, 1975), 116.

45. David Shannon, *The Socialist Party of America* (New York: Macmillan, 1936), 191.

46. Robert Moats Miller, *American Protestantism and Social Issues, 1919–1939* (Chapel Hill: University of North Carolina Press, 1958), 90.

47. Charles Chatfield and Charles DeBenedetti, "Introduction," in *Kirby Page and the Social Gospel: An Anthology*, 14.

48. Charles Chatfield, "The Life of Devere Allen," in *Devere Allen: Life and Writings*, 28.

49. Martin E. Marty, *The Noise of Conflict, 1919–1941*, vol. 2 of *Modern American Religion*, (Chicago: University of Chicago Press, 1991), 384.

50. U.S. Department of the Treasury, "History of 'In God We Trust'," accessed August 5, 2011,http://www.treasury.gov/about/education/Pages/in-god-we-trust.aspx.

51. I am adapting categories here from Charles Taylor, *Modern Social Imaginaries* (Durham, N.C.: Duke University Press, 2004), 23–24.

52. See Gamble, *The War for Righteousness*; Ruotsila, *The Origins of Christian Anti-Internationalism*.

53. Jerry Falwell, *Listen, America!* (Garden City, N.Y.: Doubleday, 1980); Sacvan Bercovitch, *The American Jeremiad* (Madison: University of Wisconsin Press, 1978).

54. See the Pew Forum on Religion and Public Life, "Many Americans Uneasy with Mix of Religion and Politics," accessed August 5, 2011, http://pewforum.org/Politics-and-Elections/Many-Americans-Uneasy-with-Mix-of-Religion-and-Politics.aspx. Based on a poll taken on August 24, 2006, Pew reports that in all demographic groups aside from those identifying as "seculars," the majority of Americans (67% overall) view America as a "Christian nation."

55. David A. Hollinger, "After Cloven Tongues of Fire: Ecumenical Protestantism and the Modern American Encounter with Diversity," *Journal of American History* 98, no. 1 (June 2011): 21–48.

56. Emil Brunner, "The Church as a Present-Day Problem and Task," Address to the Swiss Pastor's Union, May 28, 1934, cited in Graeme Smith, *Oxford 1937: The Universal Christian Council for Life and Work Conference* (Frankfurt: Peter Lang, 2004), 195.

57. On the idea of religion creating distance from a culture rather than complicity in the violence of that culture, see Miroslav Volf, "Distance and Belonging," in *Exclusion and Embrace: A Theological Exploration of Identity, Otherness, and Reconciliation* (Nashville, Tenn.: Abingdon Press, 1996), 35–55.

58. Dana L. Robert, "The First Globalization: The Internationalization of the Protestant Missionary Movement between the World Wars," *International Bulletin of Missionary Research* 26 (2002): 50.

59. On Wilson's views on race relations, see Erez Manela, *The Wilsonian Moment: Self-Determination and the International Origins of Anticolonial Nationalism* (Oxford: Oxford University Press, 2007).

60. Walter Rauschenbusch, *The Social Principles of Jesus*, reprinted in *The Social Gospel in America, 1870–1920: Gladden, Ely, Rauschenbusch*, ed. Robert T. Handy (New York: Oxford University Press, 1966), 375.

61. Walter Rauschenbusch, *A Theology for the Social Gospel*, in *A Rauschenbusch Reader*, ed. Benson Y. Landis (New York: Harper and Brothers, 1957), 106.

62. Josiah Strong, *Our Country: Its Possible Future and Present Crisis* (New York: Baker and Taylor, 1885), 174, 173.

63. Washington Gladden, *The Nation and the Kingdom*, reprinted in *The Social Gospel in America, 1870–1920*, 145–46.

64. Rauschenbusch, *A Theology for the Social Gospel*, 106. "Seething yellow flocks" is from a fundraising letter for the German Department at Rochester Seminary, cited in Gary Dorrien, *Social Ethics in the Making: Interpreting an American Tradition* (Chichester, UK: Wiley-Blackwell, 2009), 93.

65. George C. Herring is right to identify post–World War I internationalism as, on the whole, strikingly Eurocentric and North Atlantic in focus. See *From Colony to Superpower: U.S. Foreign Relations Since 1776* (New York: Oxford University Press, 2008), 436. Sluga's *Internationalism in the Age of Nationalism* highlights exceptions to such Eurocentrism in her coverage of the Universal Races Congress of 1911, see 28–30.

66. On the institute, see Tomoko Akami, *Internationalizing the Pacific: The United States, Japan, and the Institute of Pacific Relations in War and Peace, 1919–45* (London: Routledge, 2003).

67. The following section on missiological crisis is adapted, with the permission of Cambridge University Press, from Michael G. Thompson, "Sherwood Eddy, the missionary enterprise, and the rise of Christian internationalism in 1920s America." *Modern Intellectual History* 12, no. 1 (2015): 65–93.

68. Charles W. Forman, "A History of Foreign Mission Theory in America," in *American Missions in Bicentennial Perspective: Papers Presented at the Fourth Annual Meeting of the American Society of Missiology at Trinity Evangelical Divinity School, Deerfield, Illinois, June 18–20, 1976*, ed. R. P. Beaver and Catherine L. Albanese (South Pasadena, Calif.: William Carey Library, 1977), 69–137; William R. Hutchison, *Errand to the World: American Protestant Thought and Foreign Missions* (Chicago: University of Chicago Press, 1987); Grant Wacker, "Second Thoughts on the Great Commission: Liberal Protestants and Foreign Missions, 1890–1940," in *Earthen Vessels: American Evangelicals and Foreign Missions, 1880–1980*, ed. Joel A. Carpenter and Wilbert R. Shenk (Grand Rapids, Mich.: W. B. Eerdmans, 1990), 281–300.

69. William E. Hocking, ed., *Re-thinking Missions: A Laymen's Inquiry after One Hundred Years* (New York: Harper & Bros., 1932). On Rockefeller and Hocking, see Hutchison, *Errand*, 148–49, 158–64.

70. Grant Wacker, "Pearl S. Buck and the Waning of the Missionary Impulse," *Church History* 72, no. 4 (2003): 852–74.

71. On Machen's criticisms, see Hutchison, *Errand*, 173–75.

72. Hutchison rightly points out that the most important debates occurred between the liberal Hocking end of the spectrum and the middle ground of Speer. Hutchison, *Errand*, 175. Robert E. Speer, *The Finality of Jesus Christ* (New York: Fleming H. Revell, 1933), 372.

73. Forman, "A History of Foreign Mission Theory in America," 98.

74. All quotations here are from the King James version of the Bible. Another text commonly cited was Acts 17:26, in which the Apostle Paul argues to listeners in Athens that God "hath made of one blood all nations of men."

75. Joseph H. Oldham, *The World and the Gospel* (London: United Council for Missionary Education, 1916) and *Christianity and the Race Problem* (London: Student Christian Movement, 1924).

76. Robert E. Speer, *Of One Blood: A Short Study of the Race Problem* (New York: Council of Women for Home Missions and Missionary Education Movement of the United States and Canada, 1924). On Lothrop Stoddard, see John F. Piper, *Robert E. Speer: Prophet of the American Church* (Louisville, Ky.: Geneva Press, 2000), 339.

77. Cited in Philip Potter and Thomas Wieser, *Seeking and Serving the Truth: The First Hundred Years of the World Student Christian Federation* (Geneva: WCC Publications, 1997), 70. On Japanese influence, see Michael Parker, *The Kingdom of Character: The Student Volunteer Movement for Foreign Missions, 1886–1926* (Lanham, Md.: American Society of Missiology, 1998), 157. The Peking Resolutions were likely a deliberate redressing of U.S. President Woodrow Wilson's and Australian Prime Minister Billy Hughes's rejection of the proposed Japanese-authored racial equality clause in the treaty deliberations at Versailles. On this rejection, well known at the time, see N. K. A. Meaney, *Australia and World Crisis, 1914–1923*, vol. 2 of *History of Australian Defence and Foreign Policy 1901–23* (Sydney: Sydney University Press, 2009), 376–78.

78. International Missionary Council, "Statement Adopted by the Council: Racial Relationships," in *The Christian Mission in the Light of Race Conflict*, vol. 4 of *Report of the Jerusalem Meeting of the International Missionary Council, March 24th–April 8th, 1928*, (London: Oxford University Press, 1928), 237–45, 237, 238.

79. This was the implication of Sherwood Eddy, *The New Era in Asia* (New York: Missionary Education Movement of the United States and Canada, 1913), for example. As Forman notes, nineteenth-century mission theory was characterized by an "appreciation for American life and the desire to reproduce it everywhere." Forman, "A History of Foreign Mission Theory in America," 97.

80. Daniel Johnson Fleming, *Whither Bound in Missions* (New York: Association Press, 1925), 47. On Fleming's missionary internationalism, see Robert, "The First Globalization."

81. Volf, *Exclusion and Embrace*, 29.

1. Anti-imperialism for Jesus

1. Kirby Page, *Kirby Page, Social Evangelist: The Autobiography of a 20th Century Prophet for Peace*, ed. Harold E. Fey (Nyack, N.Y.: Fellowship Press, 1975), 23.

2. Basil Matthews, *John R. Mott: World Citizen* (New York: Harper & Brothers, 1934), 436. See also Charles H. Hopkins, *John R. Mott, 1865–1955: A Biography* (Grand Rapids, Mich.: Eerdmans, 1979).

3. For "bullfighters," see David A. Hollinger, "William James, Ecumenical Protestantism, and the Dynamics of Secularization," in Martin Halliwell and Joel D. S. Rasmussen, eds., *William James and the Transatlantic Conversation* (Oxford: Oxford University Press, 2014): 31–47, 42.

4. Vanderbilt University's Oscar E. Brown remarked in 1914 that there were six global powers in the world: "The British Empire, the Russian Empire, the Japanese Empire, the Chinese Republic, the American Republic, and the Young Men's Christian Association." Cited in Emily S. Rosenberg, *Spreading the American Dream: American Economic and Cultural Expansion, 1890–1945* (New York: Hill and Wang, 1982), 28.

5. Andrew Preston, *Sword of the Spirit, Shield of Faith: Religion in American War and Diplomacy* (New York: Alfred A. Knopf, 2012), 298.

6. On the wider pattern of applying muckraking journalism to foreign affairs in the 1920s, see Warren I. Cohen, *Empire without Tears: America's Foreign Relations, 1921–1933* (Philadelphia: Temple University Press, 1987), 70.

7. Page, *Social Evangelist*, 26.

8. Eddy, *The Right to Fight*, cited in "Personal Testimony," in Sherwood Eddy and Kirby Page, *The Abolition of War: The Case against War and Questions and Answers Concerning War*, Christianity and World Problems Series, no. 7 (New York: Doubleday, Doran and Co., 1924), 14.

9. Eddy, "Personal Testimony," 16. See also later his appeal to Hegelian teleology in Sherwood Eddy, *Everybody's World* (London: Religious Tract Society, 1920), 12.

10. Page, *Social Evangelist*, 26.

11. For a helpful introduction to Alexander Campbell and the Disciples of Christ's primitivism, see Nathan O. Hatch, *The Democratization of American Christianity* (New Haven: Yale University Press, 1989), 167–68.

12. Page, *Social Evangelist*, 28.

13. Page, *Social Evangelist*, 33.

14. For example, one pamphlet advertised Sherwood Eddy as "World Traveler–Religious Statesman–Author–Speaker." See "University of North Carolina Y.M.C.A. Presents Sherwood Eddy in Six Public Addresses," in Box 6, Folder 114, George Sherwood Eddy Papers (Record Group No 32) Special Collections, Yale Divinity School Library, (hereafter cited as "Eddy Papers").

15. On Eddy's inheritance deriving from his father's earlier railway interests, see Rick L. Nutt, *The Whole Gospel for the Whole World: Sherwood Eddy and the American Protestant Mission* (Macon, Ga.: Mercer University Press, 1997), 11.

16. Page calculated that over his lifetime he received amounts totaling around $100,000 from Eddy. Page, *Social Evangelist*, 150.

17. Devere Allen, "The Irrepressible Pamphleteers," *The World Tomorrow*, December 1926, 272–73.

18. On the republication of Moorfield Storey and Marcial P. Lichauco's *The Philippines and the United States*, see Page, *Social Evangelist*, 87. The original text was Moorfield Storey and Marcial P. Lichauco, *The Conquest of the Philippines by the United States, 1898–1925* (New York: G.P. Putnam's Sons, 1926). On petition for Russian recognition, see, for example, the open letter to President Coolidge, published as "For Russian Recognition" in *The World Tomorrow*, October 1926, 180.

19. Kirby Page, *The Sword or the Cross: An Examination of War in the Light of Jesus' Way of Life* (New York: Doran, 1921); *Christianity and Economic Problems, Facts, Principles, Programs; A Discussion Group Text-Book* (New York: Association Press, 1922); and *Something More: A Consideration of the Vast, Undeveloped Resources of Life* (New York: Association Press, 1920).

20. Page, *Social Evangelist*, 73.

21. Kirby Page, *The Personality of Jesus* (New York: Association Press, 1932), 173.

22. Page, *Social Evangelist*, 17.

23. See, for example, Walter Lippmann, *The Stakes of Diplomacy* (New York: Holt, 1915); Lippmann, *Public Opinion* (New York: Harcourt, Brace and Co, 1922); and Lippmann, *The Phantom Public* (New York: Harcourt, Brace, 1925).

24. Kirby Page, *International Relations in the Light of the Religion of Jesus: An Address Delivered at the National Student Conference, Milwaukee, Wisconsin, December 30, 1926* (New York: K. Page, 1927), 9.

25. Kirby Page, *Jesus or Christianity: A Study in Contrasts* (Garden City, N.Y.: Doubleday, Doran & Co, 1929), 267–71.

26. Vladimir G. Simkhovitch, *Toward the Understanding of Jesus* (New York: Macmillan [1921], 1925). In his own widely read work, *War: Its Causes, Consequences and Cure* (New York: George H. Doran company, 1923), Page even placed his personal address in the footnotes so anyone wanting a copy of Simkhovitch's work could contact him to obtain one.

27. Page, *War*, 175–77.

28. See W. T. Stead, *If Christ Came to Chicago: A Plea for the Union of All Who Love in the Service of All Who Suffer* (Chicago: Laird & Lee, 1894); Charles Sheldon, *In His Steps, What Would Jesus Do?*

(Chicago: Advance Pub Co., 1898); and Richard W. Fox, *Jesus in America: Personal Savior, Cultural Hero, National Obsession* (San Francisco: HarperSanFrancisco, 2004), 313.

29. Bruce Barton, *The Man Nobody Knows: A Discovery of the Real Jesus* (Indianapolis: Bobbs-Merrill, 1925), 140–43. See Fox, *Jesus in America,* 318.

30. Kirby Page, "Was Jesus a Patriot?" 1925, in *Kirby Page and the Social Gospel: An Anthology,* ed. Charles Chatfield and Charles DeBenedetti (New York: Garland, 1976), 393. The "Above all nations is humanity" quotation was the motto of the Cosmopolitan Clubs, organizations established by liberal Protestant and YMCA figures to reach out to foreign students studying at American colleges in the early twentieth century. For a rendering of such efforts as part of a campaign of Americanisation, see Liping Bu, *Making the World Like Us: Education, Cultural Expansion, and the American Century* (Westport, Conn.: Praeger, 2003). The phrase was used more widely as shorthand for the cosmopolitanism of the Christian internationalist movement. A note in the guestbook of the Eddy seminar for 1921 read: " 'Above all nations is humanity': so teaches the Eddy Seminar." Box 23, Eddy Papers.

31. See advertisement for magazine, including series of articles, "Would Jesus be a Christian Today?," in *The World Tomorrow,* October 1928, 431.

32. Page, *Jesus or Christianity.*

33. Page's work appeared before the major revisionist monographs published by Sidney Fay and Harry Elmer Barnes. See Harry Elmer Barnes, *The Genesis of the World War: An Introduction to the Problem of War Guilt* (New York: A.A. Knopf, 1926), and Sidney Bradshaw Fay, *The Origins of the World War* (New York: Macmillan, 1930), whose first edition was published in 1929 in two volumes. On the wider intellectual currents of revisionism in the period, see Warren I. Cohen, *The American Revisionists: The Lessons of Intervention in World War I* (Chicago: University of Chicago Press, 1967).

34. Harry Elmer Barnes, "Review: Some Recent Books on International Relations," *Social Forces* 4 (1926): 665–67. In his major revisionist text, *Genesis of the World War,* Barnes praised Page and Eddy's role, among others, in checking the tendency toward a "Pollyanna" view of American history. Harry Elmer Barnes, *The Genesis of the World War* (New York & London: Knopf, 1927), 707.

35. Charles Chatfield, *For Peace and Justice: Pacifism in America 1914–1941* (Knoxville: University of Tennessee Press, 1971), 123.

36. Cited in Chatfield, *For Peace and Justice,* 124.

37. The Versailles Treaty, June 28, 1919, Part VIII: Reparation, Section 1, Article 231, "The Allied and Associated Governments affirm and Germany accepts the responsibility of Germany and her allies for causing all the loss and damage to which the Allied and Associated Governments and their nationals have been subjected as a consequence of the war imposed upon them by the aggression of Germany and her allies." Yale Law School, The Avalon Project, accessed August 9, 2011, http://avalon.law.yale.edu/imt/partviii.asp.

38. Eddy and Page, *The Abolition of War,* 125–26.

39. Eddy and Page, *The Abolition of War,* 126.

40. Eddy and Page, *The Abolition of War,* 167.

41. On Roosevelt's corollary to the Monroe Doctrine, see Serge Ricard, "The Roosevelt Corollary," *Presidential Studies Quarterly* 36, no. 1 (2006): 17–26.

42. Eddy and Page, *The Abolition of War,* 168.

43. Page, *Social Evangelist,* 140.

44. Page cites Theodore Roosevelt in *The Outlook,* September 23, 1914, in *Imperialism and Nationalism,* 55.

45. Cf. Samuel Flagg Bemis's famous "aberration" thesis, *A Diplomatic History of the United States* (New York: Henry Holt, 1936), 463ff.

46. Page, *Imperialism and Nationalism,* 54–80.

47. Page, *Imperialism and Nationalism,* 82.

48. Paul Kramer, "Thinking with Empire in Modern U. S. History," paper given at the Annual Meeting of the Society for Historians of American Foreign Relations, Falls Church, Virginia, 2009. See also Kramer's discussion of the jeremiad in Kramer, "Power and Connection: Imperial Histories of the United States in the World," *The American Historical Review* 116, no. 5 (December 2011): 1348–91, 1390–91. For examples of the range of such earlier anti-imperialist arguments, see Robert L. Beisner, *Twelve against Empire: The Anti-Imperialists, 1898–1900* (New York: McGraw-Hill, 1968). Ian Tyrrell's *Reforming the World: The Creation of America's Moral Empire* (Princeton, N.J.: Princeton University Press, 2010) documents moral critiques of empire in which vices such as prostitution were seen as being linked to the outgrowth of militarism and imperialism, 139–40.

49. J. A. Hobson, *Imperialism: A Study* (New York: J. Pott & Co, 1902). Cited in Page, *Imperialism and Nationalism*, 91–92.

50. Page, *Imperialism and Nationalism*, v–vi.

51. Page, *Imperialism and Nationalism*, 84.

52. U.S. Department of State, "Memorandum on the Monroe Doctrine Prepared by J. Reuben Clark, Undersecretary of State, December 17, 1928." Reprinted with introduction in *Latin America and the United States: A Documentary History*, ed. Robert H. Holden and Eric Zolov (New York: Oxford University Press, 2011), 129–30.

53. Reflecting this priority, WILPF sent a fact-finding mission to report on conditions under the U.S. occupation of Haiti in 1926. Robert David Johnson, *The Peace Progressives and American Foreign Relations* (Cambridge, Mass: Harvard University Press, 1995), 218–19. For a *World Tomorrow* account of the mission, see Paul H. Douglas, "Haiti—A Case in Point," *The World Tomorrow*, May 1927, 222–24.

54. Samuel Guy Inman, *Trailing the Conquistadores* (New York: Friendship Press, 1930).

55. Samuel Guy Inman, "Imperialistic America," *Atlantic Monthly* 134 (1924): 107–16, 109, 107.

56. On the State Department's response to Inman's essay, see Kenneth F. Woods, " 'Imperialistic America': A Landmark in the Development of U.S. Policy toward Latin America," *Inter-American Economic Affairs* 21 (1967): 55–72.

57. See Mary A. Renda, *Taking Haiti: Military Occupation and the Culture of U.S. Imperialism, 1915–1940* (Chapel Hill: University of North Carolina Press, 2001), esp., 270–73; and Virginia S. Williams, "Samuel Guy Inman: Unorthodox Missionary-Scholar," in *Radical Journalists, Generalist Intellectuals, and U.S.-Latin American Relations* (Lewiston, N.Y.: E. Mellen Press, 2001).

58. Charles W. Forman, "A History of Foreign Mission Theory in America," in *American Missions in Bicentennial Perspective: Papers Presented at the Fourth Annual Meeting of the American Society of Missiology at Trinity Evangelical Divinity School, Deerfield, Illinois, June 18-20, 1976*, ed. R. P. Beaver and Catherine L. Albanese (South Pasadena, Calif: William Carey Library, 1977), 97.

59. Page, *International Relations in the Light of the Religion of Jesus*, 4.

60. "Appendix C: Informal Discussion Groups," in *Religion on the Campus, The Report of the National Student Conference, Milwaukee, Dec. 28, 1926 to Jan. 1, 1927*, ed. Francis Pickens Miller (New York: Association Press, 1927), 193–94.

61. Johnson, *Peace Progressives*, 221. See also Advertisement, Committee on Militarism in Education, in *The World Tomorrow*, October 1926, 188.

62. John Nevin Sayre, "The Altars of Freedom," *The World Tomorrow*, October 1926, 156–59.

63. Page, *International Relations*, 6.

64. Page, *Imperialism and Nationalism*, 23–24.

65. Page, *International Relations*, 8.

66. Page, *International Relations*, 8.

67. Kirby Page, *National Defense: A Study of the Origins, Results and Prevention of War* (New York: Farrar & Rinehart, 1931), 4.

68. John Nevin Sayre to Grace Hutchins, May 19, 1926, 1, in Devere Allen Papers, Swarthmore College Peace Collection, DG 53, Series C-4, Box 2.

69. The Garland Fund rejected *The World Tomorrow's* application for funding, claiming they weren't radical enough. Despite having just granted $17,000 to the *New Masses* magazine the previous year, the committee rejected *The World Tomorrow's* request for $7,000 on the grounds that they needed to be more consistently pro-labor, or otherwise go and seek help from their liberal, pacifist, or religious supporters. Details outlined in draft manuscript, "To All Friends, Enemies, Contributors, Supporters, and Subscribers," [April 1926], 2. For "new deal," see Sayre to Hutchins, May 19, 1926, 3. On the Garland Fund, see Gloria G. Samson, *The American Fund for Public Service: Charles Garland and Radical Philanthropy, 1922–1941* (Westport, Conn.: Greenwood Press, 1996).

70. Cited in Sherwood Eddy, *Facing the Crisis: A Study in Present Day Social and Religious Problems* (New York: G.H. Doran Co, 1922), 233–34.

71. Page, *Social Evangelist,* 99.

72. Point V of Principles, cited in Eddy, *Facing the Crisis,* 233–34.

2. *The World Tomorrow* as a Foreign Policy Counterpublic

1. Gen. Douglas MacArthur to Kirby Page, reprinted in "Reverberations!," *The World Tomorrow,* June 1931, 192–93.

2. For "a clean sweep," see John Nevin Sayre to Grace Hutchins, May 19, 1926, 3, in Devere Allen Papers, Swarthmore College Peace Collection, DG 53, Series C-4, Box 2 (hereafter cited as DAP).

3. Grace Hutchins to John Nevin Sayre, May 21, 1926, 2, DAP.

4. Devere Allen, Notes, "If I were to consider taking a definite position on the new World Tomorrow under Kirby Page's editorship I should want light on these important points," [1926], 1, DAP.

5. John Nevin Sayre, Untitled Memorandum (pencil-marked "W.T. reorganization"), [1921], 1, DAP.

6. Sayre, Untitled Memorandum, [1921], 2, DAP. Sayre's broad picture of *The World Tomorrow's* positioning among other journals remained a fair one in the Page years. Page's *World Tomorrow* was closer to the Socialist Party and third-party politics in general than *Christian Century*, and was more likely to feature reflections on a Christian reception of Marx. It showed comparatively little interest in Prohibition compared to its liberal counterpart and offered as much scepticism as it did support for legalist programs such as the Outlawry of War campaign, in which Charles Clayton Morrison, *Christian Century's* editor, played a leading role. And, while *World Tomorrow* writers and contributors contributed to the *Nation, New Republic,* and *Survey Graphic,* they articulated their approach in political-theological terms most fully and forthrightly in the smaller Christian monthly.

7. Ernest R. May, *American Imperialism: A Speculative Essay* (New York: Atheneum, 1968). The delimiting logic was explicated in Gabriel A. Almond, *The American People and Foreign Policy* (New York: Praeger, 1960).

8. By one estimate, during the imperialism debates of the 1890s–1900s, the foreign policy public population was no more than around 10–20 percent of the voting public (i.e., around 1.5–3 million people), notwithstanding the heightened role of the Hearst press. Thomas G. Paterson, John Garry Clifford, and Kenneth J. Hagan, *A History since 1895,* vol. 2 of *American Foreign Relations* (Boston: Houghton Mifflin, 2000), 10.

9. See, for example, Nancy Fraser, "Rethinking the Public Sphere: A Contribution to the Critique of Actually Existing Democracy," in *Habermas and the Public Sphere,* ed. Craig Calhoun (Cambridge,

Mass.: MIT Press, 1992), 109–42; Michael Warner, *Publics and Counterpublics* (New York: Zone Books, 2002); Robert Asen and Daniel C. Brouwer, "Introduction: Reconfigurations of the Public Sphere," in *Counterpublics and the State*, eds. Robert Asen and Daniel C. Brouwer (Albany: State University of New York Press, 2001), 1–32. Jürgen Habermas, *The structural transformation of the public sphere: an inquiry into a category of bourgeois society* (Cambridge, Mass: MIT Press, 1989).

10. Robert Asen, "Seeking the 'Counter' in Counterpublics," *Communication Theory* 10 (2000): 424–46, 425, 424, 444.

11. Elesha Coffman's *The Christian Century and the Rise of the Protestant Mainline* (New York: Oxford University Press, 2013) and Mark Hulsether's *Building a Protestant Left: Christianity and Crisis Magazine, 1941–1993* (Knoxville: University of Tennessee Press, 1999) are notable exceptions to this trend and highlight a welcome broadening of methodology. A classic example of the older method was Robert M. Miller, *American Protestantism and Social Issues, 1919–1939* (Chapel Hill: University of North Carolina Press, 1958).

12. Sean Latham and Robert Scholes, "The Rise of Periodical Studies," *PMLA* 121, no. 2 (March 2006): 517–31, 517–18.

13. Kirby Page, "The Point of View," *The World Tomorrow*, May 1927, 196.

14. Herbert Adams Gibbons, "How We Got the Philippines," *The World Tomorrow*, February 1927, 64–65.

15. Leland H. Jenks, "A Waterway to What?," *The World Tomorrow*, May 1927, 214–16.

16. Edwin M. Borchard, "From Monroe to Coolidge," *The World Tomorrow*, May 1927, 218–20.

17. Paul H. Douglas, "Haiti—A Case in Point," *The World Tomorrow*, May 1927, 222–24.

18. Maps of the Philippines were provided in the February 1927 edition, 62, and of the Caribbean in the May, 1927 edition, with tables showing regional trade statistics, 221.

19. For example, see Commission on International Relations of the National Conference on the Christian Way of Life, *Missions and World Problems: A Syllabus of Questions for Use by Discussion Classes* (New York: Association Press, 1925). On the rising emphasis on social concern and education in the YMCA, see Charles Howard Hopkins, *History of the Y.M.C.A. in North America* (New York: Association Press, 1951), 642–45. On the influence of YMCA educational innovator Harrison Sacker Elliott, see Mark Thomas Edwards, *The Right of the Protestant Left: God's Totalitarianism* (New York: Palgrave Macmillan, 2012), 48.

20. Advertisement, "World Tomorrow Discussion Groups," *The World Tomorrow*, January 1927, 2.

21. Advertisement, "World Tomorrow Discussion Groups," 2.

22. Joan S. Rubin, *The Making of Middle/brow Culture* (Chapel Hill: University of North Carolina Press, 1992), 93ff. For a recent and important discussion of the way liberal religion related to middlebrow book culture in the mid-twentieth century, see Matthew Hedstrom, *The Rise of Liberal Religion: Book Culture and American Spirituality in the Twentieth Century* (Oxford: Oxford University Press, 2013).

23. Grace Loucks, "For Group Discussion," *The World Tomorrow*, May, 1927, 236.

24. Page, "The Point of View," *The World Tomorrow*, May 1927, 196.

25. From *New York World*, reprinted on the editorial page with the title "Comments on Our Imperialism," *The World Tomorrow*, February 1927, 54.

26. Cover, *The World Tomorrow*, October 1926, 141. Attribution to Committee on Militarism in Education given on page 142.

27. Ludwig Quidde, "European Militarism Before the War: Can We Discover Any 'Deadly Parallels'?," *The World Tomorrow*, October 1926, 161–62.

28. Kirby Page, "The Point of View," *The World Tomorrow*, October 1926, 142.

29. Reinhold Niebuhr, "The Threat of the R.O.T.C.," *The World Tomorrow*, October 1926, 154–56.

30. George A. Coe, "Training Citizens–For What?," *The World Tomorrow* October 1926, 151–54, 152.

31. Coe, "Training Citizens–For What?," 152.

32. Harry Overstreet, "Militarizing Our Minds," *The World Tomorrow*, October 1926, 144–47, 146, 147.

33. Overstreet, "Militarizing Our Minds," 144.

34. "Militarizing our Youth," *The World Tomorrow*, November 1927, 453.

35. John Nevin Sayre, "Suggested Points of Difference between the Old and the New World Tomorrow," [1921], 4, DAP.

36. "Not in the Headlines," *The World Tomorrow*, November 1926, 212.

37. Published in "Correspondence," *The World Tomorrow*, February 1927, 368.

38. As Nancy Fraser explains, "on the one hand, [counterpublics] function as spaces of withdrawal and regroupment; on the other hand, they also function as bases and training grounds for agitational activities directed toward wider publics." See "Rethinking the Public Sphere," 124. See also Asen and Brouwer, "Introduction: Reconfigurations of the Public Sphere."

39. Kirby Page, "The Monroe Doctrine and World Peace," *The World Tomorrow*, October 1928, 403–8, 403.

40. Ibid., 404.

41. Ibid., 403.

42. Ibid., 408.

43. Robert H. Holden and Eric Zolov, Introduction to Clark Memorandum, in *Latin America and the United States: A Documentary History*, ed. Robert H. Holden and Eric Zolov (New York: Oxford University Press, 2011), 129.

44. Kirby Page, "The Monroe Doctrine and Arbitration," *Annals of the American Academy of Political and Social Science* 138 (1928): 140–45.

45. Harry Elmer Barnes, *The Genesis of the World War* (New York: Knopf, 1927), 707.

46. Sidney B. Fay, "Economic and Psychological Release for Germany," *The World Tomorrow*, November 1931, 352–54.

47. "Public Opinion Shifts on German War Guilt," *New York Times*, September 27, 1930, 12.

48. Sarah E. Igo, *The Averaged American: Surveys, Citizens, and the Making of a Mass Public* (Cambridge, Mass.: Harvard University Press, 2007), 20, 21.

49. Igo, *The Averaged American*, 13–15. See also Melvin G. Holli, *The Wizard of Washington: Emil Hurja, Franklin Roosevelt, and the Birth of Public Opinion Polling* (New York: Palgrave, 2002).

50. For example, see "The Digest's 20,000,000–Vote Prohibition Poll," *Literary Digest*, March 8, 1930, 5. On this point I am indebted to historian Julie Yarwood.

51. Devere Allen, "War Resistance Old and New," *The World Tomorrow*, November 1931, 363–64.

52. Albert Einstein, Address Delivered before the New History Society, New York City, December 14, 1930, trans. Rosika Schwimmer, reprinted under the title "Militant Pacifism" in *The World Tomorrow*, January 1931, 9.

53. Editorial, [Kirby Page], "Can the Church Stop War?," *The World Tomorrow*, May 1931, 133.

54. Table of data included in feature article by Kirby Page, "Nineteen Thousand Clergymen on War and Peace," *The World Tomorrow*, May 1931, 138–49, 140–41.

55. For data on theological students, see *The World Tomorrow*, May 1931, 171. Page's comment is from the introduction to the results in Kirby Page, "Nineteen Thousand Clergymen on War and Peace," 138.

56. "10,427 Pastors 'Wouldn't Fight in Any War': Most of 19,372 Oppose Military Training," *Chicago Daily Tribune*, April 24, 1931, 23.

57. "Summary of Replies from 19,780 Clergymen," *The World Tomorrow*, May 1931, 140.

58. Bertrand Russell to Kirby Page, reprinted in "Reverberations!," *The World Tomorrow*, June 1931, 196.

59. Editorial, *Nation*, May 6, 1931, reprinted in "Re-Reverberations," *The World Tomorrow*, July 1931, 225.

60. Harry Elmer Barnes, in *New York World-Telegram*, April 24, 1931, reprinted in "Reverberations!," 196.

61. Albert Einstein to Kirby Page, reprinted in *The World Tomorrow*, June 1931, 193.

62. Bruce Barton to Kirby Page, reprinted in "Reverberations!," 196. Page's earlier proposals were published as *An American Peace Policy* (New York: George H. Doran Company, 1925).

63. Gen. Douglas MacArthur to Kirby Page, reprinted in "Reverberations!," 192–93.

64. "Gen MacArthur Lashes Pacifism of Clergymen: Refusal to Fight Peril," *Chicago Daily Tribune*, June 3, 1931, 18.

65. William Randolph Hearst in *New York American*, June 5, 1931, reprinted in "Re-Reverberations," 224.

66. "Sees Armaments as Peace Insurance: Rear Admiral Fiske, Retired, Says," *New York Times*, November 12, 1928, 12.

67. Bradley A. Fiske to Kirby Page, reprinted in "Reverberations!," 194.

68. On Legion opposition, see William Pencak, *For God & Country: The American Legion, 1919–1941* (Boston: Northeastern University Press, 1989), 3, 167ff.

69. Edward E. Spafford to Page, reprinted in "Re-Reverberations," 223. On Spafford, see Pencak, *For God & Country*.

70. Editorial, *Iowa Legionnaire*, May 8, 1931, reprinted in "Reverberations!," 194.

71. Editorial, *Pennsylvania Manufacturer's Journal*, April 1931, reprinted in "Reverberations!," 197.

72. Editorial, "Radical Truth Goes off the Air," *The World Tomorrow*, March 22, 1933, 272.

73. Cited in Kirby Page, *Kirby Page, Social Evangelist: The Autobiography of a 20th Century Prophet for Peace,* ed. Harold E. Fey (Nyack, N.Y.: Fellowship Press, 1975), 132.

74. Ibid.

75. George C. Herring, *From Colony to Superpower: U.S. Foreign Relations Since 1776* (New York: Oxford University Press, 2008), 436, 484.

3. A Funeral and Two Legacies

1. Untitled Pamphlet Advertising *The World Tomorrow*, [1921], 1; "Remarks about Proposed Editorials," September 22, 1925, 2, both in Devere Allen Papers, Swarthmore College Peace Collection, DG 53, Series C-4, Box 2 (hereafter cited as DAP).

2. Mrs. Louis F. Post, reprinted in Advertisement, "The Tide Has Turned," *The World Tomorrow*, December 1928, 482.

3. Reinhold Niebuhr, "Ex Cathedra," *The World Tomorrow*, January 4, 1933, 2.

4. Reinhold Niebuhr, "Ex Cathedra," *The World Tomorrow*, December 14, 1932, 554.

5. Helena Flam, "Emotion's Map: A Research Agenda," in *Emotions and Social Movements,* ed. Helena Flam and Debra King (London: Routledge, 2005), 19.

6. Kirby Page to Devere Allen [August 7] 1934, DAP.

7. On the efforts to secure donations from a Socialist figure, see Kirby Page to Devere Allen, July 24, 1934, DAP.

8. "The Press: Faster World Tomorrow," *Time*, August 15, 1932, accessed February 4, 2011, http://www.time.com/time/printout/0,8816,744212,00.html.

9. Kirby Page, *Kirby Page, Social Evangelist: The Autobiography of a 20th Century Prophet for Peace*, ed. Harold E. Fey (Nyack, N.Y.: Fellowship Press, 1975), 125.

10. George C. Herring, *From Colony to Superpower: U.S. Foreign Relations Since 1776* (New York: Oxford University Press, 2008), 436, 484.

11. Franklin D. Roosevelt, "Address at Madison Square Garden, New York City," October 31, 1936. Online by Gerhard Peters and John T. Woolley, *The American Presidency Project*, http://www.presidency.ucsb.edu/ws/?pid=15219.

12. Robert David Johnson, "The Decline of Anti-Imperialism," in *The Peace Progressives and American Foreign Relations* (Cambridge, Mass: Harvard University Press, 1995).

13. Editorial, "Hands off Cuba," *The World Tomorrow*, September 28, 1933, 534–35.

14. Sec. Hull and President Roosevelt both cited at Office of the Historian, U.S. Department of State, "Milestones: 1921–1936, Good Neighbor Policy," accessed August, 23, 2011, http://history.state.gov/milestones/1921-1936/GoodNeighbor.

15. Editorial, "Filipinos: We Apologize," *The World Tomorrow*, January 25, 1933, 75.

16. Kirby Page, "If War Is to Be Abolished," *The World Tomorrow*, July 26, 1934, 371–73.

17. Editorial, "Religious Radicalism Is News," *The World Tomorrow*, June 14, 1934, 291.

18. "Religion: Churchmen on War," *Time*, May 21, 1934, accessed February 4, 2011, http://www.time.com/time/printout/0,8816,747448,00.html. Fosdick cited in Editorial, "Religious Radicalism Is News," 291.

19. Announcement, "Changes in Editorial Staff," *The World Tomorrow*, October 1928, 390.

20. H. C. Engelbrecht, "The Traffic in Death," *The World Tomorrow*, October 5, 1932, 330–31.

21. H. C. Engelbrecht, "The Arms Industry: An Appraisal," *The World Tomorrow*, December 7, 1933, 661–33.

22. "Book Notes," *New York Times*, April 2, 1934, 15.

23. John Chamberlain, "Books of the Times," *New York Times*, April 25, 1934, 19. Chamberlain placed *Merchants of Death* alongside George Seldes's *Iron, Blood and Profits* (Harpers: New York, 1934) in its pertinence to the Nye Committee's activities.

24. U.S. Senate, "September 4, 1934: 'Merchants of Death,'" accessed May 12, 2014, http://www.senate.gov/artandhistory/history/minute/merchants_of_death.htm.

25. Dorothy Detzer, "Looking Toward Disarmament, Rev. of Benjamin Williams, *The United States and Disarmament*," *The World Tomorrow*, February 1932, 56.

26. Matthew W. Coulter, *The Senate Munitions Inquiry of the 1930s: Beyond the Merchants of Death* (Westport, Conn.: Greenwood Press, 1997), 20. See also Dorothy Detzer, *Appointment on the Hill* (New York: H. Holt, 1948).

27. *Recent Gains in American Civilization, by a Group of Distinguished Critics of Contemporary Life*, ed. Kirby Page (New York: Harcourt, 1928).

28. C. A. Beard, "In Time of Peace, Prepare for Peace," *New Republic*, March 18, 1936, cited in R. A. Kennedy, "The Ideology of American Isolationism," *Cercles* 5 (2002): 68.

29. Page, *Social Evangelist*, 111.

30. Ibid., 106.

31. Kirby Page, *How to Keep America out of War*, published jointly by American Friends Service Committee, Fellowship of Reconciliation, General Conference Commission on World Peace of the Methodist Episcopal Church, Keep America Out of War Congress, National Council for Prevention of War, War Resisters League, Women's International League for Peace and Freedom, 1939. On circulation, see Page, *Social Evangelist*, 106.

32. Page, *How to Keep America Out of War*, 10.

33. Ibid., 23. According to a footnote in his text, the "map" Page cited was one outlining the history of expansion in the *Chicago Tribune*, May 3, 1936.

34. Page, *How to Keep America Out of War*, 29.

35. See Leilah Danielson, "Christianity, Dissent, and the Cold War: A. J. Muste's Challenge to Realism and U.S. Empire," *Diplomatic History* 30, no. 4 (September 2006): 645–69, 650; Dan McKanan, *Prophetic Encounters: Religion and the American Radical Tradition* (Boston: Beacon Press, 2011), 174–75.

36. Danielson, "Christianity, Dissent, and the Cold War," 647–48.

37. McKanan, *Prophetic Encounters*, 174ff. For Niebuhr as "father" to cold war liberals (a phrase attributed to George Kennan, but later disputed), see the discussion in William Inboden, "The Prophetic Conflict: Reinhold Niebuhr, Christian Realism, and World War II," *Diplomatic History* 38, no. 1 (2014): 49–82, 50.

38. For language of little leagues and fellowships, see Martin Marty, *The Noise of Conflict, 1919–1941*, vol. 2 of *Modern American Religion* (Chicago: University of Chicago Press, 1991), 384.

39. Niebuhr joined the FCSO in 1921 when he was still working in his parish at Detroit and was appointed a traveling secretary for the fellowship in 1924. This was such a consuming position that Eddy and Page financed an assistant minister for Niebuhr's Detroit church in order to enable Niebuhr to fulfill his FCSO role. Richard Wightman Fox, *Reinhold Niebuhr: A Biography, with a New Introduction and Afterword* (Ithaca: Cornell University Press, 1996), 75–76, 81. This foreshadowed Niebuhr's connection to *The World Tomorrow*. In 1928, Eddy and Page jointly arranged (with Eddy's finance) for Niebuhr's appointment at the magazine and at Union Theological Seminary, also in New York. Fox, *Reinhold Niebuhr*, 105–6.

40. Editorial, "Build a New Party!," *The World Tomorrow*, December 1929, 483–84.

41. Editorial, "Synagogue and Church Awaken," *The World Tomorrow*, November 1931, 344.

42. For the fellowship's founding statement of principles, see Editorial, "Fellowship of Socialist Christians," *The World Tomorrow*, February 1932, 39. For details of the Fellowship retreat in September 1933, see Editorial, "Fellowship of Socialist Christians," *The World Tomorrow*, September 28, 1933, 533. The most developed explanation of the FSC's philosophy came from Reinhold Niebuhr, "The Fellowship of Socialist Christians," *The World Tomorrow*, June 14, 1934, 297–98.

43. Fox, *Reinhold Niebuhr*, 167–68.

44. Editorial, "Fellowship of Socialist Christians," 39.

45. Niebuhr, "The Fellowship of Socialist Christians," 297–98.

46. Editorial, "Fellowship of Socialist Christians," 39.

47. Examples of the argument to reject organized Christianity included Harry F. Ward, "Jesus' Significance in our Modern Age," *The World Tomorrow*, January 1931, 15–17, and Ernest Fremont Tittle, "What Will the Church do with Jesus?," *The World Tomorrow*, March 1931, 75–76.

48. Reinhold Niebuhr, *Reflections on the End of an Era* (New York: C. Scribner's Sons, [1934] 1936), ix.

49. Henry P. Van Dusen, "The Sickness of Liberal Religion," *The World Tomorrow*, August 1931, 256–59.

50. Reinhold Niebuhr, "Radicalism and Religion," *The World Tomorrow*, October 1931, 324.

51. John C. Bennett, "Religion: Opiate or Stimulant," *The World Tomorrow*, June 1932, 178–80, 180.

52. Reinhold Niebuhr, "Property and the Ethical Life," *The World Tomorrow*, January 1931, 19–21, 19.

53. Ibid., 20.

54. Ibid., 21.

55. Ibid., 20.

56. On historical catastrophism and Marx, see Reinhold Niebuhr, "Intellectual Autobiography," in *Reinhold Niebuhr: His Religious, Social, and Political Thought*, ed. C. W. Kegley and R. W. Bretall (New York: Macmillan, 1961), 1–23.

57. Reinhold Niebuhr, *Moral Man and Immoral Society* (1932; repr. London: Continuum, 2005), xii–xiii.

58. Ibid., xvii.

59. Ibid., xvi–xvii.

60. Helena Flam, "Emotion's Map: A Research Agenda," in *Emotions and Social Movements*, ed. Helena Flam and Debra King (London: Routledge, 2005), 19.

61. Norman Thomas, "Moral Man and Immoral Society: A Review by Norman Thomas," *The World Tomorrow*, December 14, 1932, 565.

62. F. Ernest Johnson, "Religion and Social Work," review of *The Contribution of Religion to Social Work*, by Reinhold Niebuhr, *The World Tomorrow*, March 1, 1933, 213.

63. E. G. Homrighausen in "Correspondence: Inspired by Niebuhr's Book," *The World Tomorrow*, February 1, 1933, 118.

64. Ralph H. Read, "Who Are the Defeatists?," *The World Tomorrow*, April 5, 1933, 328.

65. Editorial, "Fellowship of Socialist Christians," *The World Tomorrow*, February 1932, 39.

66. Reinhold Niebuhr, "Is Peace or Justice the Goal?," *The World Tomorrow*, September 21, 1932, 275–77, 277.

67. As well as clarifying the position of the group, a secondary purpose of the survey was to work out what to do with its Executive Secretary J. B. Matthews, who had been advocating violence in the case of class warfare, who was openly secular in his reasons for doing so, and who was known to have become enmeshed in several Communist-front organizations (before later reversing his position and assisting HUAC enquiries). In a meeting of the FOR executive in October, the leadership voted 18–13 to accept the resignation he had offered earlier. For details of the questionnaire, and an emerging realist's interpretation of it, see John C. Bennett, "That Fellowship Questionnaire," *The World Tomorrow*, December 21, 1933, 690–92. For a detailed discussion of the results of the questionnaire, in the form of correspondence between interested parties, see "Fellowship Reverberations," *The World Tomorrow*, January 18, 1934, 40–46. A thorough treatment of the background to Matthews and the FOR controversy, including the results of the vote on Matthews's resignation, is given by Charles Chatfield in *For Peace and Justice: Pacifism in America 1914–1941* (Knoxville: University of Tennessee Press, 1971), 191–97.

68. Reinhold Niebuhr, "Why I Leave the F.O.R.," *Christian Century*, January 3, 1934, reprinted in *Love and Justice: Selections from the Shorter Writings of Reinhold Niebuhr*, ed. D. B. Robertson (Cleveland, Ohio: Meridian Books, World Publishing, 1967), 254, 258.

69. Inboden, "The Prophetic Conflict," 49, 54–55.

70. Reinhold Niebuhr, "Pacifism against the Wall," *American Scholar* (Spring 1936), reprinted in *Love and Justice*, 267.

71. Reinhold Niebuhr, "Why the Christian Church Is Not Pacifist," in *The Essential Reinhold Niebuhr*, ed. Robert McAfee Brown (New Haven, Conn.: Yale University Press, 1986). See p. 110 for his rebuttal of the moral equivalence argument.

72. See Inboden, "The Prophetic Conflict"; Fox, *Reinhold Niebuhr*; Andrew Preston, *Sword of the Spirit, Shield of Faith: Religion in American War and Diplomacy* (New York: Anchor, 2012), 303–14; and Michael G. Thompson, "An Exception to Exceptionalism: A Reflection on Reinhold Niebuhr's Vision of 'Prophetic' Christianity and the Problem of Religion and U.S. Foreign Policy," *American Quarterly* 59 (2007): 833–55.

73. See, for example, Niebuhr's close colleague Kirby Page's reading of these forces in *Imperialism and Nationalism* (New York: George H. Doran, 1925), 23–24. On the intellectual history of nationalism as a psychological phenomenon, see Glenda Sluga, *The Nation, Psychology, and International Politics, 1870–1919* (Basingstoke: Palgrave Macmillan, 2006).

74. Carlton J. H. Hayes, *Essays on Nationalism* (New York: Macmillan, 1926). See also Hans Kohn, *The Idea of Nationalism: A Study in Its Origins and Background* (New York: Macmillan, 1958 [1944]); and Benedict Anderson, *Imagined Communities: Reflections on the Origin and Spread of Nationalism* (London: Verso, 1983).

75. For example, see Norman Thomas, "So This Is Nationalism," review of *Essays on Nationalism*, by Carlton Hayes, *The World Tomorrow*, October 1926, 171.

76. For an excellent and recent treatment of Miller, see Mark Thomas Edwards, *Right of the Protestant Left: God's Totalitarianism* (New York: Palgrave Macmillan, 2012).

77. Francis P. Miller, "These Sovereign United States," *The World Tomorrow*, November 1926, 197–98.

78. Kirby Page, *National Defense: A Study of the Origins, Results and Prevention of War* (New York: Farrar & Rinehart, 1931), 190. For Page's documenting of examples of the "vices" and excesses of nationalism, see chap. 1, 3–24, and chap. 8, 189–204.

79. Cited in Page, *National Defense*, 204.

80. Niebuhr, *Moral Man and Immoral Society*, 64.

81. Ibid.

82. Robert A. Divine, *Second Chance; The Triumph of Internationalism in America during World War II* (New York: Atheneum, 1967).

83. Robert H. Ferrell, *Peace in Their Time: The Origins of the Kellogg-Briand Pact* (New Haven, Conn.: Yale University Press, 1952).

84. For example, see John Haynes Holmes, "Outlawry of War—A Policy of Abolition," *The World Tomorrow*, November, 1926, 204–7.

85. On internationalist culture and league "fever," see Sluga, *Internationalism*, 58. On league internationalism as "religious," see Alfred Zimmern, "The Ethical Presuppositions of a World Order," in *The Universal Church and the World of Nations*, ed. Philip Henry Kerr et al., vol. 7 of *Church, Community, and State* (London: Allen & Unwin, 1938), 27–56, 40.

86. Kirby Page, "War as an Institution: A Review of 'The Outlawry of War,'" *The World Tomorrow*, November 1927, 447–50; Charles Clayton Morrison, "Dr. Morrison Replies," *The World Tomorrow*, November 1927, 451–52.

87. Page, "War as an Institution," 450.

88. Morrison, "Dr. Morrison Replies," 452.

89. On the Delta Farm Cooperative, see Rick L. Nutt, *The Whole Gospel for the Whole World: Sherwood Eddy and the American Protestant Mission* (Macon, Ga.: Mercer University Press, 1997), 275–80. On the Highlander Folk School, see Frank T. Adams, *James A. Dombrowski: An American Heretic, 1897–1983* (Knoxville: University of Tennessee Press, 1992), 65–77. Dombrowski was employed by Sherwood Eddy as a guide through Russia for the 1932 Eddy Seminar, and he later invited Kirby Page and Reinhold Niebuhr to give speeches at the new Folk School in Tennessee in 1934 (44–49, 77).

90. See Mark Edwards, "'God Has Chosen Us:' Re-Membering Christian Realism, Rescuing Christendom, and the Contest of Responsibilities during the Cold War," *Diplomatic History* 33 (2009): 67–94; David Zietsma, "'Sin Has No History': Religion, National Identity, and U.S. Intervention, 1937–1941," *Diplomatic History* 31, no. 3 (2007): 531–65; John Fousek, *To Lead the Free World: American Nationalism and the Cultural Roots of the Cold War* (Chapel Hill: University of North Carolina Press, 2000); and Dianne Kirby, *Religion and the Cold War* (Houndmills: Palgrave, 2003).

91. Ernest Lee Tuveson, *Redeemer Nation: The Idea of America's Millennial Role* (Chicago: University of Chicago Press, 1968), vii.

4. All God's Household

1. Henry Smith Leiper, *World Chaos or World Christianity, A Popular Interpretation of Oxford and Edinburgh, 1937* (Chicago: Willett, Clark & Co, 1937). For Lang, see 24; for Niemöller, 23. Journalists reported Lang as calling for "supernatural religion." See "Canterbury Asks for a Stronger Church," *New York Times,* July 13, 1937, 21; "Council of the Churches," *The Times* (London), July 13, 1937, 16.

2. In attendance were two delegates of the Federation of Protestant Free Churches in Germany (*Vereinigung Evangelischer Freikirken Deutschlands*), Otto Melle and Paul Schmidt, plus other German intellectuals in exile, notably Professor Paul Tillich and Otto Piper. Conference on Church, Community and State, Oxford, July 12 to 26, 1937, "List of Delegates" (Geneva: The Universal Christian Council for Life and Work, 1937), in Box 16, Life and Work Collection, Ecumenical Library, Interchurch Center, New York City.

3. The term "demonic" was used in the Marquess of Lothian, Philip Kerr's preparatory paper, published as "The Demonic Influence of National Sovereignty," in *The Universal Church and the World of Nations,* ed. Philip Henry Kerr et al., vol. 7 of the Official Oxford Conference books (London: Allen & Unwin, 1938), 3–23. "Demonic" was also used throughout reports of the conference, such as "Church and Community," *Official Reports of the Oxford Conference* [Federal Council of Churches], in Box 14, Life and Work Collection.

4. J. H. Oldham, "General Introduction," in *The Universal Church and the World of Nations,* viii.

5. Keith Clements, *Faith on the Frontier: A Life of J. H. Oldham* (Edinburgh: T&T Clark, 1999), 311.

6. Daniel T. Rodgers, *Atlantic Crossings: Social Politics in a Progressive Age* (Cambridge, Mass.: Belknap Press of Harvard University Press), 1998.

7. Warren F. Kuehl, *Biographical Dictionary of Internationalists* (Westport, Conn.: Greenwood Press, 1983).

8. See, for example, Ruth Rouse and Stephen Neill, *A History of the Ecumenical Movement 1517–1948* (Philadelphia: Westminster Press, 1954); Michael Kinnamon and Brian E. Cope, *The Ecumenical Movement: An Anthology of Key Texts and Voices* (Geneva: WCC Publications, 1997); G. K. A. Bell, *The Kingship of Christ: The Story of the World Council of Churches* (Middlesex: Penguin, 1954); and Willem Adolph Visser 't Hooft, *The Genesis and Formation of the World Council of Churches* (Geneva: World Council of Churches, 1982). John Nurser's *For All Peoples and All Nations: Christian Churches and Human Rights* (Geneva: WCC Publications, 2005) narrates the involvement of ecumenists in the drafting of the UN Declaration of Human Rights. Nurser recognizes that Christian involvement in the establishment of the UN and its human rights charter has to be set against the impulse at the founding of the World Council of Churches, namely the Oxford 1937 conference. "There was from the beginning a sense that the ecumenical movement had a properly theological commitment to 'global order,'" Nurser writes (5). Here I seek to go beyond Nurser's helpful focus on the theme and language of "Christendom" (chap. 1, "The Idea: To Universalize 'Christendom'") and explore the wider thematic landscape of ecumenical reflection on world affairs, in which notions of Christendom were but one part.

9. Graeme Smith, *Oxford 1937: The Universal Christian Council for Life and Work Conference* (Frankfurt am Main: Peter Lang, 2004), 26–27.

10. Darril Hudson, *The Ecumenical Movement in World Affairs* (London: Weidenfeld & Nicolson for the London School of Economics & Political Science, 1969), esp. chap. 8, "Christian Social Research and Labour," and chap. 10, "Oikumene and the League."

11. Hudson's brief treatment of Oxford is helpful in that it gathers several critical editorials published at the time of the conference. Yet, contrary to opinion then and since, Hudson sees Stockholm as the more important conference and Oxford as failing to live up to its forebear's legacy. Hudson, *Ecumenical Movement in World Affairs,* 157–62, 161.

12. See Heather A. Warren, *Theologians of a New World Order: Reinhold Niebuhr and the Christian Realists* (New York: Oxford University Press, 1997); Mark Thomas Edwards, *Right of the Protestant Left: God's Totalitarianism* (New York: Palgrave Macmillan, 2012), 73.

13. Delegates at world conferences often represented national units and thus were in one sense part of an "international" phenomenon. Yet the way that ideas and people circulated within the ecumenical movement is better understood within a "transnational" framework, that is, as not pertaining to any one nation-state and moving with fluidity across borders.

14. For scholarly works that place nonstate actors within such a framework of American cultural expansion and power, see, for example, Frank Costigliola, *Awkward Dominion: American Political, Economic, and Cultural Relations with Europe, 1919–1933* (Ithaca: Cornell University Press, 1984); Emily S. Rosenberg, *Spreading the American Dream: American Economic and Cultural Expansion, 1890–1945* (New York: Hill and Wang, 1982); and Victoria De Grazia, *Irresistible Empire: America's Advance through Twentieth-Century Europe* (Cambridge, Mass.: Belknap Press of Harvard University Press, 2005). For an account of international thought in the period that stresses the expanding influence of American *ideas*, see Elizabeth Borgwardt, *A New Deal for the World: America's Vision for Human Rights* (Cambridge, Mass.: Belknap Press of Harvard University Press, 2005).

15. Ronald W. Pruessen, *John Foster Dulles: The Road to Power* (New York: Free Press, 1982), 187–88.

16. Richard Wightman Fox, *Reinhold Niebuhr: A Biography, with a New Introduction and Afterword* (Ithaca: Cornell University Press, 1996), 78–81.

17. Eric Fenn, cited in Fox, *Reinhold Niebuhr*, 180.

18. Edwin E. Aubrey, "The Oxford Conference, 1937," *Journal of Religion* 17 (1937): 385.

19. Mark G. Toulouse, *The Transformation of John Foster Dulles: From Prophet of Realism to Priest of Nationalism* (Macon, Ga.: Mercer University Press, 1985), 50.

20. Barbara Dianne Savage, "Benjamin Mays, Global Ecumenism, and Local Religious Segregation," in *Religion and Politics in the Contemporary United States*, ed. R. Marie Griffith and Melani McAlister (Baltimore, Md.: Johns Hopkins University Press, 2008), 259–80.

21. Daniel Johnson Fleming, *Whither Bound in Missions* (New York: Association Press, 1925), 33.

22. In 1945, for example, John Foster Dulles consulted for the Department of State at the San Francisco conference and, apart from a few weeks' reprieve, maintained his leadership of the Federal Council of Churches' Commission on a Just and Durable Peace. In 1946 he was a delegate to the Foreign Ministers' Conference appointed by Harry Truman, a delegate (with Niebuhr) at the inaugural Churches' Commission on International Affairs meeting held in Cambridge, and also maintained leadership of the Commission on a Just and Durable Peace. See correspondence files for United Nations and Federal Council of Churches of Christ in America for 1944–1946, Series 1, John Foster Dulles Papers, 1860–1988 (bulk 1945–1960), MC016, Seeley G. Mudd Manuscript Library, Princeton University. Such connections are explored in depth in chapter 7 in this volume. On the church lobby to the deliberations on the Declaration of Human Rights, see Nurser, *For All Peoples*, and correspondence from O. F. Nolde to the Commission on a Just and Durable Peace in Box 5, Folder 91, Series 1, Issues of Peace and War Pamphlet Collection, Record Group 61, Special Collections, Yale Divinity School Library. For Niebuhr's involvement with UNESCO, see Fox, *Reinhold Niebuhr*, 239.

23. Galatians 6:10.

24. For example, *Ecumenical Missionary Conference, New York, 1900: Report of the Ecumenical Conference on Foreign Missions, Held in Carnegie Hall and Neighboring Churches, April 21 to May 1*, vol. 1 (American Tract Society, 1900). See Brian Stanley, *The World Missionary Conference, Edinburgh 1910* (Grand Rapids, Mich.: William B. Eerdmans, 2009), 18.

25. David A. Hollinger, "After Cloven Tongues of Fire: Ecumenical Protestantism and the Modern American Encounter with Diversity," *Journal of American History* 98, no. 1 (June 2011): 21–48.

A recent and important work on the changing legacy and meaning of the term as it relates to the political project of European unification after World War II is Lucian Leuştean, *The Ecumenical Movement and the Making of the European Community* (Oxford: Oxford University Press, 2014).

26. In *A Cautious Patriotism: The American Churches and the Second World War* (Chapel Hill: University of North Carolina Press, 1997), Gerald Sittser argues American churches were marked by a more "cautious" and tempered patriotism than in previous wars. In a 1948 essay, John C. Bennett linked support of the United Nations and general "antimilitarism" among American churches to the influence of interwar ecumenism: "The American Churches in the Ecumenical Situation," *Ecumenical Review: A Quarterly* 1 (1948): 57–64, 62.

27. Richard John Neuhaus, *American Babylon: Notes of a Christian Exile* (New York: Basic Books, 2009), 41.

28. Victor Turner and Edith Turner, *Image and Pilgrimage in Christian Culture* (New York: Columbia University Press, 1978), 13. Also see entry in the glossary, appendix A, "Communitas, or social antistructure," 250.

29. Turner and Turner, *Image and Pilgrimage*, 13.

30. Akira Iriye, *The Globalizing of America, 1913–1945*, vol. 3 of *The Cambridge History of American Foreign Relations* (Cambridge: Cambridge University Press, 1993), 107–10. More broadly, see Iriye's later work *Cultural Internationalism and World Order* (Baltimore and London: The Johns Hopkins University Press, 1997).

31. Cited in Iriye, *Globalizing of America*, 107.

32. On preparations for Edinburgh, see W. H. T. Gairdner and John R. Mott, *Echoes from Edinburgh, 1910: An Account and Interpretation of the World Missionary Conference* (New York: Fleming H. Revell, 1910), 18–26; and Stanley, *World Missionary Conference*, chap. 2, "Origins and Preparations."

33. Leiper, *World Chaos or World Christianity*, 53.

34. For a brief overview of the Faith and Order movement, especially as it arose from the American response to Edinburgh 1910 under the auspices of Bishop Charles Brent, see Thomas E. Fitzgerald, *The Ecumenical Movement: An Introductory History* (Westport, Conn.: Praeger, 2004), 83–87.

35. Smith, *Oxford 1937*, 55.

36. Charles H. Hopkins, *John R. Mott, 1865–1955: A Biography* (Grand Rapids, Mich.: Eerdmans, 1979), 127–209. On the broader context of world travel through Christian agencies in the 1880s and 1890s, see Ian R. Tyrrell, *Woman's World/Woman's Empire: The Woman's Christian Temperance Union in International Perspective, 1880–1930* (Chapel Hill: University of North Carolina Press, 1991), and his later *Reforming the World: The Creation of America's Moral Empire* (Princeton, N.J.: Princeton University Press, 2010).

37. Hopkins, *John R. Mott*, 208.

38. Ibid.

39. On anxieties over Japan's victory, see Marilyn Lake and Henry Reynolds, *Drawing the Global Colour Line: White Men's Countries and the International Challenge of Racial Equality* (Cambridge: Cambridge University Press, 2008).

40. Cited in Philip Potter and Thomas Wieser, *Seeking and Serving the Truth: The First Hundred Years of the World Student Christian Federation* (Geneva: WCC Publications, 1997), 67.

41. Walter Littlefield, "Anti-Christians Stir China," *New York Times*, June 11, 1922, 95.

42. Cited in Potter and Wieser, *Seeking and Serving the Truth*, 70. On Japanese influence, see Michael Parker, *The Kingdom of Character: The Student Volunteer Movement for Foreign Missions, 1886–1926* (Lanham, Md.: American Society of Missiology, 1998), 157.

43. Erez Manela, *The Wilsonian Moment: Self-Determination and the International Origins of Anticolonial Nationalism* (Oxford: Oxford University Press, 2007). For the racial equality clause, see N. K. A.

Meaney, *Australia and World Crisis, 1914–1923*, vol. 2 of *History of Australian Defence and Foreign Policy 1901–23* (Sydney: Sydney University Press, 2009), 376–78.

44. Cited in Hopkins, *John R. Mott*, 626.

45. Francis P. Miller, "The Task of the Federation," *Student World*, January 1923, cited in Potter and Wieser, *Seeking and Serving the Truth*, 74.

46. W. A. Visser 't Hooft, "Nursery and Brains Trust of the Ecumenical Movement," in *Memoirs* (London: S.C.M. Press, 1973), 35–42, esp. 40, note 9.

47. Hopkins, *John R. Mott*, 603.

48. Cited in Hopkins, *John R. Mott*, 601–2, who in turns cites W. R. Hogg, *Ecumenical Foundations: A History of the International Missionary Council* (New York: Harpers, 1952).

49. Howard A. Bridgman, "As Missionaries View Their Growing World," *New York Times*, May 6, 1928, 142.

50. Hogg, *Ecumenical Foundations*, cited in Hopkins, *John R. Mott*, 659.

51. Bridgman, "As Missionaries View Their Growing World," 142.

52. Statement, "The Christian Mission and War," International Missionary Council, in *Addresses and Other Records*, vol. 8 of *Report of the Jerusalem Meeting of the International Missionary Council, March 24th–April 8th, 1928* (London: Oxford University Press, 1928), 200–1.

53. International Missionary Council, *The Christian Mission in the Light of Race Conflict*, vol. 4 of *Report of the Jerusalem Meeting of the International Missionary Council, March 24th–April 8th, 1928* (London: Oxford University Press, 1928).

54. John R. Mott, "Expectations," in International Missionary Council, *Addresses and Other Records*, 26.

55. On Yergan, David Henry Anthony's biography is especially helpful on the transnational black YMCA context in which Yergan worked. See *Max Yergan: Race Man, Internationalist, Cold Warrior* (New York: New York University Press, 2006), esp. chap. 4, "South Africa, Part II." For his later politics, see, as well as Anthony, Penny Von Eschen, *Race against Empire: Black Americans and Anticolonialism, 1937–1957* (Ithaca: Cornell University Press, 1997).

56. Davidson D. T. Jabavu, *The Segregation Fallacy and Other Papers: A Native View of Some South African Inter-Racial Problems* (Lovedale: Lovedale Institution Press, 1928).

57. Max Yergan, in "Council Discussion," in International Missionary Council, *The Christian Mission in the Light of Race Conflict*, 218.

58. Ibid., 218–19.

59. Ibid., 220.

60. Cited in Bridgman, "As Missionaries View Their Growing World," 142.

61. Jorge Bocobo, in James A. Dobson, "Account of the Discussion," in *The Christian Mission in the Light of Race Conflict*, 228.

62. Samuel Guy Inman, "Missions and Economics in Latin America," in *Christianity and the Growth of Industrialism in Asia, Africa, & South America*, vol. 5 of *Report of the Jerusalem Meeting of the International Missionary Council, March 24th–April 8th, 1928* (London: Oxford University Press, 1928), 135.

63. Ibid., 139.

64. Bridgman, "As Missionaries View Their Growing World," 142.

65. "The Protection of Missionaries," in *Addresses and Other Records*, 201–2.

66. Samuel McCrea Cavert, "Jerusalem Looks at the World," *The World Tomorrow*, June 1928, 251–53.

67. International Missionary Council, "Statement Adopted by the Council: Racial Relationships," in *The Christian Mission in the Light of Race Conflict*, vol. 4 of *Report of the Jerusalem Meeting of the International Missionary Council, March 24th–April 8th, 1928* (London: Oxford University Press, 1928), 237–45, 237.

68. Ibid., 238.

69. Ibid., 237.

70. Glenda E. Gilmore, *Defying Dixie: The Radical Roots of Civil Rights, 1919–1950* (New York: W. W. Norton, 2008). Also see Anthony, *Max Yergan,* esp. chap. 4.

71. "Statement Adopted by the Council: Racial Relationships," 238–39. Compare, for example, a characteristic speech from John R. Mott in 1925 to the Foreign Missions Convention of North America at Washington, in which he argued "because He [Christ] is all of them so the Church which is His Body cannot be perfected until 'they shall bring the glory and the honor of the nations into it,' that is to say, until the spiritual characteristics of every race and Christian name have been, not submerged, but brought to their individual perfection in a perfect whole." Mott, "New Forces Released by Cooperation," in *The Foreign Missions Convention at Washington,* ed. Fennel P. Turner and Frank Knight Sanders (New York: Fleming H. Revell Company, 1925), 209–10, 216.

72. "Statement Adopted by the Council: Racial Relationships," 238.

73. Ibid., 239.

74. Ibid.

75. Ibid.

76. Ibid., 241.

77. Sidney Gulick, untitled address, in G. K. A. Bell, *The Stockholm Conference 1925: The Official Report to the Universal Christian Conference on Life and Work Held in Stockholm, 19–30 August 1925* (London: Oxford University Press, 1926), 489–500, 498.

78. See Fitzgerald, *Ecumenical Movement,* 104–5.

79. For a general biography of Söderblom available in English, see Bengt Sundkler, *Nathan Söderblom: His Life and Work* (Lund: Gleerup, 1968).

80. The phrase "as if" is used by Visser 't Hooft in *Memoirs,* 25.

81. Fitzgerald, *Ecumenical Movement,* 90; Visser 't Hooft, *Memoirs,* 25.

82. Bell, *Stockholm Conference 1925,* 2.

83. Visser 't Hooft, *Memoirs,* 25.

84. *International Relations: Being the Report Presented to the Conference on Christian Politics, Economics and Citizenship at Birmingham, April 5–12, 1924,* vol. 7 (London: Longmans Green, 1924), 88.

85. Sundkler, *Nathan Söderblom,* 376.

86. M. le Pasteur Jézéquel, in Bell, *Stockholm Conference 1925,* 474–75.

87. Sundkler, *Nathan Söderblom,* 374.

88. Visser 't Hooft, *Memoirs,* 25.

89. D. Klingemann, in Bell, *Stockholm Conference 1925,* 452.

90. Sundkler, *Nathan Söderblom,* 373.

91. Bell, *Kingship of Christ,* 28.

92. Willoughby Dickinson, "International Friendship through the Churches," in Bell, *Stockholm Conference 1925,* 507.

93. Charles Brent, in Bell, *Stockholm Conference 1925,* 444.

94. Adolf Diessmann in Bell, *Stockholm Conference 1925,* 481.

95. Diessmann, in Bell, *Stockholm Conference 1925,* 479–80.

96. Cited in Visser 't Hooft, *Memoirs,* 26.

97. Nils Ehrenström, "Movements for International Friendship and Life and Work, 1925–1948," cited in Fitzgerald, *Ecumenical Movement,* 90.

98. Graeme Smith also argues that a report from Rufus Jones to the Jerusalem 1928 conference inspired, and helped frame, Oldham's approach to setting the research parameters for Oxford 1937. Smith, *Oxford 1937,* 119–21.

5. Race, Nation, and Globe at Oxford 1937

1. Henry Smith Leiper, *Highlights of Oxford* (New York: Universal Christian Council for Life and Work, 1937), 5, in Box 14, Life and Work Collection, Ecumenical Library, Interchurch Center, New York City (hereafter cited as Life and Work Collection).

2. On devotions being treated as free time at other conferences, see Henry Smith Leiper, *World Chaos or World Christianity, A Popular Interpretation of Oxford and Edinburgh, 1937* (Chicago: Willett, Clark & Co, 1937), 33.

3. *Conference on Church, Community and State, Oxford, July 12–26, 1937, Notes on Devotional Sessions and Suggestions for Prayer* (Geneva: Universal Christian Council for Life and Work, 1937), 4, in Life and Work Collection.

4. "Suggestions for Prayer," from A Call to Prayer, in Box 14, Life and Work Collection.

5. Edwin E. Aubrey, "The Oxford Conference, 1937," *Journal of Religion* 17 (1937): 384.

6. On the German Confessing Church's struggle against Reich church policies, see Eberhard Bethge and Victoria Barnett, *Dietrich Bonhoeffer: A Biography*. Trans. Eric Mosbacher (Minneapolis: Fortress Press, 2000), 257–406. The year 1934 was also the year in which the Confessing Church—technically the Free Synod of Barmen—promulgated the internationally famous "Barmen Declaration," declaring political and theological independence from Nazi church policies. Keith Clements, "Barmen and the Ecumenical Movement," *Ecumenical Review* 61 (2009): 6–16.

7. "Nazi Church Defies All World Critics," *New York Times*, August 28, 1934, 6. Bethge and Barnett, *Dietrich Bonhoeffer*, 380–85.

8. W. A. Visser 't Hooft, *Memoirs* (London: S.C.M. Press, 1973), 71; Nils Ehrenström, cited in Keith Clements, *Faith on the Frontier: A Life of J. H. Oldham* (Edinburgh: T&T Clark, 1999), 308.

9. Joseph H. Oldham, *Church, Community and State: A World Issue* (New York: Harper, 1935), 26.

10. Ibid., 29.

11. Although my designation might differ from his in its precise deployment, I am indebted here to Gary Dorrien's excellent critique of the term "neoorthodoxy" and his use of "postliberal thinking" to describe the currents in theology often wrongly bagged together as neoorthodox. Gary J. Dorrien, *The Barthian Revolt in Modern Theology: Theology without Weapons* (Louisville, Ky.: Westminster John Knox Press, 2000). On page 2, Dorrien writes, "In the 1930s these thinkers [Eduard Thurneysen, Friedrich Gogarten, Emil Brunner, Rudolf Bultmann and Paul Tillich] and numerous others, notably Dietrich Bonhoeffer, Reinhold Niebuhr, H. Richard Niebuhr, Regin Prenter, Gustav Aulen, and Helmut Thielicke worked out their own forms of theologically postliberal thinking while highlighting their differences from Barth and each other." As Dorrien notes, Barth rejected the terms "neoorthodox," "dialectical," and "Barthian." It should also be noted here that I do not use the term "postliberal" to refer to the specific genealogy of theologians associated with Yale Divinity School in the late twentieth century, although there may be some overlap between their concerns and those of 1930s theologians. On the later movement, see Ronald T. Michener, *Postliberal Theology: A Guide for the Perplexed* (London: Bloomsbury, 2013).

12. See Mark Thomas Edwards, *Right of the Protestant Left: God's Totalitarianism* (New York: Palgrave Macmillan, 2012).

13. Dorrien, "Introduction: Neoorthodoxy Reconsidered," in *The Barthian Revolt in Modern Theology*. On Reinhold Niebuhr's criticisms of Barth and Barthianism as lacking social and ethical effectiveness—especially as a resource for Christian socialism, see "Barth—Apostle of the Absolute," *Christian Century*, December 13, 1928; "Barthianism and the Kingdom," *Christian Century*, July 15, 1931; and "Barthianism and Political Reaction," all in *Essays in Applied Christianity*, ed. D. B. Robertson (New York: Meridian Books, 1959), 141–56. As Richard Fox notes, Niebuhr's engagement

with the dialectical elements in Barth's theology became increasingly theological (as opposed to merely ethical) in the mid-1930s. While he still stated his differences, Niebuhr himself took up the dialectical style, and argued that Barth ought to be more truly dialectical—recognizing the tension in Hebrew prophetism—than he was. Richard Wightman Fox, *Reinhold Niebuhr: A Biography, with a New Introduction and Afterword* (Ithaca: Cornell University Press, 1996), 164–65.

14. Visser 't Hooft, *Memoirs*, 36.

15. See, for example, Karl Barth, *Protestant Thought: From Rousseau to Ritschl*, trans. Brian Cozens (New York: Harper, 1959); Barth, "Introductory Essay," in Ludwig Feuerbach, *The Essence of Christianity*, trans. George Eliot (New York: Harper Torchbooks, 1957).

16. Karl Barth, *The Epistle to the Romans*, 2nd. ed., 1922, reprinted in *Karl Barth: Theologian of Freedom*, ed. Clifford Green (Minneapolis: Fortress Press, 1991), 116. According to Barth scholar Eberhard Busch, the publication of successive translations of this commentary into English throughout the 1920s–1930s defined Barth's notoriety even though he later softened his position in his multivolume *Church Dogmatics* over ensuing decades. Cited in *Karl Barth: Theologian of Freedom*, 115.

17. Karl Barth, "No! Answer to Emil Brunner," reprinted in *Karl Barth: Theologian of Freedom*, 154.

18. See Edwards, *Right of the Protestant Left*.

19. On Niebuhr's criticisms of Barth and Barthianism as lacking social and ethical effectiveness, see sources listed in note 13.

20. See Langdon Gilkey, *On Niebuhr: A Theological Study* (Chicago: University of Chicago Press, 2001); Stanley Hauerwas, *With the Grain of the Universe: The Church's Witness and Natural Theology: Being the Gifford Lectures Delivered at the University of St. Andrews in 2001* (London: SCM Press, 2002).

21. Reinhold Niebuhr, "Why I Leave the F.O.R.," *Christian Century*, January 3, 1934, reprinted in *Love and Justice: Selections from the Shorter Writings of Reinhold Niebuhr*, ed. D. B. Robertson, (Cleveland, Ohio: Meridian Books, World Publishing, 1967), 261.

22. Reinhold Niebuhr, *Human Nature*, vol. 1 of *The Nature and Destiny of Man* (New York: C. Scribner's Sons, 1941).

23. Clements, *Faith on the Frontier*, 63.

24. Graeme Smith, *Oxford 1937: The Universal Christian Council for Life and Work Conference* (Frankfurt am Main: Peter Lang, 2004), 194; Barth, "No! Answer to Emil Brunner," 154. As Clements has shown, Brunner was seen as being so close to Barth's position that it caused anxiety to intending American Oxford delegates. Clements, *Faith on the Frontier*, 317–18.

25. Henry P. Van Dusen, "To the Members of the Theological Discussion Group," October 9, 1936, Box 1, Folder 7, Theological Discussion Group Papers, Burke Library, Union Theological Seminary (hereafter, TDG Papers).

26. "The Church" was the theme of the November 1936 meeting of the Theological Discussion Group. See Van Dusen, "To the Members of the Theological Discussion Group," October 9, 1936, Box 1, Folder 7, TDG Papers. "The Christian Philosophy of History" was the theme of the February 1936 meeting. See Van Dusen, "To the Members of the Theological Discussion Group," December 11, 1935, Box 1, Folder 6, TDG Papers. "The Christian Doctrine of Man" was the subject of February 1935 meeting. See Van Dusen, "To the Members of the Theological Discussion Group," December 14, 1934, Box 1, Folder 4, TDG Papers.

27. Reinhold Niebuhr, "The Christian Church in a Secular Age," in *The Essential Reinhold Niebuhr*, ed. Robert McAfee Brown (New Haven, Conn.: Yale University Press, 1986), 80ff.

28. This emphasis was increasingly clear in Reinhold Niebuhr, *An Interpretation of Christian Ethics* (1935, repr., San Francisco: Harper San Francisco, 1963), in which he dabbled in Continental theology with the help of new émigré to New York Paul Tillich, and it was made emphatic in Karl Barth's famous "Nein" to all forms of natural and historical immanentism.

29. For poems coined by British clergy and students about Niebuhr, see Fox, *Reinhold Niebuhr*, 181.

30. Charles W. Hurd, "Militant Program Urged for Religion," *New York Times*, July 14, 1937, 12.

31. F. Ernest Johnston's initials appear on the front cover of the Delegates Handbook. On page 22 he has made notes next to the list of speakers on the conference program. Box 14, Life and Work Collection.

32. Cited in "Introduction to the Programme," *Conference on Church, Community and State, Oxford, July 12–26, 1937: Delegates' Handbook*, 19–20, in Box 14, Life and Work Collection.

33. Leiper, *World Chaos*, 53.

34. Aubrey, "The Oxford Conference," 390–91. For the typical process of drafting and review within each section, see Leiper, *World Chaos*, 51–56.

35. William Adams Brown, *What the Oxford Conference of 1937 May Mean for the Life of the Church: A Paper* (New York: Universal Christian Council for Life and Work, 1937), 7, in Box 13, Life and Work Collection.

36. Ernest Barker, "Church and Community," in *Church and Community*, vol. 5 of *Church, Community, and State*, ed. Kenneth S. Latourette et al. (London: G. Allen & Unwin, 1938), 21–60, 27–29.

37. Ibid., 32.

38. Hanns Lilje, "Church and Nation," in *Church and Community*, vol. 5 of *Church, Community, and State*, ed. Kenneth S. Latourette et al. (London: G. Allen & Unwin, 1938), 85–114, 87.

39. Ibid., 88.

40. Ibid.

41. Ibid., 90.

42. Ibid., 91.

43. Ibid., 109.

44. "Church and Community," *Official Reports of the Oxford Conference*, [Federal Council of Churches], 58, in Box 14, Life and Work Collection.

45. For the president of the Fédération Protestante de France, Pastor Marc Boegner (later a member of the French resistance and a postwar ecumenist), the latter position was true: Nationality was not to be considered part of the orders of creation but part of the results of sin. "The nations . . . do not appear till after the Fall, and even after the Flood," Boegner asserted, referring to the narrative sequence of Genesis 1–11. Marc Boegner, "The Church and the Nation," in *Church and Community*, vol. 5 of *Church, Community, and State*, ed. Latourette et al. (London: G. Allen & Unwin, 1938), 63–81, 71.

46. "Church and Community," *Official Reports of the Oxford Conference*, 55–60.

47. Compare, for example, Ernest Gellner, *Nations and Nationalism* (Ithaca: Cornell University Press, 1983) and Anthony Giddens, *A Contemporary Critique of Historical Materialism* (Berkeley: University of California Press, 1981), 13.

48. "Church and Community," *Official Reports of the Oxford Conference*, 55–56.

49. See the address of Rt. Rev. E. J. Palmer, bishop of Bombay, who argued, "Our Lord also recognized inequality of privilege between races, but drew from it the lesson that the races which have been privileged to receive more enlightenment have heavier responsibilities." In G. K. A. Bell, *The Stockholm Conference 1925: The Official Report to the Universal Christian Conference on Life and Work Held in Stockholm, 19–30 August 1925* (London: Oxford University Press, 1926), 461.

50. "Church and Community," *Official Reports of the Oxford Conference*, 60.

51. See Barbara Dianne Savage, "Benjamin Mays, Global Ecumenism, and Local Religious Segregation," in *Religion and Politics in the Contemporary United States*, ed. R. Marie Griffith and Melani McAlister (Baltimore. Md.: Johns Hopkins University Press, 2008), 261.

52. "Church and Community," *Official Reports of the Oxford Conference*, 62.

53. Leiper, *Highlights of Oxford*, 7.

54. For Henry Smith Leiper's list of those involved in the World of Nations section, see *World Chaos*, 54–56.

55. "The Universal Church and the World of Nations," *Official Reports of the Oxford Conference*, 10.

56. The particular text from Wells provoking discussion in ecumenical circles was H. G. Wells, *The Shape of Things to Come* (New York: The Macmillan Co, 1933). See John S. Partington, *Building Cosmopolis: The Political Thought of H.G. Wells* (Aldershot: Ashgate, 2003). The marquess of Lothian, Phillip Kerr, who was sympathetic with Wells's reasoning, also later lauded Clarence Streit's related plan for a federal superstate encompassing the democratic nations, elaborated in Clarence K. Streit, *Union Now: A Proposal for a Federal Union of the Democracies of the North Atlantic* (New York: Harper & Bros, 1939). See "New Peace Plan Hailed by Lothian," *New York Times*, March 6, 1939, 3.

57. Philip Kerr, "The Demonic Influence of National Sovereignty," *The Universal Church and the World of Nations*, ed. Philip Henry Kerr et al., vol. 7 of the Official Oxford Conference books (London: Allen & Unwin, 1938), 18.

58. Ibid., 23.

59. Ibid., 20.

60. See "Part IV: Inherent Difficulties in the Establishment of International Order," in Report, "The Universal Church and the World of Nations," in *The Universal Church and the World of Nations*, Oxford Conference Study Series (New York: Universal Christian Council), 10, in Box 17, Life and Work Collection.

61. On the background to Zimmern's idea of an "international commonwealth—establishing global harmony in a world of national sentiments," see Mark Mazower, "Zimmern and the Empire of Freedom," in *No Enchanted Palace: The End of Empire and the Ideological Origins of the United Nations* (Princeton, N.J.: Princeton University Press, 2009), chap. 2, 66ff.

62. Alfred Zimmern, "The Ethical Presuppositions of a World Order," in *The Universal Church and the World of Nations*, ed. Philip Henry Kerr et al., vol. 7 of *Church Community and State* (London: Allen & Unwin, 1938), 27–57, 45.

63. From Augustine, Zimmern claimed to draw the idea that peace proceeds from order, and that order is found primarily in the City of God. The earthly state could approximate, in a distant way, the order and righteousness of the heavenly city, but (and here Zimmern is quoting from Barker's introduction to the Temple Classics edition of *City of God*), "granted the defect of sin . . . it is only a second best." Zimmern, "The Ethical Presuppositions of a World Order," 43. Compare Reinhold Niebuhr, "Augustine's Political Realism," in *Christian Realism and Political Problems* (New York: Scribner, 1953), chap. 9. See also Roger Ivan Epp, *The Augustinian Moment in International Politics: Niebuhr, Butterfield, Wight and the Reclaiming of a Tradition* (Aberystwyth: Dept. of International Politics, University College of Wales, 1991).

64. John Foster Dulles, "The Problem of Peace in a Dynamic World," in *The Universal Church and the World of Nations*. ed. Philip Henry Kerr et al., vol. 7 of *Church Community and State* (London: Allen & Unwin, 1938), 145–68, 152.

65. Ibid., 155.

66. "The Universal Church and the World of Nations," *Official Reports of the Oxford Conference*, 11.

67. Ibid.

68. Wilhelm Menn, "The Church of Christ and the International Order," in *The Universal Church and the World of Nations*, ed. Philip Henry Kerr et al., vol. 7 of *Church Community and State* (London: Allen & Unwin, 1938), 203–38.

69. Ibid., 208.

70. Ibid., 209.

71. "The Universal Church and the World of Nations," *Official Reports of the Oxford Conference*, 8.

72. Ibid.

73. Ibid., 16.

74. The report of the subsection on war recognized three basic positions on war: those who saw war as "always sin"; those who would only participate in "just wars"—whether the justness was determined by international law or by a criterion of "essential Christian principle"; and finally those who "while also stressing the Christian obligation to work for peace and mutual understanding among the nations, hold nevertheless that no such effort can end war in the world." The latter held that the state was a divinely appointed tool for the prevention of anarchy and crime, and thus it was "a Christian's duty to obey the political authority as far as possible." Despite the differences in opinion over what to do about war, the report managed to agree on an important consensus paragraph containing a theological description of war:

> Wars, the occasions of wars, and all situations which conceal the fact of conflict under the guise of outward peace are marks of a world to which the Church is charged to proclaim the gospel of redemption. War involves compulsory enmity, diabolical outrage against human personality, and a wanton distortion of the truth. War is a particular demonstration of the power of sin in this world, and a defiance of the righteousness of God as revealed in Jesus Christ and Him crucified. No justification of war must be allowed to conceal or minimize this fact.

Such description—marked for special attention in the original report with the use of italics—left little room for a triumphalist nationalistic justification for war. "The Universal Church and the World of Nations," *Official Reports of the Oxford Conference*, 13–16.

75. "The Universal Church and the World of Nations," *Official Reports of the Oxford Conference*, 9.

76. On internationalist culture and league "fever," see Glenda Sluga, *Internationalism in the Age of Nationalism* (Philadelphia: University of Pennsylvania Press, 2013), 58.

77. Zimmern, "The Ethical Presuppositions of a World Order," 40.

78. Ibid., 38.

79. Ibid., 41.

80. Notes on League of Nations in "Study Two: Obstacles to International Order," in *The Universal Church and the World of Nations*, Oxford Conference Study Series (New York: Universal Christian Council), 26, in Box 17, Life and Work Collection.

81. "The Universal Church and the World of Nations," part 6, "Attempts to Organize an International Order," *Official Reports of the Oxford Conference*, 12.

82. Ibid.

83. Huber's major work outlining his view of the sociological basis of international law was *Die soziologischen grundlagen des völkerrechts* (Berlin-Grunewald: W. Rothschild, 1928). For an introduction to and analysis of Huber's life and legacy, see the special edition of the *European Journal of International Law* 18, no. 1 (2007), where Huber's views are seen to hold special topical relevance to debates over the limits of state power in the international sphere in the 2000s. See especially Daniel Thürer, "Max Huber: A Portrait in Outline," *European Journal of International Law* 18 (2007): 69–80.

84. Jost Delbrück, "Max Huber's Sociological Approach to International Law Revisited," *European Journal of International Law* 18 (2007): 97–113, 102.

85. "Study Two: Obstacles to International Order," *The Universal Church and the World of Nations*, Oxford Conference Study Series (New York: Universal Christian Council), 25, in Box 17, Life and Work Collection.

86. Huber's paper was not listed on the provisional contents list in the conference handbook, but it was included in the final edition that went to press that same year.

87. Max Huber, "Some Observations upon the Christian Understanding of International Law," in *The Universal Church and the World of Nations*. ed. Philip Henry Kerr et al., vol. 7 of *Church Community and State* (London: Allen & Unwin, 1938), 95–141, 131.

88. "The Universal Church and the World of Nations," *Official Reports of the Oxford Conference*, 10.

89. Huber, "Some Observations," 138.

90. Ibid., 102–3. For the double aspect, Huber, after lengthy biblical exegesis, cited Romans 13 for the divinely willed necessity, and Revelation 15 for the demonic character of the state, although his use of the latter passage was oblique.

91. Huber, "Some Observations," 116.

92. "The Universal Church and the World of Nations," *Official Reports of the Oxford Conference*, 10.

93. Ibid., 11.

94. Ibid., 10.

95. Ibid., 8.

96. "The Universal Church and the World of Nations," part 7, "The Church and War," *Official Reports of the Oxford Conference*, 13.

97. Leiper, *World Chaos*, 31.

98. "Church Spirit Here Scored at Oxford," *New York Times*, July 17, 1937, 16.

99. "The Universal Church and the World of Nations," *Official Reports of the Oxford Conference*, 18.

100. "The Universal Church and the World of Nations," part 8: "The Church's Witness"; part 7, "Ecumenical Organization," *Official Reports of the Oxford Conference*, 19.

101. Aubrey, "The Oxford Conference," 388.

102. "The Proposal for a World Council of Churches," in *The Universal Church and the World of Nations,* Oxford Conference Study Series (New York: Universal Christian Council), 20–21, in Box 17, Life and Work Collection.

103. "Message from the Oxford Conference to the Christian Churches," in Leiper, *Highlights of Oxford*, 13–14.

104. Ibid., 13.

105. Ibid.

106. Ibid., 13–14.

107. See Dorothy V. Jones, *Toward a Just World: The Critical Years in the Search for International Justice* (Chicago: University of Chicago Press, 2002); Akira Iriye, *Cultural Internationalism and World Order* (Baltimore, Md.: Johns Hopkins University Press, 1997); Cecelia Lynch, *Beyond Appeasement: Interpreting Interwar Peace Movements in World Politics* (Ithaca: Cornell University Press, 1999).

6. Oxford's Atlantic Crossing

1. "A Word from Henry Smith Leiper, Executive Secretary for the Universal Christian Council, New York City," accompanying Pamphlet for American delegates, Amerop Travel Service, "The World Conference on Life and Work, Oxford, July 12 to July 26," in Box 13, Life and Work Collection, Ecumenical Library, Interchurch Center, New York City (hereafter, cited as Life and Work Collection).

2. Edwin E. Aubrey, "The Oxford Conference, 1937," *Journal of Religion* 17 (1937): 396.

3. Brochure, Amerop Travel Service, "The World Conference on Life and Work, Oxford, July 12 to July 26," in Box 13, Life and Work Collection.

4. Daniel T. Rodgers, *Atlantic Crossings: Social Politics in a Progressive Age* (Cambridge, Mass.: Belknap Press of Harvard University Press, 1998).

5. Joint Executive Committee [of the American sections of the Life and Work and Faith and Order movements], "On from Oxford and Edinburgh: What communities have done to present the message of these world conferences of 1937," in Box 17, Life and Work Collection.

6. For NBC, see Heather A. Warren, *Theologians of a New World Order: Reinhold Niebuhr and the Christian Realists* (New York: Oxford University Press, 1997), 87.

7. Walter Van Kirk, cited in Henry Smith Leiper, *Highlights of Oxford* (New York: Universal Christian Council for Life and Work, 1937), 3, in Box 14, Life and Work Collection.

8. Charles W. Hurd, "Fellowship Urged to Reclaim Church: Oxford Conference Hears Pleas for Vigorous Christian Band to Offset Nationalism," *New York Times*, July 15, 1937, 7.

9. Aubrey, "The Oxford Conference," 395.

10. Reinhold Niebuhr, "The Oxford Conference on Church and State," *Radical Religion* (Autumn 1937), reprinted in *Essays in Applied Christianity*, ed. D. B. Robertson (New York: Meridian Books, 1959), 295–97.

11. Benjamin Mays, "The Church Surveys World Problems"; "World Churchmen Score Prejudice," *Crisis* (November 1937): 340–41.

12. I am drawing here on Elesha J. Coffman's excellent exploration of the meaning of "mainline" in *The Christian Century and the Rise of the Protestant Mainline* (New York: Oxford University Press, 2013), 6.

13. "Study One," in *The Universal Church and the World of Nations*, Oxford Conference Study Series, (New York: Universal Christian Council), 23–24, in Box 17, Life and Work Collection.

14. "Study Two," *The Universal Church and the World of Nations*, 28.

15. "Study Three," *The Universal Church and the World of Nations*, 31.

16. Cited in *The Church and Race: What Was Said at the World Conference on Church, Community and State* (New York: Department of Race Relations, Federal Council of the Churches of Christ in America, Interracial Publications, no. 36, 1937), n.p., in Box 14, Life and Work Collection.

17. *The Church and Race*, front cover.

18. Mark Thomas Edwards, *Right of the Protestant Left: God's Totalitarianism* (New York: Palgrave Macmillan, 2012), 80.

19. Attachment (B), "Evanston Illinois," Joint Executive Committee, "On from Oxford and Edinburgh."

20. Ibid.

21. Exchange between Morrison and Van Dusen cited in Richard Wightman Fox, *Reinhold Niebuhr: A Biography, with a New Introduction and Afterword* (Ithaca: Cornell University Press, 1996), 180.

22. For example, see "Religion: Justification of Justice," [review of Reinhold Niebuhr's work], *Time*, Monday, March 1, 1943, accessed August 27, 2011, http://www.time.com/time/magazine/article/0,9171,932978,00.html; "Religion: Faith for a Lenten Age," [feature story on Reinhold Niebuhr with front cover image], *Time*, Monday, March 8, 1948, accessed August 27, 2011, http://www.time.com/time/magazine/article/0,9171,853293,00.html; "Religion: The Liberal," [on a new professorship at Union Seminary], *Time*, Monday, May 25, 1953, accessed August 27, 2011, http://www.time.com/time/magazine/article/0,9171,890580,00.html; "Religion: Heart First" [profile of former Seminary President Henry Sloane Coffin], *Time*, Monday, December 6, 1954, accessed August 27, 2011, http://www.time.com/time/magazine/article/0,9171,820962,00.html; "Religion: New Head for Union," [on appointment of Henry Pit Van Dusen as new president], *Time*, Monday, May 29, 1944, accessed August 27, 2011, http://www.time.com/time/magazine/article/0,9171,850922,00.html. Countless other profiles and stories referring to Van Dusen, Niebuhr, and Bennett are to be found in *Time* archives throughout the 1940s–1960s.

23. Fox, *Reinhold Niebuhr*, 211–12.

24. Henry Sloane Coffin, *A Half Century of Union Theological Seminary, 1896–1945: An Informal History* (New York: Scribner, 1954), 226.

25. Mark Edwards, "'God Has Chosen Us': Re-Membering Christian Realism, Rescuing Christendom, and the Contest of Responsibilities during the Cold War," *Diplomatic History* 33 (2009): 72.

26. For Leiper's position, see Union Theological Seminary, *Catalogue: 1944*, 16, in Box 10, Group 14, Series 2: UTS Records, Union Theological Seminary Archives, The Burke Library (Columbia University Libraries) at Union Theological Seminary, New York (hereafter UTS Records).

27. Union Theological Seminary, *Catalogue: 1945*, 92, in Box 10, Group 14, Series 2: UTS Records. Note that "Amsterdam" was not a reference to the future 1948 conference, but the 1939 gathering of Christian youth through the World Council of Churches.

28. John C. Bennett, "Christian Ethics 337: The Church and the World," in Union Theological Seminary, *Catalogue: 1945*, 95.

29. Reinhold Niebuhr to John C. Bennett, March 13 [1943], Folder for John C. Bennett Correspondence, Box 42, Reinhold Niebuhr Papers, Library of Congress.

30. Union Theological Seminary, *Catalogue: 1944*, 90, 17.

31. Union Theological Seminary, *Catalogue: 1945*, 94.

32. John M. Graham, "Problems of To-day : VII. What Is Meant by the Social Gospel?," *The Expository Times* 50 (1939): 301–5. On *Radical Religion* as a personal mouthpiece, see Fox, *Reinhold Niebuhr*, 167–68.

33. Mark Hulsether, *Building a Protestant Left: Christianity and Crisis Magazine, 1941–1993* (Knoxville: University of Tennessee Press, 1999), 26.

34. Niebuhr to John C. Bennett, May 31, 1940, Folder for John C. Bennett Correspondence, Box 42, Reinhold Niebuhr Papers, Library of Congress.

35. Reinhold Niebuhr, "The Christian Faith and the World Crisis," *Christianity and Crisis*, February 10, 1941, 4–5.

36. Editorial, "The Lend-Lease Bill," *Christianity and Crisis*, February 10, 1941, 2.

37. Editorial, "The World after the War," *Christianity and Crisis*, February 10, 1941, 3.

38. Editorial, "Holy Wars," *Christianity and Crisis*, February 10, 1941, 2.

39. "Universal Church and World of Nations, part 8: The Church's Witness," *Official Reports of the Oxford Conference*, [Federal Council of Churches], 58, in Box 14, Life and Work Collection, 18.

40. Editorial, "British Churchmen and Peace Aims," *Christianity and Crisis*, February 10, 1941, 3.

41. The distinctly "nonscientific" approach of Martin Wight and Niebuhr, which Hedley Bull recalled nostalgically as he contrasted it to university study in the 1960s, should be seen, to a significant extent, as a legacy of the theological mode of enquiry generated by ecumenists at the Oxford 1937 conference. See Hedley Bull, "The Theory of International Politics 1919–1969," in *International Politics, 1919–1969*, ed. Brian Porter (London: Oxford University Press, 1972), 30–55.

42. Roger Ivan Epp, *The Augustinian Moment in International Politics: Niebuhr, Butterfield, Wight and the Reclaiming of a Tradition* (Aberystwyth: Dept. of International Politics, University College of Wales, 1991).

43. Martin Wight, "The Church, Russia and the West," *The Ecumenical Review* 1 (1948): 25–45.

44. On Tillich's influence on Niebuhr's *Interpretation of Christian Ethics*, see Fox, *Reinhold Niebuhr*, 161–64.

45. "Message from the Oxford Conference to the Christian Churches," in Leiper, *Highlights of Oxford*, 13–14.

46. Reinhold Niebuhr, *Human Nature*, vol. 1 of *The Nature and Destiny of Man* (New York: C. Scribner's Sons, 1941), 222.

47. Niebuhr, *Human Nature*, 226.

48. Reinhold Niebuhr, "Democracy as a Religion," *Christianity and Crisis*, August 4, 1947, 1.

49. Reinhold Niebuhr, *The Children of Light and the Children of Darkness: A Vindication of Democracy and a Critique of Its Traditional Defence* (New York: C. Scribner's Sons, 1944), xi.

50. Niebuhr, "Democracy as a Religion," 1.

51. Reinhold Niebuhr, "Ten Fateful Years," *Christianity and Crisis*, February 5, 1951, 2. See also Reinhold Niebuhr, "The Idolatry of America," *Christianity and Society* (spring 1950), reprinted in *Love and Justice: Selections from the Shorter Writings of Reinhold Niebuhr*, ed. D. B. Robertson, (Cleveland, Ohio: Meridian Books, World Publishing, 1967), 94–97.

52. Reinhold Niebuhr, "The Illusion of World Government," *Foreign Affairs* (April 1949), reprinted in Niebuhr, *Christian Realism and Political Problems* (New York: Scribner, 1953), 15–31. For critique of rationalism and social contract, see 18. For quote on "community," see 22.

53. Max Huber, "Some Observations upon the Christian Understanding of International Law," in *The Universal Church and the World of Nations*. ed. Philip Henry Kerr et al., vol. 7 of *Church Community and State* (London: Allen & Unwin, 1938), 131.

54. "Universal Church and the World of Nations," *Official Reports of the Oxford Conference*, 10.

55. Henry P. Van Dusen, "The Ecumenical (World-Wide) Character of the Church Enables It and Its Members to Make a Unique Contribution to World Order," in *A Just and Durable Peace: A Discussion by Leaders of the American Churches*, ed. John Foster Dulles et al. (London: Student Christian Movement Press, 1943), 31.

56. Reinhold Niebuhr, *Human Destiny*, vol. 2 of *The Nature and Destiny of Man* (New York: C. Scribner's Sons, 1943), 294–96.

57. Reinhold Niebuhr, "Plans for World Reorganization," *Christianity and Crisis*, October 19, 1942, 3–6, 6.

58. Fox, *Reinhold Niebuhr*, 234. See also the account of Barth's speech in which he made such an accusation, "Plenary Session, Concertgebouw, 3pm," Monday August 23, 1948, in *The First Assembly of the World Council of Churches: The Official Report*, ed. W. A. Visser 't Hooft (London: SCM Press, 1948), 32–33.

59. Karl Barth, "The Church between East and West," first translated into English by Stanley Godman in *World Review*, 1949, reprinted in *Karl Barth: Theologian of Freedom*, ed. Clifford Green (Minneapolis: Fortress Press, 1991), 302–18, 309.

60. Barth, "The Church between East and West," 315.

61. Reinhold Niebuhr, Class Lecture Notes: "Barth's Neutralism," 1. Niebuhr's notes discuss Barth's text, "The Christian Community in Political Change," Class Lectures, Box 24: Miscellany, Reinhold Niebuhr Papers, Library of Congress.

62. Reinhold Niebuhr, "Anglo-Saxon Destiny and Responsibility," *Christianity and Crisis*, October 4, 1943, 2–4.

63. Reinhold Niebuhr, "The Moral and Spiritual Content of the Atlantic Community," in *Five Years of the North Atlantic Alliance: A Symposium* (New York: American Council on N.A.T.O., 1954). For drafts and correspondence with commissioning editor David Martin, see Box 16, Reinhold Niebuhr Papers, Library of Congress. On the USIA "marketing the Atlantic Community in Europe," see Kenneth A. Osgood, *Total Cold War: Eisenhower's Secret Propaganda Battle at Home and Abroad* (Lawrence: University of Kansas, 2006), 107ff.

64. Reinhold Niebuhr, *The Irony of American History* (London: Nisbet & Co., 1952), 145.

65. Richard John Neuhaus, *American Babylon: Notes of a Christian Exile* (New York: Basic Books, 2009), 41.

66. In Edwards, *Right of the Protestant Left*, 36.

67. Ronald W. Pruessen, *John Foster Dulles: The Road to Power* (New York: Free Press, 1982), 189. For realists and pacifists reorienting themselves so as to cooperate in deliberations on the postwar future, see David A. Hollinger, "The Realist–Pacifist Summit Meeting of March 1942 and the Political Reorientation of Ecumenical Protestantism in the United States," *Church History* 79 (2010): 654–77, esp. 654–56.

68. "Message of the National Study Conference on the Churches and the International Situation, 1940," reprinted in *A Just and Durable Peace, Data Material and Discussion Questions*, 14.

69. Ibid., 14–15.

70. Hollinger, "The Realist–Pacifist Summit Meeting of March 1942," 665.

71. On Muste's role, see Hollinger, "The Realist–Pacifist Summit Meeting of March 1942," 664–65.

72. "A Message from the National Study Conference on the Churches and a Just and Durable Peace, 1942," 29, in Box 5, Folder 91, FCCCA: Commission to Study the Basis of a Just and Durable Peace-Miscellaneous 1941–1947, Series 1, Issues of Peace and War Pamphlet Collection, Record Group 61, Special Collections, Yale Divinity School Library.

73. Hollinger, "The Realist–Pacifist Summit Meeting of March 1942," 660.

74. Ibid.

75. *A Message to the Churches from the National Study Conference on the Churches and a Just and Durable Peace, Cleveland, Ohio, January 16–19, 1945* (New York: [Federal Council of Churches], 1945), 13.

76. Hollinger, "The Realist–Pacifist Summit Meeting of March 1942," 659.

77. "A Message from the National Study Conference, 1942," 15.

78. A. J. Muste, "The True International," *Christian Century*, May 24, 1939, in A. J. Muste and Nat Hentoff, *The Essays of A. J. Muste* (Indianapolis: Bobbs-Merrill, 1967), 213–14.

7. The Dulles Commission, the UN, and the Americanization of Christian Internationalism

1. Pamphlet, "The Christian Mission on World Order," 1943, Box 5, Series 1, Issues of Peace and War Pamphlet Collection, Record Group No. 61, Special Collections, Yale Divinity School Library (hereafter cited as Issues of Peace and War Pamphlet Collection).

2. "Mission for World Order: U.S. Church Campaign," *New York Times*, October 30, 1943, 3. On Ball's resolution, see Townsend Hoopes and Douglas Brinkley, *FDR and the Creation of the UN* (New Haven, Conn.: Yale University Press, 1997), 65–67.

3. Cited in Martin Erdmann, *Building the Kingdom of God on Earth: The Churches' Contribution to Marshal Public Support for World Order and Peace, 1919–1945* (Eugene, Ore.: Wipf and Stock, 2005), 297.

4. On the "presumption of a proprietary relationship between Protestant Christianity and the American nation," see David A. Hollinger, "The Realist–Pacifist Summit Meeting of March 1942 and the Political Reorientation of Ecumenical Protestantism in the United States," *Church History* 79 (2010): 658.

5. On the State Department's increased desire to instrumentalize cultural and public-opinion-shaping agencies in service of the state during the late 1930s and 1940s, see Justin Hart, *Empire of Ideas: The Origins of Public Diplomacy and the Transformation of U.S. Foreign Policy* (Oxford: Oxford University Press, 2013), particularly chapters 1 and 2.

6. Cited in Cecelia Lynch, *Beyond Appeasement: Interpreting Interwar Peace Movements in World Politics* (Ithaca: Cornell University Press, 1999), 205.

7. On the state's courting of morale-building civilian agencies as part of wartime mobilization and the growth of big government, see James T. Sparrow's *Warfare State: World War II Americans and the Age of Big Government* (New York: Oxford University Press, 2011). Sparrow gives coverage to the small, far-right, anti-Semitic "Christian Nationalist Crusade" political movement of 1944 (90), but does not discuss the more influential Christian internationalism of the Dulles Commission, nor mainline or liberal Protestantism in general.

8. On FDR's political imperatives, see Andrew Preston, *Sword of the Spirit, Shield of Faith: Religion in American War and Diplomacy* (New York: Alfred A. Knopf, 2012), 396–97.

9. Henry Pit Van Dusen, cited in Ronald W. Pruessen, *John Foster Dulles: The Road to Power* (New York: Free Press, 1982), 190.

10. Mark G. Toulouse, *The Transformation of John Foster Dulles: From Prophet of Realism to Priest of Nationalism* (Macon, Ga.: Mercer University Press, 1985), 58.

11. Pruessen, *John Foster Dulles*, 190.

12. Preston, *Sword of the Spirit, Shield of Faith*, 386–88. More generally, see also chap. 21, "John Foster Dulles and the Quest for a Just and Durable Peace."

13. Toulouse, *Transformation of John Foster Dulles*, 56–58.

14. Ibid., 50.

15. Dulles, "The Churches and World Order," cited in Toulouse, *Transformation of John Foster Dulles*, 52.

16. Dulles, "The Problem of Peace in a Dynamic World," *Religion in Life* 6 (spring 1937): 207, cited in Toulouse, *Transformation of John Foster Dulles*, 53.

17. John Foster Dulles, *War, Peace and Change* (New York: Harper & Brothers, 1939), 56–64, and 116–17.

18. "Principles of a Just and Durable Peace Recommended by Responsible Christian Leaders: Statement adopted at the Biennial Meeting of the Federal Council of the Churches in Christ in America at Atlantic City, December 10–13, 1940." Reprinted in *A Just and Durable Peace, Data Material and Discussion Questions* (New York: The Commission to Study the Bases of a Just and Durable Peace of the Federal Council of the Churches of Christ in America, 1941), 10.

19. *A Just and Durable Peace*, 28.

20. "Memoranda of Study Department, Prepared under Auspices of the Provisional Committee of World Council of Churches (1939–1941)," in *A Just and Durable Peace, Data*, 34.

21. Aims listed in "The Commission to Study the Bases of a Just and Durable Peace," chap. 1 of *A Just and Durable Peace, Data*, 3.

22. John Foster Dulles, "The American People Need Now to Be Imbued with a Righteous Faith," in John Foster Dulles et al., *A Just and Durable Peace: A Discussion by Leaders of the American Churches* (London: Student Christian Movement Press, 1943), 15.

23. Malcolm D. Magee, *What the World Should Be: Woodrow Wilson and the Crafting of a Faith-Based Foreign Policy* (Waco, Tex.: Baylor University Press, 2008). The heavy influence of Dulles and other Presbyterians such as John Mackay in the commission may have accounted for the resonance of its ideas with Reformed Calvinist notions of common grace, moral law, and the totalizing impulse to reform all of life. John A. Mackay, former missionary, delegate at Oxford 1937, president of Princeton Theological Seminary, and commission member, concurred with Dulles's approach, arguing that the laws of world order "will be truest when they are transcripts of moral law," in *A Just and Durable Peace: A Discussion*, 60.

24. The Commission to Study the Bases of A Just and Durable Peace and the Federal Council of Churches of Christ in America, "A Message from the National Study Conference on The Churches and A Just and Durable Peace, 1942," 10–11, in Issues of Peace and War Pamphlet Collection.

25. Hollinger, "The Realist–Pacifist Summit Meeting of March 1942," 665–66.

26. "A Message from the National Study Conference, 1942," 12.

27. Ibid.

28. Woodrow Wilson, "Address at Independence Hall: 'The Meaning of Liberty,' July 4, 1914," *The American Presidency Project*, ed. Gerhard Peters and John T. Woolley, http://www.presidency.ucsb.edu/ws/?pid=65381.

29. "A Message from the National Study Conference, 1942," 14.

30. "A Message from the National Study Conference, 1942," 6.

31. Otto A. Piper, in "Minutes of Meeting Held at Murray Hill Hotel, June 20, 1941," Federal Council of Churches to Committee of Direction, July 25, 1941, 5, Box 5, Issues of Peace and War Pamphlet Collection.

32. Adolf Keller, in "Minutes of Meeting Held at Murray Hill Hotel, June 20, 1941," 5.

33. "Minutes of Committee Meeting of Commission to Study the Bases of a Just and Durable Peace, September 16–17, 1942," 11, Box 5, Issues of Peace and War Pamphlet Collection.

34. Ibid., 3.

35. Ibid., 17.

36. Ibid., 3.

37. One version, consisting of six headings, read:

I. The peace must provide the political framework for a continuing collaboration of the United Nations and, in due course, of neutral and enemy nations.

II. The peace must make provision for bringing under international supervision those economic and financial acts of national governments which have widespread international repercussions.

III. The peace must make provision for an organization to adapt the treaty structure of the world to changing underlying conditions.

IV. The peace must proclaim the goal of autonomy for subject peoples, and it must establish international organization to assure and to supervise the realization of that end.

V. The peace must establish procedures for controlling military establishments everywhere.

VI. The peace must establish in principle, and seek to achieve in practice, the right of individuals everywhere to religious and intellectual liberty.

The first release of the pillars came in March 1943 in a pamphlet called "A Just and Durable Peace: Statement of Political Propositions Which Underlie a Just and Durable Peace and Which the United States Ought Now to Accept for Itself and Begin Forthwith to Realize in Cooperation with Others" (New York: The Commission to Study the Bases of a Just and Durable Peace of the Federal Council of the Churches of Christ in America).

38. "A Just and Durable Peace: Statement of Political Propositions," 5.

39. Commission on a Just and Durable Peace, *Six Pillars of Peace: A Study Guide Based on "A Statement of Political Propositions"* (New York, 1943).

40. Circular Letter, Walter Van Kirk to Commission Members, April 12, 1942 [actually 1943], Box 5, Issues of Peace and War Pamphlet Collection.

41. See Preston, *Sword of the Spirit, Shield of Faith*, 394–95.

42. "U.S. Churches' Peace Plan Moral Basis for World Order," *The Times* (London), Friday, March 19, 1943, 3.

43. John Foster Dulles, "Introductory Article," in *"A Just and Durable Peace": Discussion of Political Propositions (Six Pillars of Peace)* (New York: Commission to Study the Bases of a Just and Durable Peace, 1943), 9–10, 10, Issues of Peace and War Pamphlet Collection.

44. Erdmann, *Building the Kingdom of God on Earth,* 252.

45. John Foster Dulles, "Report on Conference with President, February 15, 1944," in Box 24 (Correspondence, Federal Council of the Churches of Christ in America, 1944), Series 1: Selected Correspondence, 1891–1960; John Foster Dulles Papers, Public Policy Papers, Department of Rare Books and Special Collections, Princeton University Library (hereafter cited as Dulles Papers). See also Commission on a Just and Durable Peace, "World Organization: Curative and Creative," January 1944, 1–2, Box 5, Issues of Peace and War Pamphlet Collection; and Preston, *Sword of the Spirit, Shield of Faith*, 396. On the secretive State Department postwar planning in the early years of the

war—mainly led by Cordell Hull, Sumner Welles, and Leo Pasvolsky—see Hoopes and Brinkley, *FDR and the Creation of the UN*, 43–54. See also Cordell Hull, *The Memoirs of Cordell Hull*, vol. 2 (London: Hodder & Stoughton, 1948), chaps. 116, 118.

46. Wendell L. Willkie, *One World* (New York: Simon & Schuster, 1943).

47. United Nations, "Dumbarton Oaks and Yalta," *History of the Charter of the United Nations*, accessed April 29, 2015, http://www.un.org/en/aboutun/history/dumbarton_yalta.shtml.

48. Untitled press release, Box 25 (1944 UN Correspondence), Series 1, Dulles Papers.

49. Edward T. Folliard, "Hull, Dulles, Leave Peace Open to Debate," *Washington Post*, n.d., Box 25 (1944 UN Correspondence), Series 1, Dulles Papers.

50. "Dulles Says Goal Is Basic Unity Here on Plan for World," *New York Times*, August 20, 1944, Box 25 (1944 UN Correspondence), Series 1, Dulles Papers.

51. Preston, *Sword of the Spirit, Shield of Faith*, 397. For Hull's account—expressed in terms of political defense of the UN and eventual triumph—see Hull, *Memoirs of Cordell Hull*, vol. 2, 1690–91.

52. "Secret: Results to Date of the Dumbarton Oaks Discussion," September 11, 1944; "Secret: Proposals for the Establishment of a General International Organization," Conv. A, Document 3, September 27, 1944; Hugh R. Wilson to Dulles, September 7, 1944; all in Box 23 (Correspondence, Dumbarton Oaks Proposals, 1944), Series 1, Dulles Papers.

53. Cited in Luman J. Shafer, "Editorials to Appear in *Post-War World*," October 15, 1944, 1, in Box 24, (Correspondence, Federal Council of the Churches of Christ in America, 1944), Series 1, Dulles Papers.

54. See Henry St. George Tucker to Dulles, May 17, 1944; John Mackay to Dulles, September 27, 1944, in Box 24 (Correspondence, Federal Council of the Churches of Christ in America, 1944), Series 1, Dulles Papers.

55. Dulles to Charles Clayton Morrison, March 1, 1944, Box 24 (Correspondence, Federal Council of the Churches of Christ in America, 1944), Series 1, Dulles Papers.

56. In attendance, according to the conference records, were "481 delegates from 34 church communions, 18 allied religious bodies and 70 city and state councils of churches." The Commission on a Just and Durable Peace, *A Message to the Churches from the National Study Conference on the Churches and a Just and Durable Peace, Cleveland, Ohio, January 16–19, 1945* (New York: [Federal Council of Churches], 1945), 3.

57. Ibid., 8.

58. Ibid., 15.

59. Dulles to Geoffrey Parsons, January 22, 1945, Box 27 (Correspondence, UN, 1945), Series 1, Dulles Papers.

60. "Radio Address by John Foster Dulles, Station WJW, Cleveland, Ohio, 9:00–9:15, January 16, 1945," 11, Box 26 (Dumbarton Oaks Proposals, 1945), Series 1, Dulles Papers.

61. The Commission on a Just and Durable Peace, *A Message to the Churches . . . Cleveland, Ohio, January 16–19, 1945*, 9–10.

62. Telegram, Edward Stettinius Jr. to Dulles, March 31, 1945, Box 25 (Correspondence, Stettinius, Edward R., Jr., Mrs., 1945), Series 1, Dulles Papers.

63. Dulles to Edward Stettinius Jr., April 4, 1945, Box 25, Dulles Papers.

64. Edward Stettinius Jr. to Dulles, April 7, 1945, Box 25, Dulles Papers.

65. Dulles to G. Bromley Oxnam, April 6, 1945, Box 26 (Correspondence, Federal Council of the Churches of Christ in America, 1945), Series 1, Dulles Papers.

66. On Vandenberg, see Preston, *Sword of the Spirit, Shield of Faith*, 405–8. See also Arthur H. Vandenberg and Joe A. Morris, *The Private Papers of Senator Vandenberg* (Boston: Houghton Mifflin, 1952), 188.

67. Pamphlet, "Program: The Dulles Meeting, April 22, 1945," Box 27 (Correspondence, UN, 1945), Series 1, Dulles Papers.

68. Notes found in Box 27 (Correspondence, UN, 1945), Series 1, Dulles Papers.

69. Manuscript, "Article by John Foster Dulles for the *Dallas Morning News*," August 13, 1945, 2–5, 5, JFD papers, Box 27 (Correspondence, UN, 1945), Series 1, Dulles Papers.

70. "Extract from notes dictated in advance of meeting of Commission on a Just and Durable Peace and, in substance, used in J.F.D. opening 'off-the-record' statement to Commission on November 8, 1945," Box 26 (Correspondence, Federal Council of the Churches of Christ in America, 1945), Series 1, Dulles Papers.

71. Dulles to Harry Truman, March 8, 1946, in Box 29, (Correspondence, Federal Council of the Churches of Christ in America, 1946), Series 1, Dulles Papers.

72. Truman to Dulles, November 6, 1945, Box 26 (Correspondence, Federal Council of the Churches of Christ in America, 1945), Series 1, Dulles Papers.

73. Toulouse, *Transformation of John Foster Dulles*.

74. John Foster Dulles, "The Problem of Peace in a Dynamic World," in *The Universal Church and the World of Nations*, ed. Philip Henry Kerr et al., vol. 7 of *Church Community and State* (London: Allen & Unwin, 1938), 145–68, 168.

75. "Minutes of Committee Meeting of Commission to Study the Bases of a Just and Durable Peace, September 16–17, 1942," 4, Box 5, Issues of Peace and War Pamphlet Collection.

76. Ibid., 5.

77. John Foster Dulles, "Foreword," in *A Just and Durable Peace: A Discussion*, 10.

78. John Foster Dulles, "The American People Need Now to Be Imbued with a Righteous Faith," in *A Just and Durable Peace: A Discussion*, 11–20, 11.

79. Dulles, *War, Peace and Change*, 124.

80. Ralph B. Levering, *The Public and American Foreign Policy, 1918–1978* (New York: Published for the Foreign Policy Association by Morrow, 1978), 89. Here Levering is quoting John Morton Blum.

81. Henry R. Luce, "America's War and America's Peace," *Life*, February 16, 1942, 85, cited in Levering, *The Public and American Foreign Policy*, 90.

82. [Henry Luce] Editorial, " 'Getting Tough' with Russia," *Life*, March 18, 1946, 36.

83. Ibid., 36.

84. Richard John Neuhaus, *American Babylon: Notes of a Christian Exile* (New York: Basic Books, 2009), 41.

Conclusion: Neglected Genealogies

1. Jon Butler, "Jack-in-the-Box Faith: The Religion Problem in Modern American History," *Journal of American History* 90 (2004): 1357–78.

2. See Andrew Preston, *Sword of the Spirit, Shield of Faith: Religion in American War and Diplomacy* (New York: Alfred A. Knopf, 2012); Mark Thomas Edwards, *Right of the Protestant Left: God's Totalitarianism* (New York: Palgrave Macmillan, 2012); David A. Hollinger, *After Cloven Tongues of Fire: Protestant Liberalism in Modern American History* (Princeton, N.J.: Princeton University Press, 2013).

3. Andrew Preston, "Bridging the Gap between the Sacred and the Secular in the History of American Foreign Relations," *Diplomatic History* 30 (2006): 803, note on 804.

4. Arthur Schlesinger Jr., "The Missionary Enterprise and Theories of Imperialism," in *The Missionary Enterprise in China and America*, ed. John K. Fairbank (Cambridge, Mass.: Harvard University Press, 1974), 336–73.

5. Frank A. Ninkovich, *The United States and Imperialism* (Malden, Mass.: Blackwell Publishers, 2001), 160–63, 222–27.

6. Robert David Johnson, *The Peace Progressives and American Foreign Relations* (Cambridge, Mass.: Harvard University Press, 1995), esp. chap. 6: "Anti-Imperialism and the Peace Movement." See, for example, Page's "authorized and approved" interview with Senator Borah, published as "Borah Tells Views on Anti-War Treaty," *New York Times*, March 25, 1928, 1, 8.

7. See, for example, Mary A. Renda, *Taking Haiti: Military Occupation and the Culture of U.S. Imperialism, 1915–1940* (Chapel Hill: University of North Carolina Press, 2001), 270–73; Virginia S. Williams, *Radical Journalists, Generalist Intellectuals, and U.S.–Latin American Relations* (Lewiston, N.Y.: E. Mellen Press, 2001), chap. 3, "Samuel Guy Inman: Unorthodox Missionary-Scholar."

8. See, for example, Andrew Carnegie's "Distant Possessions: The Parting of the Ways," originally published in the *North American Review* (August 1898), accessed August 28, 2011, http://web.viu.ca/davies/h324war/carnegie.distant.1898.htm. On anti-imperialist arguments following the Spanish-American War generally, see Robert L. Beisner, *Twelve against Empire: The Anti-Imperialists, 1898–1900* (New York: McGraw-Hill, 1968) and Michael P. Cullinane, *Liberty and American Anti-Imperialism, 1898–1909* (New York: Palgrave Macmillan, 2012).

9. See, for example, Ernest H. Gruening, "The Senators Visit Haiti and Santo Domingo," *Nation* 294, no. 2948 (January 4, 1922): 7–10.

10. Glenda Elizabeth Gilmore, *Defying Dixie: The Radical Roots of Civil Rights, 1919–1950* (New York: W. W. Norton & Co, 2008).

11. Jacquelyn Dowd Hall, "The Long Civil Rights Movement and the Political Uses of the Past," *Journal of American History* 91 (2005): 1233–63.

12. For example, see Agnes A. Sharp, "The Shame of America," *The World Tomorrow* (part of "Not in the Headlines" column), December 1926, 262.

13. Anonymous, "Wings for God's Chillun: The Story of Burghardt Du Bois," *The World Tomorrow*, August 1929, 333–36.

14. Published later as Kirby Page, *Recent Gains in American Civilization, by a Group of Distinguished Critics of Contemporary Life* (New York: Harcourt, 1928).

15. Published in "Correspondence," *The World Tomorrow*, February 1927, 368.

16. Kirby Page, "Building Tomorrow's World," *The World Tomorrow*, June 1927, 253–55.

17. Roland A. Gibson, "The 'New Negro' Takes Another Step," *The World Tomorrow*, February 1927, 81–82.

18. Alain Locke, "Negro Contributions to America," *The World Tomorrow*, June 1929, 255–57.

19. Wallace Thurman, "Harlem Facets," *The World Tomorrow*, November 1927, 465–67.

20. N. K. A. Meaney, *Australia and World Crisis, 1914–1923*, vol. 2 of *History of Australian Defence and Foreign Policy 1901–23* (Sydney: Sydney University Press, 2009), 376–78.

21. Marilyn Lake and Henry Reynolds, *Drawing the Global Colour Line: White Men's Countries and the Question of Racial Equality* (Melbourne: Melbourne University Press, 2008), 311.

22. Ibid., 312.

23. Charles H. Hopkins, *John R. Mott, 1865–1955: A Biography* (Grand Rapids, Mich.: Eerdmans, 1979), 627.

24. Cited in *The International Missionary Council*, vol. 5 of *Addresses and Papers of John R. Mott* (New York: Association Press, 1946), 407–8.

25. Mott, "The Race Problem," in *The International Missionary Council*, 610.

26. Ibid., 620.

27. Ibid., 619.

28. Joseph H. Oldham, *Christianity and the Race Problem* (London: SCM Press, 1924).

29. J. H. Oldham, *The World and the Gospel* (London: United Council for Missionary Education, 1916), 190–91.

30. Oldham, *Christianity and the Race Problem*, 17–18.

31. Cited in Philip Potter and Thomas Wieser, *Seeking and Serving the Truth: The First Hundred Years of the World Student Christian Federation* (Geneva: WCC Publications, 1997), 70.

32. "Statement Adopted by the Council: Racial Relationships," in International Missionary Council, *The Christian Mission in the Light of Race Conflict,* vol. 4 of *Report of the Jerusalem Meeting of the International Missionary Council, March 24th–April 8th, 1928* (London: Oxford University Press, 1928), 238.

33. "Statement Adopted by the Council: Racial Relationships," 237.

34. "Message from the Oxford Conference to the Christian Churches," in Henry Smith Leiper, *Highlights of Oxford* (New York: Universal Christian Council for Life and Work, 1937), 13–14, in Box 14, Life and Work Collection, Ecumenical Library, Interchurch Center, New York City.

35. Cf. W. E. B. Du Bois, "The Souls of White Folk," in *Darkwater* (New York: Schocken Books, 1920), 29–55.

36. Benjamin Mays, "The Church amidst Ethnic and Racial Tensions," Speech to the Second Assembly of the World Council of Churches, August 21, 1954, cited in Barbara Dianne Savage, "Benjamin Mays, Global Ecumenism, and Local Religious Segregation," in *Religion and Politics in the Contemporary United States*, ed. R. Marie Griffith and Melani McAlister (Baltimore, Md.: Johns Hopkins University Press, 2008), 266.

37. Cemil Aydin, *The Politics of Anti-Westernism in Asia: Visions of World Order in Pan-Islamic and Pan-Asian Thought* (New York: Columbia University Press, 2007), 6.

38. *International Relations: Being the Report Presented to the Conference on Christian Politics, Economics and Citizenship at Birmingham, April 5–12, 1924*, vol. 7 (London: Longmans Green & Co., 1924), 6.

39. "Church and Community," *Official Reports of the Oxford Conference*, [Federal Council of Churches], 55–60, in Box 14, Life and Work Collection, Ecumenical Library, Interchurch Center, New York City.

40. Daniel T. Rodgers, *Atlantic Crossings: Social Politics in a Progressive Age* (Cambridge, Mass.: Belknap Press of Harvard University Press, 1998), 4.

41. For more on the "apogee of internationalism," see Glenda Sluga, *Internationalism in the Age of Nationalism* (Philadelphia: University of Pennsylvania Press, 2013), 79.

42. Walter LaFeber, *America, Russia, and the Cold War, 1945–66* (John Wiley & Sons, 1967), 40–41.

43. Richard Wightman Fox, *Reinhold Niebuhr: A Biography, with a New Introduction and Afterword* (Ithaca: Cornell University Press, 1996), 238–39.

44. Morgenthau, cited in Ronald H. Stone, *Prophetic Realism: Beyond Militarism and Pacifism in an Age of Terror* (New York: T & T Clark International, 2005), 60. See also Andrew Bacevich, "Introduction," in Reinhold Niebuhr, *The Irony of American History* (Chicago: University of Chicago Press, 2008), ix.

45. See Andrew J. Bacevich, *The Limits of Power: The End of American Exceptionalism* (New York: Metropolitan Books, 2008); Anatol Lieven and John Hulsman, *Ethical Realism: A Vision for America's Role in the World* (New York: Pantheon Books, 2006).

46. Mark Mazower, *Governing the World: The History of an Idea, 1815 to the Present* (New York: Penguin Books, 2012), 237–38.

47. Richard H. Immerman, *Empire for Liberty: A History of American Imperialism from Benjamin Franklin to Paul Wolfowitz* (Princeton, N.J.: Princeton University Press, 2010), 178ff.

48. Preston, *Sword of the Spirit, Shield of Faith*, 460.

49. Reinhold Niebuhr, *The Structure of Nations and Empires: A Study of the Recurring Patterns and Problems of the Political Order in Relation to the Unique Problems of the Nuclear Age* (New York: Scribner, 1959).

50. For his most abstract, psychological, rendering of imperialism, with shades of Carl Jung and Friedrich Nietzche, see Reinhold Niebuhr, *Reflections on the End of an Era* (New York: C. Scribner's Sons, 1936), 6–7. Niebuhr's earlier, landmark "Awkward Imperialists" essay simply ignored American imperialism before the Great War and left out contemporary U.S. relations with Western hemispheric countries entirely, focusing instead on the apparent uniqueness and awkward unknowingness of America's economic and cultural—as opposed to military or territorial—forms of domination in Europe. Reinhold Niebuhr, "Awkward Imperialists," *Atlantic Monthly*, May 1930, 670–75.

51. For example, Reinhold Niebuhr, "Leaves from the Notebook of a War-Bound American," *Christian Century*, September 3, 1939, cited in Charles C. Brown, *Niebuhr and His Age: Reinhold Niebuhr's Prophetic Role and Legacy* (Harrisburg, Pa.: Trinity Press International, 2002), 97; Reinhold Niebuhr, "Imperialism and Responsibility," *Christianity and Crisis*, February 24, 1941, 6.

52. Matthew John Paul Tan, "Eucharistic Worship and Peacemaking," *Case* 22 (2010): 25–28, 27.

53. Andrew Chandler, review of *Oxford 1937: The Universal Christian Council for Life and Work Conference*, by Graeme Smith, *Journal of Ecclesiastic History* 57 (2006): 413.

54. Raymond J. Haberski, *God and War: American Civil Religion Since 1945* (New Brunswick, N.J.: Rutgers University Press, 2012).

Index

Addams, Jane, 8, 73
Africa: Max Yergan on, 110; and missionary enterprise, 18–19. *See also* South Africa
Allen, Devere, 10–11, 48, 65
American Friends Service Committee, 45, 73, 164
American Legion, 55, 57, 64, 72
Anti-Imperialist League, 31
Army and Navy Journal, 55, 72
Army and Navy Register, 55
The Atlantic Monthly, 41, 48
Aubrey, Edwin E., 120, 126, 128, 145, 148

Balch, Emily Greene, 73
Ball, Joseph H., 167
Barker, Ernest, 128–29, 134
Barnes, Harry Elmer, 12, 35–36, 59, 63
Barth, Karl, 121–25, 160–62
Barthianism, 123–24, 140, 173
Barton, Bruce, 34, 63
Beard, Charles A.: citation in Reinhold Niebuhr's work, 85; contributor at *The World Tomorrow*, 12, 48, 58–59, 193; and neutralism, 71, 73
Beard, Mary, 59–60, 73, 85
Bell, George K. A., 95, 116, 143, 156
Bennett, John C.: Christian realism of, 9, 76–79, 81; involvement with Commission on a Just and Durable Peace, 169; participa-

tion in Oxford 1937, 126, 143; at Union Theological Seminary, 152–56
Bocobo, Jorge, 110–11
Boegner, Marc, 227n45
Bonhoeffer, Dietrich, 121
Borah, William E., 40, 191–92
Borchard, Edwin, 52
Brailsford, Henry Noel, 48
Brent, Charles H., 115–16
Bretton Woods Conference, 173
Britain. *See* Great Britain
Brown, William Adams, 80, 152–53
Brunner, Emil, 12, 14, 22, 94, 125
Buck, Pearl, 17
Butterfield, Herbert, 12, 157

Campbell, Alexander, Disciples of Christ movement, 30
Catholic Association for International Peace, 5
Catt, Carrie Chapman, 73
Cavert, Samuel McCrea, 36, 45, 126, 141, 169
Cherrington, Ben M., 3
The Chicago Tribune, 64, 72
China: Anti-Christian Association, 106; conference delegates, 105–6, 121, 141; missionaries in, 2, 17, 20, 191. *See also* Manchurian Crisis; World Student Christian Federation Conference 1922 (Peking)
Christian Century, 2–3, 49, 68–69, 86–87, 155